50 Z1035 A2 M49

Caldecott Medal Books

edited *by* BERTHA MAHONY MILLER

and ELINOR WHITNEY FIELD

Caldecott

Medal Books: 1938-1957

with the Artist's Acceptance Papers

& Related Material chiefly from the

HORN BOOK MAGAZINE

HORN BOOK PAPERS  VOLUME II

THE HORN BOOK, INCORPORATED · BOSTON · 1957

Contents

In Conclusion

by *The Editors*

Preface

The first volume of Horn Book Papers — *Newbery Medal Books,* 1955 — had so cordial a reception, that we resolved to bring out at once Volume II — *Caldecott Medal Books.*

Both these volumes should be read in conjunction with Irene Smith Green's *History of the Newbery and Caldecott Awards,* published by Viking in the fall of 1957. Mrs. Green's book gives a complete account of the founding of the Medals and of the librarians' function in awarding them, with emphasis on the human history of these events.

This volume we now present is also filled with human history and interest. The artists' own Acceptance papers are rich in the creative aspects of their work. The reading of them is the next best thing to listening in to their discussion of picture books. The biographical papers are warm-hearted, intelligent and discriminating stories of the lives of the artists. Without artists there would be no picture books.

The time of the biographical papers, as of the Acceptance papers, is the time of the Award. The two exceptions are the papers written specially for this volume, one on Dorothy P. Lathrop by her sculptor-sister, Gertrude Lathrop; and the other on Robert McCloskey written by his wife, Margaret Durand McCloskey.

Throughout our work on this volume we have wished we had for inclusion from each Awards Committee a statement telling why the particular picture book was chosen. So far as we know such statements do not exist. They seem so important as records that we hope they may become established practice with future Awards Committees.

We do not attempt to tell our readers what they should think about these twenty books honored with the Caldecott Medal. The only way to enjoy and to judge picture books is to look at them. As a basis for the examination or re-examination of the books, we present a stimulating final chapter on one such examination by Esther Averill, long interested in art and artists, publisher of the Domino Press, and one who has illustrated some of her own books.

Miss Averill places her emphasis upon the picture book as a graphic unit, a " work of visual art," although she does not go into the aspects of printing or discuss what poor colors and faulty registration on the printer's part can do to an artist's intentions. She raises, but does not attempt to answer, the question as to whether literary distinction is required in an Award picture book. While writing her chapter, Miss Averill had access to picture book collections in some of the larger public libraries and because of this, it was possible for her to make comparative studies of some of the books mentioned in her chapter.

We long to see more critical discussion of the Awards each year as they are announced, and also of the runners-up, for it is through comparisons that we can sharpen our wits and our taste and determine whether the best has really been chosen. We need, too, to hear directly from more libraries, public, school and home, as to children's enjoyment of the Medal books.

Picture books are not an isolated area of art, they are a part of the main stream. They are important. They may " break down the divisions of time, place and circumstance, and set the spirit free to go on its voyages." They may plant in their readers " a seed from which their own imagination shall spring; fertilize their earth that of it they may be reborn." *

* Charles Morgan, *Liberties of the Mind*, page 95. Macmillan, 1951.

Acknowledgments

The editors of this volume wish to thank the Children's Library Association for the privilege of reprinting from *The Horn Book* the annual Caldecott Acceptance papers from 1938 on. We thank also the illustrators themselves for permission to publish their addresses. We thank the authors of the biographies, written to accompany the Acceptance papers in *The Horn Book*, for permission to include their papers in this volume. We thank Miss Dorothy Waugh for permission to reprint here from *The Horn Book* her paper on Roger Duvoisin which was not originally written in connection with the award of the Medal. We give our thanks, too, to Miss Mildred Fish for permission to use a portion of Helen Dean Fish's paper on Robert Lawson; and to Mrs. Elmer E. Bailey, Thomas Handforth's sister-in-law, for permission to reprint his Acceptance paper and his autobiographical paper, "Personal Progress to the Orient." We thank the various publishers for permission to reproduce the illustrations in this volume. Individual acknowledgment will be found opposite each picture. We thank Miss Dorothy Abbe for her willingness to answer various questions, to advise on many points in the preparation of this volume for the press, since in its making we are following her design for *Newbery Medal Books;* and for her design for its jacket.

The editors wish to thank Norma R. Fryatt for her many services in the preparation of this manuscript for the press, including the choice of illustrations, and for her care in watching it through the press.

Caldecott Medal Books

by *Bertha Mahony Miller*

Randolph Caldecott
For Whom the Award Is Named

ONE night in the spring of 1888 there gathered at the Brasenose Club in Manchester, England, an eminent group of members to honor the memory of one of their number who had died — Randolph Caldecott. The Club was showing at that time a memorial exhibition of his work which included not only water colors, oils, pen-and-ink sketches, but also bas-reliefs and bronzes.

If Caldecott's friends could have been told then that his *Picture Books* would be children's favorites half a century later, and that an annual award for the best picture book published yearly in America would bear his name, they would have said, "But of course! How could it be otherwise?" Several spoke that night of his love for children, one speaking of a sketch of Caldecott's showing himself surrounded by children as he drew.

No one could study Caldecott's *Picture Books* without realizing the deep interest and regard with which he had observed children, and had drawn them for themselves. But he did more than that. Caldecott put into his *Picture Books* all that rural England he knew so well, with its village folk, its horses and dogs, its birds, and creatures of the barnyard and wood; scenes through which he had moved all his life so happily and so gaily.

There were two other famous illustrators at work in England at the same time as Caldecott who, together with him, are considered to have founded the Nursery Academy. They were Kate Greenaway and Walter Crane. Both had genius and contributed much to art and to children's books, but Caldecott's work had a spontaneous quality of reality and fun lacking in theirs. Country life *flowed* through his drawings. Of this vitality, F. J. Harvey Darton has written:

"Of the three, Caldecott had the most robust and, so to speak, humane personality. The other two seem like artists first and ordinary people afterwards. You always feel that Caldecott is not thinking of a picture, but of folk and lovable dogs and horses and flesh-and-blood hybrids like his fellow Englishmen."

One of his friends said of Caldecott, "His qualities were so bright, so new, so versatile, as to appeal at once to young and old. To a mind singularly frank and open, and a shrewd but kindly humor, he united a rare grace and a delicate and refined sympathy which gave a distinctive and peculiar charm to all his artistic work; and to the poetic temperament with which he was also so richly endowed by nature was added an enthusiastic enjoyment of robust life, and a hearty liking for field sport."

We know from the record of his life written by his friend, Henry Blackburn, that Randolph Caldecott was a charming boy and man; tall, with light-brown hair, gray-blue eyes, and "a gay good humor." He was born March 22, 1846, in Chester, and educated there at King's School. He did well at school and in his school days was always sketching and modeling animals in wood. He loved above everything to wander over the countryside; and he delighted in riding.

At fifteen Caldecott began work in a bank at Whitchurch in Shropshire, and stayed there six years, living in an old farmhouse about two miles from the town. It is easy to picture him, going fishing and shooting in his free time, riding to hounds, visiting with his sketch book markets and cattle fairs, *seeing so much* and enjoying it with all his being.

It was an important characteristic of Caldecott's that, just as he did well at school although he was not a scholar, so he did his bank work well. In 1867, when he was twenty-one, he went to Manchester and worked five years more in the Salford Bank. It was in Manchester that his work began appearing in journals, although his very first published drawing, of the burning of Queen's Hotel, Chester, is said to have appeared in the *Illustrated London News*, November, 1861, when Caldecott was fifteen. Now his work began to be seen in such local journals as *The Will-o'-the-Wisp* and *The Sphinx*, and one of his pictures was shown at the Manchester Royal Institution.

In 1871 Caldecott's drawings were printed in London newspapers and journals. Some appeared in *London Society*, which counted many notable names among its contributors at that time. Early in 1872 Caldecott gave up his assured position and income and went up to London to try his fortune as an artist. He joined a life class at the Slade School and made studies of birds at the Zoölogical Gardens. Mr. Thomas Armstrong, Director of the South Kensington Museum, became his best friend. George Du Maurier and M. Dalou, the sculptor, were also among his close friends.

His first drawing for *Punch* appeared on June 22, 1872. His contributions to a new illustrated newspaper — *The Pictorial World* — played a large part in the successful beginnings of that paper. These drawings were for the most part humorous comment upon current political incidents. In the late summer of 1872 he traveled to illustrate Henry Blackburn's book, *The Harz Mountains, A Tour in the Toy Country*, Caldecott's first piece of book illustration. It was with scenes from this journey that his name later became familiar in the pages of the *London Graphic*. Some of the Harz Mountains drawings also appeared in *Harper's Monthly Magazine* here in America to illustrate Mr. Blackburn's article. His drawings in *Harper's* brought a demand for his work from the *Daily Graphic* of New York. These *Graphic* drawings were cartoons, usually a series of amusing scenes. The titles of those reproduced in the volume, *Last Pictures for The Graphic*, are typical and are suggestive of the times and their kind: — "Scenes with the Old Mickledale Hunt," "Lovers' Quarrel," "Legend of Laughing Oak," "Strange Adventures of a Dog-Cart," "Curmudgeon's Christmas."

All will now agree that Caldecott's genius flows strongest and most permanently in his *Picture Books* and in the drawings for chapters from Irving's *Sketch Book*. It was in January, 1874, that Mr. James Cooper, engraver, went to Caldecott with this book. Caldecott liked it and immediately went to work on drawings for certain chapters. These chapters were brought out by Macmillan late in 1875 under the date 1876 and the title *Old Christmas*. At the end of the year 1876, more chapters entitled *Bracebridge Hall* were published with his drawings. Early in his work for the Washington Irving books, Mr. Blackburn reports that there came into Caldecott's drawing a new " sense of beauty and fitness in design." His complete alliance with the author's text, his creation of the genuine characters described, make a notable landmark in the history of illustrating.

Early in 1878 the wood engraver and fine, discriminating printer, Edmund Evans, proposed to Caldecott that he should illustrate some books for children to be printed in colors. Edmund Evans engraved and printed the picture books of the three members of the Nursery Academy — Caldecott, Crane and Kate Greenaway — and shares with them the honor of making the earliest of the modern picture books. He took infinite pains with every phase of his bookmaking. And so those sixteen *Picture Books* of Caldecott's, listed at the end of this chapter, came into being. For these books, his drawings were photographed onto wood blocks and then passed through the hands of engravers. Caldecott made Mrs. Ewing's acquaintance in 1879, designed the cover of *Aunt Judy's Magazine*, which she edited, and made illustrations for her *Jackanapes, Daddy Darwin's Dovecot* and *Lob Lie-by-the-Fire*.

He married in 1880 Miss Marion Brind, daughter of F. B. Brind of St. Mary's, Cray, Kent. They lived in a small house with an old-fashioned garden at Kemsing, near Sevenoaks. On February 12, 1886, when Caldecott was only forty years of age, he died at St. Augustine, Florida, and through most of his short life he had done his work in spite of delicate health and limited strength.

In our household I suppose the Caldecott *Picture Books* have had more constant examination than any others, with Leslie Brooke's three volumes about Johnny Crow and his Garden close followers. The timeless quality of the English folk tale is in them and while they have a strong and unmistakable character, which was Caldecott's own, there is a self-forgetful freedom in them as though the artist so enjoyed himself recording his observations to fit the occasion that his hand ran its way unbeknownst. "Pictures were like speech or writing to him: his natural talk," Mr. Darton has written. What one feels as one pores over these books cannot be said better than Austin Dobson has said it:

"The open air life of England, with all its freshness and breeziness, its pastoral seduction and its picturesque environment, is everywhere present in his work. He has the art, too, of being elegant without being effeminate, and of being tender without being mawkish. It is said of a great English novelist that his laugh clears the air; it may be said of these light-hearted pictures that their mirth clears not only the air but the imagination. No taint clings to them of morbid affectation or sickly sentiment: they are the genuine pictorial utterances of a manly, happy nature, delighting in beauty, delighting in innocent pleasure, and dowered as few English artists have been with the gifts of refinement and grace."

RANDOLPH CALDECOTT'S PICTURE BOOKS

1. John Gilpin
2. The House that Jack Built
3. The Babes in the Wood
4. The Mad Dog
5. Three Jovial Huntsmen
6. Sing a Song for Sixpence
7. The Queen of Hearts
8. The Farmer's Boy
9. The Milkmaid
10. Hey Diddle Diddle and Baby Bunting
11. A Frog He Would A-wooing Go
12. The Fox Jumps Over the Parson's Gate
13. Come Lasses and Lads
14. Ride a Cock-Horse to Banbury Cross, etc.
15. Mrs. Mary Blaize
16. The Great Panjandrum Himself

Randolph Caldecott's First Collection of Pictures and Songs (Nos. 1-8 mentioned above) — in one volume.
Randolph Caldecott's Second Collection of Pictures and Songs (Nos. 9-16 mentioned above) — in one volume.

(Frederick Warne & Co. All in print.)

OTHER BOOKS MENTIONED IN THIS CHAPTER

Old Christmas and Bracebridge Hall, by Washington Irving, illustrated by Randolph Caldecott. Macmillan.

Children's Books in England: Five Centuries of Social Life, by F. J. Harvey Darton. Macmillan.

Randolph Caldecott, A Personal Memoir of His Early Art Career, by Henry Blackburn. Sampson Low, Marston, Searle and Rivington, 1886. op.

Randolph Caldecott, The Complete Collection of Pictures and Songs, Engraved and Printed by Edmund Evans, with a preface by Austin Dobson. Routledge. 1887. op.

Randolph Caldecott's last "Graphic" Pictures. Routledge. 1888. op.

Catalogue of a Loan Collection of the Works of Randolph Caldecott, exhibited at the Brasenose Club, Manchester, March, 1888. Illustrated. With a report of the proceedings at the house dinner. Manchester. 1888. op.

Animals of the Bible, A Picture Book

illustrated by DOROTHY P. LATHROP

text selected by HELEN DEAN FISH

published by LIPPINCOTT*

FORMAT

SIZE: 7¼″ x 10″, 66 pp.
ARTIST'S MEDIUM: Lithographs, black and white
PRINTING PROCESS: Offset lithography
ILLUSTRATIONS: Endpapers, title page, full pages throughout
TYPE: 16/18 Deepdene

BOOK NOTE

SELECTIONS from the King James version of the Old and New Testaments. "During the drawing of these pictures, the artist studied not only the fauna but the flora of Bible lands and times, and each desert rose as well as each goat and turtle dove is as true to natural history as is possible to be." — From Foreword by Helen Dean Fish.

*Originally published by Frederick A. Stokes & Co., 1937.

ACCEPTANCE PAPER

by *Dorothy P. Lathrop*

Model Animals

You must all know how happy it makes me to receive the first medal ever given to a picture book for children, and one that bears the name of so beloved an illustrator as Caldecott. When you think that not many years ago the illustrators of children's books were as anonymous as sculptors are now at the unveiling of their own statues, you will realize how much has been done for illustration. We also hear a great deal about how much illustration has done for children's books, thanks to such people as Frederick Melcher, Anne Carroll Moore and Bertha Mahony, and no one cries "Hear! Hear!" more loudly and enthusiastically than the illustrators. It makes us feel so virtuous! For of course it is really our pleasure to draw, and, since those of us who have Puritan ancestry feel guiltily sure that all self-indulgence is sinful, we are only too relieved to find such a praiseworthy excuse for doing it. And it is especially pleasant to be encouraged in this delightful way to go on drawing.

I can't help wishing that just now all of you were animals. Of course technically you are, but if only I could look down into a sea of *furry* faces, I would know better what to say. If only your ears were the movable kind that cock forward or prick to attention, I would know what kind of sounds to make — soothing murmurs if you grew restless, little chirruping noises if your heads began to droop and your eyes to close. But what sort of sounds to pour into immobile human ears, about that I am not so sure. For drawing animals is a solitary, silent occupation, which, if persisted in too long, leads to speechlessness. A dangerous one, for what good would an illustrator be if he couldn't make a speech? An occupation in which one treads gently, moves slowly for fear of sending a timid, untamed model back to the woods or to the far corners of its cage, its fur shaking and heaving over a madly beating heart.

In such an illustrator's studio, what conversation there is is strictly one-sided, except for an occasional squeal of protest from a model prodded too often into the semblance of a position taken spontaneously just once. And on the illustrator's side also it is limited and repetitive to a pitiful degree, consisting almost entirely of such ejaculations and pleas as, " Hold still! *Please* hold still! Just for one little minute! For a second then! *That's* it! Oh dear! " Not that such conversation is of the slightest use except as a safety valve. Happily there are recesses, with nibbles of graham crackers and rubbing behind the ears. And sometimes the model actually grows a little fond of his tormentor, and the illustrator always grows fond of the model. But *you* expect more variety of thought from me than " Hold still! " And I wouldn't dare rub your ears. I don't know that I have even the equivalent of a graham cracker to offer you.

There is something soporific to man and beast alike about posing. Let the artist's victim sit still for even a few minutes, staring at a given point, and his face begins to open in a series of yawns. And for the artist to find himself continually confronted by the open countenance of even the handsomest — or perhaps especially of the handsomest — of models is something of a shock. Even a suppressed yawn does amazing and unflattering things to the human face, and the elasticity of all the features becomes something at which to wonder.

But animals, when they pose, make no bones about their sleepiness. In fact their bones seem to turn to water. Stand them up, and, like a child in a tantrum, they don't stay stood up. The little lamb who lived in our studio all one summer learned what posing meant, and more than earned her milk. For my sister modeled her, my mother painted her, and I drew her, and she knew perfectly what was expected of her. Sheep are not as silly as they are reputed to be, and she did her valiant best. She was a good little lamb. But no matter how giddily she had been gamboling, the moment she was asked to pose, her eyes began to close, her head to droop until her soft, woolly chin came to rest on a mercifully proffered arm, and there, eyes shut, chin propped, she swayed drunkenly from side to side until she went to sleep on her feet and her legs crumpled under her.

Just now my model is a baby flying squirrel. Since he has posed from the time he was pink and blind and completely hairless — though I hasten to add for the S. P. C. A. that those early poses could only have been measured by seconds — he ought by now to be an experienced model. But he too goes to sleep on the job. And his cradle is, most inconveniently, my left hand! Until deprived of it, I never realized how much I used it while drawing. But in his semi-nude state, it was the best substitute I could give him during the cold spring days for his mother's body which, with outstretched arms, she spread over them all like a soft, warm robe. Before he could see, my hand was an accepted part of his environment. With the opening of his eyes, it became the one familiar refuge in a new and frightening world, and he clung to it like a shipwrecked mariner to a spar. Since only when sleeping is he quiet, I am glad to give up the use of one hand. But settle down for a nap he never does until he has twirled around and around within my half-closed fingers like a little round top — but a top, warm, pulsating, and exquisitely furred — ending up invariably in just the wrong position — for me, at least. *He* seems quite satisfied with it. But if I have started to draw his right side, it is his left that is uppermost. If I want to see the shape of his nose, he is sleeping on it, or has wrapped his tail tightly around his head. And if I try gently to turn him over without awakening him, his eyes pop open and he starts his twirling all over again.

It is dangerous to grow too fond of one's models, for then one can hardly bear to part with them. And if one draws many animals, the studio soon begins to qualify as a zoo, and the artist as a keeper. And keepers have little time to draw. Fortunately almost all of our wild models are transients. Their brief posing ended, they go back to their woods and fields, no matter how much we may hate to see them whisk or fly out of our lives. That we are fond of them is no excuse for keeping untamed creatures confined. We may, through ignorance or carelessness, so easily love them to death. One of my little friends was enchanted by the delicate, waxen red efts that wander through the damp summer woods. She picked them up, oh so gently, and she built them a mossy house. But it never occurred to her to feed them, and day by day they shriveled and shriveled and shriveled.

> " A Robin Redbreast in a cage
> Puts all heaven in a rage . . .
> Each outcry of the hunted hare
> A fibre from the brain doth tear;
> A skylark wounded on the wing
> Doth make a cherub cease to sing . . .
> Kill not the moth nor butterfly,
> For the last judgment draweth nigh."

And these are only a few of the Blake lines.

If one is known to be fond of animals, all the maimed and dying creatures in the neighborhood are brought to one's door. But that Pippin, the young robin, came to stay with us was my fault. It was I who rescued him, somewhat tardily, alas, from the cat. For weeks he hopped about the studio with his broken wing bound up with adhesive tape. There were certain disadvantages connected with his stay. One of the greatest was the number of worms he ate. By the time he could perch on the rafters, I had a great respect for the industry and endurance of a mother robin. Do you know that that young bird could hold as many as eighteen angleworms a day?

At that time we had a maid who would very obligingly go out and dig worms for Pippin. One very hot day she came in with her face scarlet.

" Oh," we said, " you shouldn't have gotten so hot! "

" I know," she replied, " but I was getting such beautiful worms I couldn't bear to leave them! "

I have often wondered whether the life of that one robin balanced the lives of all those worms.

Yes, it is dangerous to love your models too much. On the other hand, unless you do, no one will love your pictures of them. I don't mean this in any esoteric or mystical way. I don't claim that you set into motion a force which flows between yourself and your public. That, too, may be so for all I know, but what I mean is something quite concrete. For a person who does not love what he is drawing, whatever it may be, children or animals, or anything else, will not draw them convincingly, and that, simply because he will not bother to look at them long enough really to see them. What we love, we gloat over and feast our eyes upon. And when we look again and again at any living creature, we cannot help but perceive its subtlety of line, its exquisite patterning and all its unbelievable intricacy and beauty. The artist who draws what he does not love, draws from a superficial concept. But the one who loves what he draws is very humbly trying to translate into an alien medium life itself, and it is his joy and his pain that he knows that life to be matchless.

No one, I think, is more convinced of the unity of all life than the artist, who sits before its different phases so long and silently, seeing them in a great intimacy. He not only beholds the flower, but he feels the life that, even while he draws, unfolds the petals, senses the force that pushes new leaves from the ground. He traces a network of veins in leaf and flower akin to the veining which shows under his own skin. He knows that under the microscope it is hard to tell which veins are plant and which animal, and whether that is sap or blood flowing so steadily through those channels. In that deep silence in which drawings are made, he so projects himself into the personality of any living model before him, that he becomes strangely identified with it. He not only feels himself a brother to this creature whose atoms are held together by the same mysterious force or vibration, not only feels the same life surging through them both, but, such is his intensity of interest, he *becomes* that creature. Or, as the eastern philosophers put it, he " sees all creatures in himself, himself in all creatures."

I wonder if we don't too often forget how new this natural world is to children, how fresh and unjaded their interest in it? Of course, we authors and illustrators are up against tremendous competition in trying to market our wares. No wonder we sometimes strive desperately to attract with novelty the attention of publishers who are adults and of a buying public which is also adult. But to the child himself our most novel invention is not more strange and wonderful than the living creatures of this world, and our most vivid imagination can devise nothing more enthralling than all their ways. But Thomas Traherne said it much better three hundred years ago.

"All appeared new, and strange at first, inexpressibly rare and delightful and beautiful. . . . The corn was orient and immortal wheat, which never should be reaped, nor was ever sown. I thought it had stood from everlasting to everlasting. The dust and the stones of the street were as precious as gold: the gates were at first the end of the world. The green trees when I saw them first through one of the gates transported and ravished me, their sweetness and unusual beauty made my heart to leap, and almost mad with ecstasy, they were such strange and wonderful things. The Men! O what venerable and reverend creatures did the aged seem! Immortal Cherubims! And young men glittering and sparkling angels, and maids strange seraphic pieces of life and beauty! Boys and girls tumbling in the street, and playing, were moving jewels. I knew not that they were born or should die; but all things abided eternally as they were in their proper places. Eternity was manifest in the Light of the Day, and something infinite behind everything appeared: which talked with my expectation and moved my desire."

Children feel a natural kinship with all living things. It is we adults who alienate them. When they reach out to touch the brightly colored bug or caterpillar, it is the mothers who cry, "Step on it!" When they stretch out their hands to a dog, it is the mothers who shriek, "Look out! He'll bite you!" It was not the dog who frightened the child, but the mother who yanked it back, sobbing with a new terror.

Perhaps in *Animals of the Bible* I have taken a liberty in introducing children into the picture of the family dogs. But I felt sure that, though no children were mentioned in the text, where the dogs were, even in those ancient days, there the children would be also, and helping them to more crumbs than those which normally fell from their master's table. For there is a special link in all ages between children and animals, and this is, of course, why there are so many animal stories written for them.

It never occurred to me to make a book of the animal stories of the Bible. It was Helen Dean Fish who for several years cherished that plan in secret, and when she chose me to illustrate it, I was very proud. I think that when I was little, I would have liked such a book. Whether or not I would have liked my own pictures for it, I can't begin to say. I don't even know whether I would like them now if I could look at them dispassionately, for, sad to say, one never can. But of all the stories in the Bible, those about animals were then my favorites. Repeated conferences with my editor while the book was being made, however, have convinced me that I must have been a ferocious child, for those stories that were my special delight then are much too dreadful to be given to children of the present day. Who would have believed that those young beings whose weekly fare is the animated cartoon in which great wolves with wide open mouths and dripping jowls tower in relentless pursuit like the nightmare creatures of delirium until they blot out all else and engulf at last even the beholder — who would have believed that those children would blench at the story of Elisha's two she-bears?

Nevertheless my editor was firm and I had to draw instead the bear which David slew, and draw him chasing a lamb. Then *I* was as sorry for the lamb as she was for the rude children who jeered at the prophet's bald head, and sorrier yet for the bear, which she didn't understand at all. I don't think she is sure yet that I really do like children and like them just as much as I like animals, perhaps because they act very much the same, and I see little difference between them.

Neither might I draw the Gadarene swine, though time and time again I then ran headlong down that steep place with them until the waters closed over my head. Nor might I draw Samson's foxes with the burning brands tied between their tails, though that also was one of my dreadful favorites. Still, if that story would have prompted even one small boy to try that trick on the neighborhood cats or dogs, I am glad we left it out. For my concern as a child was not for the good standing corn, and the vineyard and the olives, but only for the foxes lest they could not loose themselves from the firebrands and so perished in the flaming grain.

I wish that I had found the scapegoat when I was a child. I know that I would have rejoiced with him that it was his lot to be let go in the wilderness. For there seems to have been no Kindness to Animals Week in those ancient days. Though the pages of the Bible are filled with casual references to beasts as possessions, as food, as victims for sacrifice, I can remember no one who objected to any mistreatment of them except the angel who stood in Balaam's path and asked, " Wherefore hast thou smitten thine ass these three times? " — and, of course, the vocal ass herself! And only in the book of Job are they seen as creatures in their own right. No present-day naturalist could describe an animal more minutely than leviathan is there presented, scale by scale, and surely none could portray one with such grandeur. "He maketh the deep to boil like a pot: He maketh the sea like a pot of ointment. . . . By his neesings a light doth shine, and his eyes are like the eyelids of the morning."

It was lucky that the description was so detailed, for no leviathan visited our shores to pose for me. That, according to the reasoning of a certain English publisher, would have been an excellent reason for leaving him out of our book, for this publisher gave as his excuse for not bringing my *Who Goes There?* out in England, that they have no chipmunks in that country! Neither, except in zoos and circuses, have *we* any lions or elephants, and few can boast of having peered into the countenance of leviathan. Still, if the Bible and so many of our good sea captains claim that sea serpents do exist, who are we to doubt it? And if publishers were not always in such a hurry for drawings, and there were no such things as publication dates, I suppose I might still be sitting, pencil in hand, on the seashore hoping for a glimpse of " that great serpent of the deep."

Not all — by any means — of my favorite stories were left out of this book. In fact, most of them are in, including that of Elijah and the ravens. But not until I sat down before some caged ravens in the zoo did I realize that they have brains of a more than bird-like sort, and that that is probably why they were chosen above other birds to feed Elijah in the wilderness. For there they were, whiling away the hours of their confinement by playing with anything they could find in their cage, tossing and twirling and carrying about with them sticks and snippets of paper and, cherished above all, a bit of chain which, when they were through playing, they carefully tucked under some old straw for safe keeping. They eyed me wisely, too, and answered when spoken to. Perhaps Elijah was not, after all, too lonely in the wilderness.

For the sake of the child that I was, who wanted the foxes to escape the fire, and who hoped that the hungry lions would be fed, though not with Daniel, and for the sake of all other children who love and cherish animals — and are there many who don't? — I am glad that we ended the book with the prophecy of Isaiah:

" The wolf also shall dwell with the lamb, and the leopard shall lie down with the kid; and the calf and the young lion and the fatling together; and a little child shall lead them.

" And the cow and the bear shall feed; their young ones shall lie down together: and the lion shall eat straw like the ox.

" And the suckling child shall play on the hole of the asp, and the weaned child shall put his hand on the cockatrice' den.

"They shall not hurt nor destroy in all my holy mountain: for the earth shall be full of the knowledge of the Lord, as the waters cover the sea."

BIOGRAPHICAL PAPER

by *Gertrude K. Lathrop*

Dorothy P. Lathrop

I REMEMBER that I was a chunky, matter-of-fact child of five or six when I used to follow Dorothy through the woods. I tried to move quietly for fear of frightening away the fairies. But somehow sticks snapped under my feet and branches swished as I crashed after her. Dorothy seemed to know just how to move to avoid the twigs that cracked and the branches that reached out to grab. This may have been why it was always she who saw the fairies. When we came upon a moss-lined hole at the base of a tree, we bent down, listened and breathed lightly — listened until the roaring of our ears would have drowned out any fairy words spoken deep in the earth. Being a practical child, I wondered why fairies would want to live in the dark, damp ground, no matter how beautiful their doorway.

There were other times when Dorothy built tiny houses in the woods in the hope that the fairies might adopt them. These were made of little twigs and roofed with moss. She found fat hummocks of green moss for seats and footstools. Other sticks quickly became fences, and the flower beds bloomed with bright, red-tipped lichens. As we left the completed house and garden at dusk, she often laid a scarlet wintergreen berry inside, a special offering to the fairy queen.

The fairies must have come and been grateful, for I felt that they guided the shears of my half-grown sister as she skillfully cut their images from paper, and her paint brush, too, as she gave them long blond hair, delicate wings and many-colored dresses. And there was a golden crown for the fairy queen. I thought they were wonderful.

One of Dorothy's playmates, filled with longing to see beyond her own everyday world, wrote this wistful little note:

" Dear fairy that Dorothy Lathrop seen last night, I hope you will like our presents that we send up. My address is Miss Jessie Ryder. Please come and see me will you."

The plays that were given in my mother's studio were always fairy plays. My sister's greatest regret was that she could never be the princess or the fairy queen. She knew only too well that, because her hair was black, she must be the wicked witch.

Books have always been a large part of her life. Many miniature volumes filled the bookshelves of her doll house. Each little book was made of many tiny sheets of blank paper, but every one had a gaily colored cover bearing the name of some favorite story — *The Light Princess, The Princess and Curdie, Mopsa the Fairy* and *Sara Crewe* were among them. It is interesting that she chose some of these same books to illustrate when she grew up and made pictures for other children.

Our mother's studio is on the third floor of our house. Before civilization crowded in from every side, the windows overlooked field after field rolling back toward the distant Helderbergs and Catskills. Many mornings I would hear my mother stirring before dawn. The quiet early mornings belonged to her. No one was about to come between her and her beautiful out-of-doors as she sat with her sketch box on her lap. She loved to paint the trees and fields that were just visible through the morning mist. She worked swiftly to finish before the sun dispelled the mist and brought the hazy landscape into sharp detail. The purity and beauty of a heavy snow thrilled her as nothing else did, and she often said in a rapturous voice, " It's a fairyland! It's a fairyland!"

She loved all the beautiful little things in nature — the flowers, the mosses, the bright-colored toadstools — everything that grew. She often looked through her small magnifying glass at a miniature flower, its detail too minute for the unaided human eye to see, and marveled as the high-powered lens revealed a beauty and perfection as lovely as any orchid.

It was our mother's enthusiasm and reverence for all things beautiful that gave us the eyes to see, and gave to my sister the wish to surround the fairies and animals in her books with an almost endless variety of plants and flowers, drawn with the greatest of care, in the hope that she might catch even a little of nature's superlative beauty. Our mother encouraged us to draw all through our school days and, because of this encouragement and training, Dorothy won the medals and school honors in art all along the way.

Our father was a practical man who mistrusted art as a means of earning a living. It was he who insisted that any art training for my sister should lead to a teacher's diploma. Three years at Teachers College, Columbia, where she majored in art and also took all the English and writing courses offered, gave her such a diploma. The fourth year she chose to study illustration at the Pennsylvania Academy of the Fine Arts.

She did teach art in the Albany High School for two years. And then one day at the lunch hour as she and a fellow teacher turned the pages of an illustrated book, she said that she wished that *she* could draw like that.

"You wouldn't be here if you could," said the other teacher crisply. And my sister thought with a little shock, "I may not be a Howard Pyle, but what *am* I doing here when I want to illustrate?"

Then began the trudging from publisher to publisher with an enormous portfolio that prompted the more chivalrous editors to carry it for her back to the elevators. Her first small set of drawings was done for a Boston publisher who went bankrupt before paying for them. After that, Alfred Knopf, then a very young publisher, offered her Walter de la Mare's *The Three Mulla-Mulgars* to illustrate. Incredible good fortune for a novice illustrator! Magic and beauty to try to translate into line and color! W. H. Hudson's *A Little Boy Lost* followed, then other books from other publishers, all of which she found a joy to illustrate. But I think that she was never happier than when working with the poems and stories of Walter de la Mare.

It was Louise Seaman who encouraged her to make her own story-picture books. The first of these was *The Fairy Circus*, almost the last of her fairy work. After that her interest turned to animals, for which I perhaps am largely responsible. The animals I brought home for models for my own sculpture, quickly found their way into books — my two little lambs into *Bouncing Betsy*, my young kid into *The Little White Goat*, and my flying squirrels, that raised their families in our big outdoor cage, into *Hide and Go Seek*. This book, I think, is especially dear to her heart, possibly because we found the little creatures themselves such enchanting pets, or because of the pleasant trips we took each week to the woods to see how much farther the fern fronds had uncurled and what new flowers were in bloom, so that spring in this book keeps proper pace with the growth of the baby squirrels. Each plant is drawn with the same loving care she lavished on the squirrel portraits and shows the joy she took in leaf and animal alike.

But not all of the models were of my choosing. Lupe, the red squirrel from South America, was rescued from a pet shop by my sister. The Pekingese puppies in *Puppies for Keeps* and *Puffy and the Seven Leaf Clover* were bred, and later some of them shown to their championships, by her. They posed squirming on her lap and chewing the edges of her drawing board. Since she could not bear to toss it out into the snow, the mouse family in *The Littlest Mouse*, lived in a glass terrarium in the studio until spring. One time she rescued a turtle from almost certain death on the highway and he lived to pose and enrich some book with his grotesque beauty and intricate patterns. It is only by living with a turtle that one can know what a turtle does and why. Another time she brought home a young chipmunk that had been injured by a cat. He was nursed back to health and eventually returned to the woods a wiser chipmunk, we hope! Before leaving he paid for his peanuts and sunflower seeds by posing the best way he knew how — jumping to her drawing table for a reward and whisking away in the flick of his tail.

Whenever possible my sister likes to have models before her as she draws, but there have been no whales, lions, giraffes or sea serpents in our studio, or rarely any of the other animals found in *Animals of the Bible*. Photographs and animal anatomies had to help her construct those she could not find even in zoos. But for leviathan she relied upon her own vivid imagination. This book came after many years of careful study and drawing from nature. I think that it has one of the finest sets of drawings that she has ever done — a worthy recipient of the Caldecott Medal.

Between the making of books she has turned to wood engraving and has already won four prizes for her prints. She enjoys the cutting of the blocks and finds it a satisfaction to have the whole process from the making of the drawing to the pulling of the print from the block under her own hand. As in her books, most of her subjects have been little creatures in their natural environment — a flying squirrel in snow-capped pine branches, a couple of little red efts among rock ferns and grey lichen cups, and a snail with a group of Indian pipes towering above it. One of the most technically excellent and exquisite is that of a fantail gold-fish with its delicate, transparent tail floating across the pebbles and weeds of the aquarium. I remember thinking that this print would never be finished, for dozens of proofs were pulled and correction after correction made before she was satisfied to go ahead with the laborious task of making each print of the edition of one hundred and fifty by hand. As a result each print was as perfect as all the others.

Her life's work has been the making of books for children. She has never wanted to draw down to a child, giving him only the crude outlines which are all that he, with his limited experience and skill, is capable of producing — a practice so much the fashion these days. She has always felt that a child with his fresh vision sees more detail than we any longer remember to observe. How often a little boy, looking at one of our flying squirrels, has exclaimed, " What big eyes he has! Look at the tiny little nails on his fingers! His tail is just like a feather, isn't it?" And again, " How soft he looks! Will he mind if I touch him?" The greatest compliment, my sister says, that she ever received was when a child, looking at a drawing of one of these little squirrels, reached out and stroked the pictured fur.

Let Them Live was the outgrowth of her concern for the

creatures so hard pressed in a world which men feel belongs only to them. She has an intense desire to present animals in all the fascination of their own animal personalities and ways. I cannot help feeling that thousands of children who never have the opportunity of meeting face to face the creatures who dwell all around them in the woods and fields, are richer in their knowledge of them and their lives because of her books. Perhaps, remembering her pictures, some children will stay their hands and let their fellow creatures live. Perhaps some child may even remember that a turtle's legs are short and his steps are slow and will help him to cross the road in safety. That would please her, I know, much more than any praise of her drawings. That would make her feel that the countless hours at her drawing board had been worth while.

Mei Li

illustrated by THOMAS HANDFORTH

written by THE ILLUSTRATOR

published by DOUBLEDAY 1938

FORMAT

SIZE: 9″ x 12″, 52 pp. (unfolioed)

ARTIST'S MEDIUM: Brush and lithograph pencil

PRINTING PROCESS: Letterpress

ILLUSTRATIONS: Front matter, full-page and double-page spreads in black and white

TYPE: 18 pt. Weiss

BOOK NOTE

MEI Li goes with her brother to the New Year's Day Fair in Peking from their home in North China. The fun they had the whole day through is pictured until they ride out the city gates on camels with Uncle Wang in time to greet the Kitchen God at midnight.

ACCEPTANCE PAPER

by *Thomas Handforth*

The Story of "Mei Li"

For six years I lived in Peking, in part of a large old house which had belonged to a Chinese mandarin. It was a handsome house of grand and noble proportions, though falling into decay. To reach the part of the house which I occupied, consisting of one main courtyard and several smaller ones, it was necessary to pass, from the street, through four immense fortress-like gates. Faded red lacquered columns supported the gray tiled roofs of its paper-windowed living-rooms, which faced on the central courtyard. Tall trees shaded the paved court which on many a day was the setting for what appeared to be a one-ring circus.

Sword dancers, stiltwalkers, jugglers and archers were there, come to pose as models for the etchings and lithographs which I was making. Even camels came to have their portraits drawn, and the lowly donkey, and shaggy Mongol ponies. When it was too cold for me to sketch out-of-doors, the animals sat for their portraits in the great room which had once been a mandarin's reception hall.

Itinerant boy actors were to be seen there too. Like the puppet players and minstrels of China, they wander about from town to town, from house to house, performing little plays from Chinese folklore. Some of them, dressed as lions, would caper about the courtyard. One small boy whom I often sketched was a sword dancer. He would look at the drawing that I was doing of him, and, closing his fist, and pointing his thumb in the air in approval, would exclaim, "Hao! hao! Y ding hao kan!" meaning "Good! good! indeed good looking!"

Then he would study the drawing more critically.

" The eyes must have more spark, like this! " he would say, raising his eyebrows and showing the whites of his eyes.

" And the head must be more erect, like this! " he would say, throwing up his chin, with his little body fixed rigidly in an attitude of violent action. After all he was a sword dancer and proud of his profession though only nine years old. His two broadswords which he handled simultaneously were as large as himself. He knew better than I how they should be held, and hold them he did. He posed extremely well. His endurance in keeping still, and his patience, was certainly much greater than that of any American child of his age. The same was true of almost all the children who posed for me, and of the adults too.

A little girl acrobat, who is in many of my pictures, would amuse herself, when she was supposed to be having a rest, and no one was paying any attention to her, by tying herself up in the most amazing knots. Before I went to the Orient, I thought that the life of a child contortionist must be a pitiful existence, but I learned that in China, at least, the child acrobat enjoys his most difficult stunts.

The husky wrestlers, too, like the little sword dancer, have definite ideas about how they should appear in pictures. At temple fairs, where they wrestle, they rush at each other like bulls and sway about, exaggerating with grunts and groans their efforts to throw each other. Between their bouts they strut around with a tough dare-devil air, selling black pills the size of pigeons' eggs to give one strength like theirs. But when it comes to having their portraits painted, that is a different story! In pictures they insist upon sporting the largest fans that can be bought in the market place.

A pretty, slender girl, who sang in a tea house, in a flowered silk gown, consented to sit to me. She kept her appointment, but she was no longer slender. She had rather the shape of a sack of potatoes, having put on, for the sake of decorum, one padded robe over another, the outer one being of faded blue cotton. To get down to the inner layer of flowered silk, the price for posing went up with each padded garment removed.

But the surest way of winning the confidence and coöperation of these already cheerful people was to serve them plenty of tea, and to jolly them along with some foolish clownish acts, such as a Charlie Chaplin walk, or slapstick farce. It always brought a laugh even when performed by an odd foreigner who made drawings.

I wanted to bring all these friends of mine together in a picture book for children, but could not decide who should play the leading rôle. Then I met Mei Li. She assumed such importance, which she rightly deserved, as the leading lady, that she crowded many of my other friends out of the story. She was that kind of a girl.

During the famine in Anhwei Province, Mei Li, then an infant, had been left on the doorstep of a missionaries' home, and had spent the second year of her life in an American mission foundling asylum. Then she was adopted by a rich American lady-bountiful, and lived for two years in a luxurious home in Peking.

When the American lady found it necessary to come to the United States for a year she sensibly realized that it was an opportune moment, since Mei Li would have to spend most of her life in China anyway, to give the child a season of hardening to immune her from the dangers of Chinese germs, before she was reclaimed for her life of luxury and American sanitation.

Mei Li was left in the care of the wife of a poor gardener to play in the dust of a tiny courtyard, and to sleep on the large brick Kang which was used by the whole family. The house was seldom heated, even in the bitter cold of the North China winter, except by the clay cook stove in the one room of the house. And did Mei Li thrive on it! Sheathed in her thick padded garments, the cold and the brick bed had no terrors for her.

Often I went to see her, and, at the gate in the gray wall on the narrow lane in which she lived, Mei Li's pets, a dusty little duck and a pinkish white little dog, would greet me, standing together with just their heads peeping over the gate-sill. Whatever the hour of the day, tea was offered me by Mei Li's nurse and I stayed to gossip with her friends and neighbors who might be there: the wife of the ricksha man, the cabbage-vendor and the night watch-man. When the coalman stopped, Mei Li had intent conversa-tions with his camels, when he didn't she talked to her dusty duck. But most of her time was spent in managing the large family upon whom she had been deposited. No Empress Dowager was ever more determined than she. A career is surely ordained for her, other than being the heroine of a children's book.

Mei Li needed no urging to play this star rôle. Before long she was running the whole show. She brought her own little girl friends to be drawn, and the small boy San Yu, son of the ricksha man, and her pinkish white puppy, but if they ever weakened in this job of posing she would give them a piece of her mind.

For a long time I searched for just the right type of woman who might have been Mei Li's mother. At last after my servant too had made many futile efforts to find a person such as I de-scribed, he brought to the house a peasant woman who had just that day come from the country looking for employment. She was exactly what I wanted, but most women of her kind would have been too shy or modest to have even entered the house of a foreigner. It was Mei Li who made her feel at home, and gave her hints on behavior in an artist's studio.

The old priest in the picture book was my own lucky discovery. I noticed him just as he was disappearing in a crowd near one of the city gates. In his crazy-quilt robes, with his thick horn-rimmed spectacles slipping down his thin nose, and a large glass jewel in his black hat, he seemed to have just stepped out of an ancient Chinese scroll. He was too good to be true. As he stared vacantly at the sky, and dreamily waved his horsehair fly brush, he was like a mythical being, far, too far removed from earthly matters to ever find the address on the card which I gave him. But he arrived at my house the next day, hours before he was expected, pleased as a child, to have his picture drawn.

The toys with which Mei Li plays are personages from Chinese folklore, among them the eight immortals. There is a ninth im-mortal too, but no one knows what he looks like, for each time that he visits the earth to go about amongst the people, he assumes a different guise. If one is polite to him he will bring that person good luck. If one is discourteous, misfortune follows. It behooves one to be courteous to everybody.

And so my little models were always polite. They asked me my honorable name, my honorable age, and the honorable cost of everything in the house.

AUTOBIOGRAPHICAL PAPER

by *Thomas Handforth*

Personal Progress Toward the Orient

My progress to the Orient began apparently with my first baby steps and observations. I was born in Tacoma and spent my childhood on the Pacific Coast. I had, as early as I can remember, instinctively turned toward the East. At the age of three my favorite outing was to be taken to the lily pond in Point Defiance Park and to be allowed to climb alone across the rustic Japanese half-moon bridge. The perilous ascent and descent of its slippery slopes should have been excitement enough for any three-year-old, but for me the great experience was the sight of the arc's reflection in the lily pond forming the other half of the perfect circle. A perfect circle divided by a wave — a symbol of which I did not know the meaning, but which was soon to become familiar to me in its prosaic use as the insignia of the Northern Pacific Railway — the symbol of the Yin and Yang, the negative and positive atoms of all matter interlocked in the Ta Y, the Great Universal.

I had begun to draw even before I went to kindergarten, and at the age of seven or eight, when I was using a real artist's sketchbook, the Yin-Yang circle occurs on one of its first pages, with Chinese characters used also as magic symbols. They are followed by a page of dragons, then a Buddha in a landscape setting, copied from one of my books of Japanese fairy tales, which were dearer to me than those of Andersen or Grimm; then portraits of two Japanese dolls whose smooth and subtly smiling faces were fixed in the imagery of my childhood. One of my best efforts at realism at this time is a memory sketch in water color of three blue-gowned pigtailed Chinamen whom I had seen on a trip to Victoria, British Columbia. There were no Chinese in Tacoma, they had been driven out and their possessions burned on the tide-flats about the year that I was born. The Chinese smugglers' cave alone remained and into it I used to peer with childish fascination. It was said to continue through the hills to the sea — perhaps to China itself.

But my horizon was not to be bounded by China and Japan alone. In that first sketchbook are drawings of Egyptian pyramids and sphinxes and of far-away lands of my own creation. I conceived the idea of an immense *opus* upon which I worked intermittently until my tenth year. It was left unfinished, but I find myself working on one volume of it again at the present time. The title page proclaimed it to be " A Great, Marvelous, Misterious Circus of Birds, Beasts, Animals, Insects and *Beings* from a Far Off Planet! " I declined to have the voyages of my imagination limited to the mere oceans and continents of the geography book.

A copy in my drawing book of Hokusai's famous blue-wave expresses the same sentiment. The wave sweeps across the page in a long arc, a segment of that greater circle of the Yin and Yang, carrying one out into worlds beyond worlds. This print was my favorite of all the work of the Japanese Ukeyoie school, which I came to know at that time, thanks to Miss Katherine Ball of San Francisco, who did so much to stimulate an interest, especially among the school children of this city, in the decorative arts of the Far East. She gave a series of lectures on the Japanese printmakers to a group of club women in Tacoma and I managed to slip in behind my mother's flaring skirts of 1907.

I was very happy to meet Miss Ball again in 1934 when she spent a winter in Peking, and to be able to tell her that her talks, which the club ladies probably considered very mild afternoon diversions, had profoundly affected the whole course of my life. Now I was able to identify two little volumes which had come to me from a great-uncle who had served under General Gordon in the Taiping rebellion and had become a Chinese mandarin. These volumes were very old reprints of Hokusai's well-known *One Hundred Views of Mt. Fujiyama*. This series of little *genre* pictures of little human beings of the soil carrying on their myriad transient activities against a background of Nature, of which they remained as much an inseparable part as the leaf on the tree or the snow on the peak of Mt. Fuji, had for me a spirit which later I was ever trying to recapture in my own work.

My summers, as I grew up, were spent in wanderings about the Puget Sound country and I was never without my sketchbooks. The pine-serried hills, the snow-capped peaks, the irregular sea with its many islands insistently recalled those prints of Hokusai and those of Hiroshige. On the ocean coast of the Olympic peninsula, the great jagged rocks, jutting up from the foam-flecked sea, and striped with ribbons of mist, seemed to be a continuation of one of these masters' landscapes.

The Indians of the Far West, too, were a link with the Orient. Their totem poles, their masks, the Thunderbird and the Lightning Serpent, as we now know, have a close affinity not only with the Mayan art of this continent but with the earliest Chinese ideology. In the dream-world of my childhood they had already been fused into one.

After graduating from high school and before my one year at the University of Washington I had decided upon my profession and was trying to learn to paint. It was a rather precious period of jade and ivory towers and yellow furniture; one admired especially Edmund Dulac and Aubrey Beardsley and Kay Nielsen and the then modern Viennese decoration. During this period I painted my one and only mural — a Chinese fantasy with much Dulac influence, and produced my one and only ballet, based on the Babylonian story of Ishtar and Tamuz. I not only did the sets and costumes and arranged the choreography but danced in the chorus. It was one of my few reprehensible outbursts in this form of expression — an urge which I have since managed to preserve discreetly in the category of a suppressed desire. To the dance of others, however, I have remained one of the most ardent of devotees and have recently been investigating its various forms in India.

The first esoteric dancing that I had seen as a small child was that of Raymond Duncan, originally from San Francisco, as you know, and his wife, who were touring America in their sandals and homespun robes. Their two-year-old son, Nicoliades, also in Greek robes and sandals, was with them. Fifteen years later in Paris Raymond Duncan reported to the police that his son was lost. He described him as a youth of surpassing beauty and perfect harmony. Nicoliades was found a week later in a little café seated between two Parisian *midinettes* and dressed in vulgar modern clothes. He was on a spree – enjoying the novelty of behaving like an average youth for once.

After the mural and the Babylonian ballet I went to the San Francisco Fair of 1915 upon which legend has bestowed the epithet: the most beautiful of all expositions. For me, sentiment if not justice will always concede it that distinction. New realms of European and American art were opened up before me. However, I find myself still most absorbed in things Oriental; my notebooks record: in water color, the great green and gold Dibutsu of the Japanese pavilion against a hot blue sky; *motifs* of Chinese design seen here and there, and the curved roofs of San Francisco's Chinatown.

The curved roof, by the way, has utilitarian value, as well as esthetic, since it helps prevent malignant spirits from falling upon people. The spirits, who are fond of sliding down roofs like small boys sliding down a banister, are shot unexpectedly up into the air again by the curve at the roof edge.

While here I went timidly to Gump's wondering how much I might be able to see before I was earmarked as an unwelcome non-purchaser. To my astonishment cases of rarest porcelains were opened for me, to feel the textures of Sung celadon and white, of Peach bloom and Ox Blood Ming ware, and the fine " famille verte " porcelains of Kanghsi. On that day one youth became an amateur if not a collector of Chinese ceramics.

About two years later in New York, I saw Benrimo's play *The Yellow Jacket*, a production inspired by San Francisco's Chinatown theatre. It made a most vivid impression upon me. By what simple means the imagination of the spectator was stimulated! Four square stools placed in a row made a flower boat upon which the luscious maiden "Autumn Cloud" reclined with the august prince, Wu Hoo Git, beside her. The indifferent property-man went through the gestures of propelling the boat with a long bamboo pole across the 'most unworthy' stage while he complacently smoked a cigarette. The tremulous and scraping tones emitted by the orchestra, back center stage, suggested the lapping of wavelets and the crackling of reeds against the flower boat. Yet a picture of exquisite beauty was evoked. In another scene two stools were placed upon two tables to make a lofty mountain top over which the august prince dragged himself, while a snowstorm of white confetti, thrown by the supposedly invisible property-man, encircled his sublime legs and impeded his progress. Quite without naturalistic technique the essence of the mountain snowstorm was there before one's eyes.

Of the two principal techniques in Chinese painting one is called Hsieh Y, "to write the meaning." It is a technique related to the calligraphic and is employed by poets and therefore considered the highest form. The brush is used freely as in writing, the very pressure of the brush upon the paper, the shape of the stroke of ink, expressing the quality of the subject. Again, as in the theatre, it is the essence rather than the representation of a specific object that is being sought.

When Kenneth Hayes Miller, with whom I studied painting for a brief time, used to urge us to paint "the cosmic essence of white" or our "inner consciousness of blue," perhaps he was trying to lead us toward the same goal. But at the age of twenty I couldn't digest a precept in that form. I just didn't get it. It was easier for me to understand another of my teachers, Mahonri Young, when he said, "Draw the space about the figure rather than the figure itself."

Most of my training in draughtsmanship in New York and at the École des Beaux Arts in Paris was completely academic. Each week one did a charcoal drawing of a nude model on a large sheet of paper, beginning at 9 o'clock on Monday morning, with the head at the top of the page and finishing at the bottom of the page with the feet at exactly noon on Saturday. I often wonder how I survived it. I used to flee from the *ateliers* of Paris to the Cathedral at Chartres, seeking consolation in those quixotic faces of Gothic sculpture, smooth and subtly smiling faces, now of Madonnas instead of Japanese dolls; in those elongated figures of Gothic sculpture with tenuous flowing lines of drapery which were quickened into flame-like shapes of fresh exaltation; sharp flaming movements which come to one again in the fifth century Wei sculpture of China when Buddhism made its first impact upon the Far East.

In Paris, the Expressionists, the Cubists and the Dadaists, who were the parents of the Surrealists, were holding the center of the stage. The tender pathetic boy Harlequins of Picasso's "blue period" appealed to me especially — adolescent, supple bodies balancing upon spheres, or stepping out from groups of circus people, or in compositions with strong prancing horses. The cool sharp line of some of the modern French engravers I admired too, but I suspected many of the Modernists of being preoccupied with their manner rather than with the animating spirit. And so I welcomed the opportunity of hearing the opinions of an unbiased critic: Dr. James Cousins, who had just come from India. Some of you may remember him from his lectures given here in 1931 and '33. A large part of his life had been devoted to encouraging the so-called new renaissance in India, but for sixteen years he had been completely out of touch with the European trend. He had come to Paris to assemble a collection of contemporary Western painting for the Maharaja of Mysore, but the names and styles of even the better known Modernist painters were unknown to him. I was enlightened by his reactions, for he was always able to select without guidance examples of those painters of the ultra-modern school who were recognized as significant by the West, since, he said, they had something fundamentally in common in their abstract qualities with the great traditions of the East.

However, my interests were in present aspects of life, call it journalistic if you will, and not with the abstract or theories concerning it.

The first painter with whom I came in contact who was able

to interpret successfully the living scene, using an Eastern style of painting, was a Georgian friend of mine named Goudiachvili, which means radish. He reveled in the life of the moment, in the scenes of the cafés, in the festivities of the people, in the cabbies and their carriages and the girls of his native town of Tiflis. Yet he painted these scenes in his traditional native style which had come directly from Persia.

With Mr. Radish in mind, and Persia, and also thinking of the adventures in ports, and of what a life was that of a sailor, and a lot of other ideas muddled in my head, I sailed from Marseilles to Tunis. I had intended to go to Ragusa but I missed the boat. It really did not matter where I went. I hoped to be amused. I was hilariously so, especially while trying to etch it all on copper. From Tunis I went to Morocco. Then I jumped back to the Great Northwest, to the somber silent coast of Vancouver Island and I recalled my first love, Hokusai. Then to Mexico, breathtakingly magnificent and barbaric — and I found that Diego Rivera was doing on a grand scale and in his own manner what Hokusai had achieved in his little wood block prints. I started to do a series of etchings which were to have been called The One Hundred Views of Mt. Popocatepetl. Eleven of them were completed when I was awarded in 1931 a Guggenheim Fellowship for travel in the Orient.

I am sure that you are finding it difficult to follow my grasshopper leaps from place to place and are being quite confused by my vagueness concerning the time element. But I hope, before I finish, to have brought you to the point where the time and place no longer matter.

I sailed on a freighter which took a month and a day from New York to Yokohama and the one other passenger on board was a baker from Trenton. There were long hours to hang over the rail and wonder what I was going to do with the Orient or what it would do with me. As you may guess, I had, during my grasshopper leaps, dropped into a good many ports, both on the Atlantic and on the Pacific shores, in the Mediterranean and on the North African Coast. A collection of sketches of these ports had begun to accumulate and it seemed to me that it would be a worthy aim to continue on the same sort of theme, making a sequence of impressions of Ports of the World. Also I wanted to see more of the Dances of the World: in Java, Bali, and India. I would stop in Japan only long enough to corroborate the knowledge which I thought I already had of that country's arts.

Japan, with its passion for the perfection of arrangement, turned out to look exactly as it was expected to appear. Aside from its blatant scars of western modernization, every view in front of one, or behind, might be of Hiroshige's pictures. After all, too much was enough. Such perfectly ordered and regulated nature was unreasonable.

In the homes of the potters of Kyoto, where each family for generations had specialized in the manufacture of some special ware, one sat for restive hours while the brothers and the cousins and the fathers and the aunts discussed the decoration on a simple dish; whether the stroke of the flower stem should turn slightly more toward the right or slightly more toward the left. For business reasons, of course, it was important, because the dish was to be sold as an original Chinese piece of the 11th century!

At the Miyako Hotel I met the John Alden Carpenter family who had just come from Peking. They were all enthusiasm.

"You must go as quickly as you can to Peking," said Mrs. Carpenter. "It is inexhaustible! Peking is inexhaustible!"

"No," said I. "I am traveling to do a series of pictures of ports of the world. No more tinkling temple bells for me, thank you. Nor ivory pagodas, nor porcelain ones either, thank you. One must beware of these lands of sweet and pretty dreams — these lands of exotic fantasy. I want to be a waterfront rat and see life as it really is."

I was stubborn and went to Shanghai.

A few weeks later, on a humid drizzling day in May, I was passing by the American Express Offices near that Shanghai Bund which was already beginning to pall upon me, when I noticed a crowd of coolies gathered about a foreign lady who was having an argument — the usual one — with her ricksha man, and threatening him with her umbrella. I stepped up to watch how this financial disagreement would be settled. The foreign lady saw me and stopped with upraised umbrella. Then the blow fell, not on the ricksha man, but upon me.

" What are you doing here! " screamed the lady in good American. " Didn't I tell you to go to Peking? " It was Mrs. Carpenter. " Get out of this town at once! You go to Peking tomorrow! "

The next day I took the train to Peking.

Within the thick walls of Peking is a city which, as Mrs. Carpenter had said, is inexhaustible. Mystery, intrigue and international modernity mingle with its crumbling culture. Fabulous Ming palaces are hidden behind new little Japanese shops. A cloud of black crows flies over the yellow roofs of the Forbidden City, while cosmopolites dance on the roof garden of the French hotel to the American music of the Russian orchestra. On the dance floor might be seen a boyish Chinese woman dressed in dinner jacket and trousers from Bond Street, or in military uniform. She had become a major in the army of the notorious war lord Chang Sung-ch'iang for her services as procuress of concubines. Below on the broad avenue by the hotel, among the motor cars and rickshas, pass camels and herds of sheep and squealing pigs, and near the avenue in the hollow of a tree live two old wrinkled beggars. The smell of the dust of the Gobi Desert is in the air, the smell of caravans and of trade routes to Mongolia, Turkestan and India.

Within the walls of the Legation Quarters diplomats move complacently about from dinner party to dinner party like goldfish in an aquarium, and Chinese political offenders seek sanctuary in the German hospital. Foreigners ride Mongol ponies through the pine groves by the Temple of Heaven, whose conical blue-tiled roof is supported by pillars of Douglas pine brought from Oregon. Beside the temple is the circular white marble Altar of Heaven, so perfect in design and intention that one may stand there face to face with the Universe or dance upon it as Ruth St. Denis did. Yet around the borders of that same sacred precinct is a ditch so foul in its stench that even mangy, refuse-seeking dogs avoid it. Near the entrance to those grounds, elderly gentlemen in robes of snow-lavender velvet or moon-white gauze congregate with their birds in lacquer cages and their crickets in ivory boxes. Across the road gather a much larger throng of young and old to watch the public executions. Farther along in a dust-blown square are the coolie entertainers: jugglers, wrestlers and contortionists, men with strong-bows, and wandering child actors and lithe young acrobats with smooth and subtly smiling faces and yet, too, like Picasso's pathetic Harlequins, who here become, in these dusty streets, a part of the daily scene.

In the shade of pine trees by the Palace moat may be seen, at the propitious hours, old scholars teaching young boys the slowly postured movements of the T'ai Chi, an ancient dance especially suitable for people who read books, since it harmonizes and soothes the spirit. And gray uniformed soldiers might have been seen there too, dancing the equally ancient Woo Shoo, suitable for those who do not read books and who want to harmonize the body. Like figures from the Russian ballet they swing their flashing broadswords now to the terror of the Japanese soldiers, who wear iron collars to preserve their necks.

Mongols in greasy red brocades stomp the streets in their heavy leather boots, but those fragile Manchu girls with their ivory-white and pink complexions and flower-decked headdresses seldom appear now in their glass carriages. The mechanical canary in its gilded cage has been carried away with the other Palace treasures; the old eunuchs of the place have retired to a temple in the Hills; bolts of tribute silks and satins, and furs from the store rooms of the Palace are sold publicly on Sunday mornings, and mandarin robes are dragged in the dust of the old clothes market. When the iron-bossed gates of the city are barred and bolted for the night, the antique dealers from London and Berlin will sit up until dawn over their wine cups, with Chinese merchants, dividing the spoils of a newly opened grave, and in the icy bitterness of morning, beggars will be found frozen to death in the streets.

Gentlemen of the Embassies play the ancient game of polo on the drill grounds of the International Guard, and students from the universities, demonstrating against the Japanese, are driven bruised and bleeding from the city by the police. Funeral and wedding processions continuously block the traffic of the teeming thoroughfares — funeral processions in which officiate not only Taoists and Buddhist priests, but Lama priests and sometimes Christian clergymen as well. Being a practical people, the Chinese neglect no aids to getting on in the next world.

In the New Year season, graceful modern youth skates upon the artificial lakes of the Empress Dowager's Winter Park, and in the heat of summer white cranes stand sentinel there amongst the lotus. The sweating coolie, naked to the waist, slakes his thirst with the green striped melon freshly cut, and sleek-haired, blue-gowned women spit sunflower seeds from the balcony of the tea house.

In the spring a Manchu prince sits in his garden under a flowering crab-apple tree painting on a silken scroll, in an idiom of a thousand years ago, a nostalgic dream of mountain gorges and waterfalls. The garden is so planned that one never sees the end of it, even though it may be in the heart of the city and surrounded by a high wall. A vista of water in a valley of volcanic rocks like abstract sculpture will make a sudden turn behind a screen of artificial mountains at the foot of the garden, leading one to believe that the valley continues on indefinitely.

Young modern China is learning from American moving pictures that being modern means to kiss girls in the park. Still, in spite of the cinema, the classical drama has remained by far the more popular form of theatrical entertainment, and the female impersonator has remained a most interesting example of the Chinese point of view in the art of the theatre.

Chinese impresarios and directors of the theatre will tell you that an actress could never play a feminine rôle in the traditional drama as convincingly as a female impersonator. The boys who are to play these rôles are trained by the severest discipline from earliest childhood. They spend hours every day walking on short stilts to learn to mimic the lily-step of the bound foot. Their voices are trained in a high falsetto, and every gesture of delicacy

and grace is acquired. Their very faces are altered by the temporary face-lifting operation of stretching back the skin under the
headdress with bandages. Artifice here produces an effect of
femininity which no woman could rival, even though she should
have the same training, for she being merely a woman would in
her heart believe, no doubt, that being *feminine* was sufficient.

Neither on the stage nor in painting nor in sculpture does
allegory enter into the Chinese scheme of life interpretation.
Nothing would seem more ridiculous to them than a Rubens nude
representing " Virtue," or a marble by Rodin called " Harmony,"
or a fresco by Michelangelo representing " Peace." These qualities are not to be abstracted from the scheme of the great Universal.

Although the Chinese are especially fond of pictures of babies
one almost never sees motherhood portrayed. I personally cannot
recall ever having seen a Madonna painting by a Chinese artist.
Yet *motifs* of little children at play are most popular: the well-
known " one hundred babies " pattern is repeatedly used on textiles, ceramics, wallpapers and metal objects of art. But most
often the baby is associated with old men, with venerable and
happy old age finding immortality in the child — a continuous
flow of life without end, the convoluting circle of the Yin and
Yang.

The use of the nude in art is limited solely to the pornographic,
to the Ch'ün Hua or Spring Pictures which were used for instruction for those newly wedded. In these albums which were often
the work of some of the best artists, so little concern was given to
the correct observation of anatomy that the figures look more
often like sawdust-stuffed dolls than humans. They have no
sensuous quality whatever. They may become involved in estheti-
cally exciting patterns, but they remain manikins substituted for
the observer of the picture who becomes subjective in it, and
whose senses under such a situation would be keyed to a sharper
perception of things. One sees and feels more keenly under the
tension of the instant, suddenly becoming more sensitively aware
of the environment, focusing on the setting of the action. Every
detail of the sleeping chamber, or of the library, or the latticed

porch, or the nook in the rock garden now stands out in crystal clarity. One of the best records which exists of Ming period houses, of the arrangement and decoration of rooms, of the furniture and bric-a-brac, is from the illustrations of the erotic novel, the Hung Lou Meng — *The Dream of the Red Chamber;* and from other albums of pornography which were produced in quantity, much authentic documentation is to be derived concerning the modes and manners of the various epochs.

All the houses in Peking face south. They consist of separate one-story pavilions built around courtyards, the number of courtyards depending upon the size or wealth of the family. I rented a section, which in itself consisted of several courtyards, of one of these large old houses. The last Chinese occupant had been an official who had been active in the Boxer uprising. He had been obliged to flee and the house had been turned over by the Chinese government to an English mission school for the blind. From the mission it had been purchased by an English resident of Peking. It was a handsome house but in an advanced stage of decay. For six years I made it my home. Then came the China Incident.

For several seasons Japanese war planes had been swooping down over the houses of the city. Japanese troops had been indulging in sham battles at the most unexpected hours in the most unexpected places on the streets and the populace had courteously refrained from showing its feelings. Then the cannons began to rumble, and the rumble came closer and closer to the walls. Streets were sandbagged and trenches dug and the Chinese soldiers courteously retired from the city, leaving their dying and wounded to be picked up and washed and bandaged by the ladies and gentlemen of the foreign colony. With the streets lined by Japanese school children and hired coolies waving red-spotted white flags, the victorious army of the Mikado entered the Celestial City.

Then the most unworthy Peace Preservation Corps of the Autonomous State of Hopei and Chihli courteously massacred the entire honorable Japanese colony of four hundred men, women and children at T'ung cho twenty miles from Peking. After that we knew little of what was happening; newspapers were suppressed, there was no rail, telegraph or radio communication even with the port of Tientsin: when trains did reach Tientsin they took twenty hours instead of the normal two and a half. It seemed to me it was a very good time to take that long-postponed trip to India, and so, sealing my etching and lithograph presses into a hidden passageway in the six-foot-thick wall of my house, I went to Japan to catch a boat for India.

My departure from Japan was delayed because instead of going to the steamship office I went each day to sit on padded matting floors before the golden screens of the Buddhist temples of Kyoto, golden screens which told a story of centuries of tender, warm communion between man and nature. Here on these gold leaf screens were the chrysanthemum and the cicada, the flight of heron, the tiger drinking at the pool, the pine tree and eagle, the fish in the spray of the waterfall.

Behind the tranquil images of Buddha in these temples are auras of quick, sharp flames which had come from India to Gandara, Miran, Turfan, Tung Huan, through China and to Japan in the 7th century, burning with a freshly kindled life and awakening the spirits of the men in the lands through which they had passed, and bringing with them a passionate creative activity in the arts.

The symbols of Buddhism are here, too: the lotus, the elephant, the conch shell, the palm leaf scriptures, the ceremonial umbrella, the drums and lutes of the heavenly musicians, and the floating, wing-like scarfs of the Apsaras — all *motifs* which had come from tropical South India with those quick flames which encircle the contemplative Buddha.

Now I was about to go to the source of these symbols and to the source of Buddhistic art. At the steamship office I bought a passage to Colombo, southern port of India.

About a year ago I was alone in the temple of the Kailasa in the rock caves of Ellora in the State of Hyderabad in India. The Kailasa represents the peak of Brahman art; as one might say, Chartres Cathedral does of the Gothic. It is one of the caves excavated in the eighth century in the side of a solid rock escarpment which rises abruptly from a broad sun-bleached plain. About thirty other caves, some of them Buddhist and Jain, as well as Brahman, extend along the side of the cliff for a mile and a quarter. To approach the caves one climbs up narrow footpaths and rock-cut steps from the road below.

An emaciated Mohammedan guide with a chartreuse turban and squeaking imitation English shoes, had attached himself to me. Since he did not speak a word of English nor I of Hindustani we might have gotten along, if it had not been for his squeaky shoes. He was trying to sell me some postcard views of the caves. He seemed to insinuate that I would do better if I bought his postcards, and sat myself down comfortably under the shade of a tree and looked at them, rather than drag myself wearily around from cave to cave, merely to make sure that all the caves were there. Besides, I might have been kind enough to relieve him at once of the necessity of camping on my trail and torturing his feet in those ill-fitting shoes until he made a sale. In desperation I bought his pictures hoping to get rid of him. But when he saw that I was still determined to climb to all the caves, he thought I was mad, or else a suspicious character, and dogged every step I made. Where I looked he looked, when I looked at him he looked at me and squeaked his shoes. Simple gestures, meant to signify that he might remove his presence, made no impression. The only sign language which he understood was a hefty push down the steep trail which we had just ascended. At last I was alone.

For about ten days previously I had been living with those bright-eyed, happy children at the Theosophical College at Madanapalle. One evening at the headmaster's house their Hindu teacher of philosophy had been telling me that the only moments of real happiness for him were those when he was able to pierce the illusion of his individual separateness of existence — when he was able to identify the atoms of which he was composed with the atoms of the things about him, such as the table at which we were sitting, for instance.

I thought of the Chinese, who, being a reasonable people, sought to pierce the illusion through their art. The Hindus being an unreasonable people sought to escape more directly. But after all, it wasn't such a far cry from William Blake trying to find himself in the soul of a flea.

Now I was alone in the Kailasa with all the images of the cosmogony of the South Indian world about me, carven from the living rock; rows of stone elephants supported the temple, birds and flowers of stone adorned its roof. There must have been a flea carved in stone somewhere, but I didn't see it. On the walls danced cobra-headed demons, and slim-waisted, large-hipped goddesses; and the skeletous Kali, goddess of Vengeance, danced there too. Beside his consort Parvati, the four-armed Shiva danced his cosmic dance, creating the world with his rhythm and destroying it again by his own vibration. His face was *not* subtly smiling, but transfixed — immobile — expressionless as a mirror of polished stone.

Suddenly I felt strangely to be part of the dance. I was merely one vibration of it, yet all its vibrations were within me. Timelessness and spacelessness enveloped me. Nothing seemed to matter, not even next month's rent, or working wages, or totalitarian states. This, I suppose, was cosmic consciousness — about six seconds of it.

One might, perhaps, experience a similar six seconds without ever leaving Tacoma.

(On October 19, 1948, Thomas Handforth died in Los Angeles. On October 19, 1950, The Horn Book, Inc. published an Extra Issue devoted entirely to Thomas Schofield Handforth, Artist, Illustrator, Author. It contains a biographical paper by Carolyn Anne Schneider. Copies of this Extra Issue are still available.)

THE CALDECOTT AWARD 1940

Abraham Lincoln

illustrated by INGRI AND EDGAR D'AULAIRE

written by THE ILLUSTRATORS

published by DOUBLEDAY 1939

FORMAT

SIZE: 8½" x 12", 56 pp. (unfolioed)

ARTISTS' MEDIUM: Lithographic pencil on stone

PRINTING PROCESS: Offset lithography

ILLUSTRATIONS: Front matter, full-page and many smaller illustrations in five colors and in black and white

TYPE: Baskerville

BOOK NOTE

THE story of Abraham Lincoln's life from his birth in the lonely log cabin until his years in the White House is told briefly in text and generously in pictures.

ACCEPTANCE PAPER

by *Ingri* and *Edgar Parin d'Aulaire*

Working Together
on Books for Children

i: *by* INGRI PARIN D'AULAIRE

MR. Melcher, Members of the Committee, American Library Association! We thank you very much for the great honor you have bestowed upon us. We are deeply touched and very thankful and would only wish we could say "proud." At any other time of our lives we would have been so proud it would almost have burst our hides that the children's librarians of America have selected our *Abraham Lincoln* amongst all the other beautiful books for their Caldecott Medal. But the present moment is hardly a moment for personal pride, with half of our world in flames and everything that we have been taught to stand up for as right and just in danger of extermination.

But just for this reason the Medal means more to us at this moment than it would have meant at any other time. The happiness that it has gone to our book on Abraham Lincoln, the shining symbol of democracy, fairness and tolerance, is much more than personal pride. This book perhaps means more to us than any other book we have made. The more we studied Lincoln the closer he came to us, the greater he became, the more necessary for our present life, the closer related to us and our times. At last he was not an historical person any more, but a warm and kind and generous relative who had moved right into our studio with us. We became more and more convinced that if only we could give to our young readers a bit of the feeling we had about Abraham Lincoln we had perhaps done our tiny share to make the world a happier place, when those who are now children have grown up to run the world. And could there be any more sublime feeling for any one who had chosen for his vocation work with children and children's books?

Now, is there any vocation that could be richer and more fulfilling than work for children? You have a public with wide-open ears and eyes, without prejudices, and with a mind ready to be influenced by good or by bad. Grownups are hard to get at. They have their taste already settled; perhaps it is a good taste, perhaps it is a bad one. You just cannot do very much with it. But except for a very short period in every child's life where he has to go through a state of admiration for something that is sweet and pretty, without any inner meaning or relation to life, children have an excellent taste. You can fool grownups, give them something that is skimmed off your own surface, executed with great skill and taste and most will think — that is just wonderful. But you cannot fool a child. If a picture is cold he feels it, however beautiful the surface, and if you want to grasp and hold a child you have to give all there is in you, all your warmth and feeling. And as of course we, as does every other artist, sincerely believe that what we have to give is the only real art, we feel after having finished a book as if we had really done something to help build up society. The little book that we have just finished, we always hope, is going to help build up taste and artistic feeling in thousands of children who own this book, not only for the moment, but for the rest of their lives.

What gives us more hope than anything for the future of this country are the excellent picture books that are done here. Nowhere else in the world does there exist anything that can compare with them. Of course, many beautiful pieces pop up here and there, but those are isolated phenomena. In Europe the old saying still is, " Grownups should have beautiful books; they know how to love and respect them. But who wants to spend much effort or money on a child's book, to be torn and destroyed?" Instead of bringing up a child to respect a book, it is better, they say, to buy him a new one for a few cents, and that is all a children's book should cost.

Here is where all of you present have made your great contribution to American cultural life; and perhaps more than anybody else Miss Anne Carroll Moore, the true pioneer of the golden age of children's books, in which we are living now.

Miss Moore is the initiator of many things; she is also responsible for us. We say now, our life and our biggest pleasure is to make children's books, but she is the one who opened our eyes to it. We were painters, and after a good European art training we must confess that the thought of working for children would have seemed to us a little below our dignity. Edgar was painting murals and doing illustrations for grown-up books; I painted landscapes and portraits, especially children's portraits. As we were very young and unsettled when we were married, we were both very much afraid of becoming influenced by each other. Each kept his work strictly to himself, for we had seen too many married painting couples who painted just alike. We both had a certain respect for the sincerity of the other's work, and what we both had in common was a great interest in children, children's ways and ways of expression, children's art and psychology.

As the youngest child of a great family I was an aunt long before my skirts reached my knees. And being an aunt brings you in quite a different position to the small children of a closely related family than having a string of smaller sisters and brothers trailing you. When you are an aunt at a very young age you get a poise and an authority that very much impress your own friends — you are almost a mother yourself. I loved "my" children very much after having overcome my first jealousy of not being the tiny pet and baby myself any longer, and somehow, my own childhood melted into theirs. Though I was deeply respected and obeyed as an aunt, we spoke the same language. I remembered my childhood ways of thinking and reasoning even after I was grown up. And this has never quite left me. I still remember every one of the more important impressions and reflections ever since I was a little toddler. Perhaps an important factor also is that my own childhood was so very sunny and happy, the memory of which is a joyous and creating well from which I can draw the rest of my life. Perhaps the biggest compliment I have had in all my life came a few years ago when one of my little nieces who was in difficulties turned to me and said: " You explain it to Mother; you are the only grown-up in the whole family who is really sensible."

With Edgar it was the other way around. He had spent his life in a grown-up world, a world of art and serious discussions in Europe's art centers. So when for the first time he came home to my father's great house in Norway, where there were dogs and cats and frolicking children, a new life began for him. He had never before so much as touched a child, and now our six at that time made a ring around him — wasn't he their new uncle, so didn't they own him? As the child's world is close to me, because I never really have stepped out of it, so it is close to Edgar because it came to him like a revelation. With raptured eyes that had never seen children before, he looked at them, learned their plays and ways and even their speech. When he first met them he didn't know a word of Norwegian, so he started out with the one-year-old and learned to speak with her, simply and naturally. From Mother and Father and the necessities of life he graduated up into the bigger children, and after some years with them his vocabulary had grown from the nursery to the drawing room and we two could begin to exchange our thoughts in Norwegian.

Edgar's first violent reaction to the contact with our children never has worn off. From our children his interest spread to other children, though I must admit that every vacation of our married life, first in Paris and then in America, we rushed to Norway and the children. So when Miss Moore dropped the bomb into our lives of asking why we two didn't work together and start making our own children's books, it wasn't a bomb at all, but a match put to a heap of shavings. (We hope the fire started won't be used up for a long time yet.) We went to it. At first it was rather painful to work together. What the one proposed the other was apt to cut out as foolish, hardly willing even to listen. But we fought our ways through the fights and we began to see that perhaps as a unit our two very different selves might be able to express themselves much better than each of us alone, as long as we kept our own individualities and remembered that we were two brains and four hands, not only two half equipments put together.

So during these ten years we have been working together on children's books, we have taken aside half a year between each collaboration and have gone abroad or somewhere to a very different *milieu* from our New York home, where each of us could do his own painting and solve his own problems without the short-cut of discussing them with the other. In this way we could always return fresh to the " company " with new ideas and new outlooks.

A children's book, easy as it seems when finished, isn't only a play. There are months of research, of painstaking study and labor even before we can begin on the book itself. Would you believe that a little book like one of ours is the only output of all the working power of two people for at least a year?

After the whole conception of the book, manuscript and sketches are clear, comes the most important work of making the whole thing seem as if it had grown quite by itself without any work at all. We have worked hard. Nobody could deny that. But what a beautiful work! " Any work that isn't a play is not worth while," said Lawrence, and that is one of our few mottoes in life. So, as about our whole life is work, our whole life is also play. And we have had wonderful help. There are many people whom we have to thank, and without whom none of our books would have been possible, those of our friends who have spent night after night initiating us in writing English, all those who gave us so much of their time to help us collect material and before all, the three to whom we owe most, Anne Carroll Moore, May Massee and Peggy Lesser, who brought us here today.

ii: *by* EDGAR PARIN D'AULAIRE

Some of our friends have been wondering why we two, European born, were choosing American themes for our books, why we didn't stick to our tales of the old world which we know so well. You know that Ingri is Norwegian by birth, I only by re-birth. That is the reason, as they say in Norway, that the combination of us two can present Norway more objectively than any pure Norwegian would be able to. We know and we see Norway from the inside, every corner of it, but we are bound to see it objectively as an exotic country, not as a country of everyday life. So with the American themes. We love this country and we feel ourselves very much like Americans. We are here in this country not because we were born here but because the whole world was ours to choose from and we chose America as our home and our country. We didn't seek shelter here because we had to flee from what till then had been ours, but because this enormous continent with all its possibilities and grandeur appealed to us and caught our imagination. So here we are, with America as the home valley of our realm that stretches all over the globe. This is the country where everything we had in us could be used to its full extent, and where we could fulfill our full measures as human beings and help in building up the world.

We counted as our biggest asset just the fact that our conceptions of our American themes had never been shaped into school *clichés*, which later, through experience, must be overcome. When we started to work on George Washington and Lincoln, we had to approach the subjects as children, studying from the beginning, not hampered by standard conceptions.

Though, when I say that we set out with a purely European background, this is only partly true. From my earliest childhood I remember that the most exciting stories that could be told to me were those which my American mother told me about my grandfather. He was, for a European boy, the incorporation of an American boy with all the romantic attributes of the dangerous wilderness beyond the ocean. He was born in Texas several years after his parents had arrived there from France. When he was sixteen the Civil War began, and my grandfather, who must have been a wild boy, ran away from home and enlisted in Lincoln's army. My mother used to tell me fascinating stories about his feats. He swam across the Mississippi River, he scouted and fought until his beloved white horse was shot under him. He was taken to the worst Southern prison camp, where he spent the rest of the war, wounded and miserable. There my great-grandmother found him after the war was over.

In my childhood recollections I see Lincoln's huge figure towering above everything, and my grandfather fighting like a real frontiersman. I was never quite sure whether it was Indians or Southerners he fought and I drew glorifying hero pictures of him fighting single-handed against swarms of half-naked Indians. Then, later, from my mother's stories I saw my grandfather as a doctor driving on the endless, rolling prairie in his big-wheeled prairie buggy. I saw the picture of the strange carriage that looked to me with its tiny body on huge wheels like an enormous mosquito. I imagined the vast American prairies where brilliant flowers stood as tall as the head of a man on horseback, where the hooves of horses were tinted red from strawberries, where sudden fires swept across as far as the eye could reach, with burning grass tufts shooting like rockets into the sky, where lonely farms with their small fields stood as tiny specks in the immense expanse of a yellow ocean, where the first crop of corn stood fifteen feet high. Gigantic electric storms would sweep over the country, the huge yellow rivers that cut across the prairie would swell up and carry with them everything that came in their way. It was the most perfect dreamland for a boy, living in a European metropolis. The fact that I never saw my grandfather, he died before I was born, let my imagination about him and his country run wild. I exaggerated and painted out this picture of my mother's land to my friends and I became in their eyes, to my great satisfaction, a slightly adventurous person myself.

This was my early childhood's America. Later, when I had studied architecture for a year and had begun my work as a mural painter, America changed for me into a land of green lawns with huge shade trees and white houses with massive columns, the picture of Colonial America. So when I first came to America, today eleven years ago, my main reason, besides seeing the land of my mother, was to study Colonial style. But as I stood on the Brooklyn Bridge and watched the sunset behind the Statue of Liberty where the flaming red sky melted into the flat horizon of New Jersey, my childhood's stories woke up again in me. I felt America again as the pioneer country.

And we certainly were not far away from the hardships of the pioneers when innocently, five years later, we set off to explore the Washington country by foot. We envied the pioneers for their comfort, for they had walked soft, untrodden soil, while we trudged along burning concrete roads. The idea of driving a car hadn't entered our minds yet. That was something terrific and far beyond our abilities. We set off as we were accustomed to in Europe — you take a train to where you want to start and you walk across the country you want to explore. Already in Fredericksburg Ingri's toes looked like red and round Bermuda potatoes, and we shall never forget with what envy we gazed at the most decrepit cars dashing lightly by on the endless cement roads that would take us to Wakefield, while we had to trudge along under a merciless sun with our heavy paint boxes on our backs. We suffered, but we saw more intensely all the little corners where Washington had been, and it certainly cannot be denied that we have been in touch with his soil. But when we later started out in Washington's trail to New England, we had broken down and gone out and bought ourselves a car. It wasn't much of a car; we named it " Maybe," because you were never sure whether it wanted to start or not. But nobody could expect more for $25.

As the head of the family I had the privilege of learning to drive a car first, as we had to have one driver's license before we could start. But we hadn't taken into consideration that only once in a while did " Maybe " start of its own free will, so as I was the one who was licensed to hold the wheel, Ingri was the one to run behind and push until the engine started. All during that trip people were wonderful to us. Even policemen looked at us full of kindness and understanding when we did something not quite according to the motor vehicle law.

But " Maybe " brought us to all the places where we wanted to go, and we found all we looked for. " Maybe " was a very good experience to have, for when we were ready to set off for the much more formidable distances of the Lincoln country, we had learned how to combine European and American tramping. Now we could both drive without ruining a gear shift, so we had a good car with a huge luggage compartment. When we started off from New York we vowed that as long as we were off we would not once sleep in a hotel, only in the tent that we had brought along from Norway. In this way we would get into close contact with the country.

We have a big, snow-white tent that looks like a real house, with four walls and a roof. And when you walk into it you have the feeling of entering a home. There is a carpet on the floor, a low table in the middle with a candle and a bunch of wild flowers. And along three of the walls there are soft green mattresses with red silk cushions. The kitchen equipment is excellent; we have a fast burning stove, colorful plates, two pots, a pan and a coffee kettle.

Except for one instance we kept our promise. As long as we were in the prairie states we lived in our tent, and let me tell you that when you live in a tent you see that the prairie of the time of Lincoln is still alive. When we set off people promised us that we would find nothing of Lincoln's prairie country, except in the museums — that we would find nothing but straight concrete roads crossing each other at right angles with some green patches of grass between. That voyage turned out to be one of the most unforgettable experiences we ever had. We took all the little mud roads and there we found plenty of wild country. Every night our tent was pitched in a different place, sometimes under a clump of trees, sometimes at the brink of a fast-flowing river, sometimes right in the open prairie. Every morning we were awakened by the overwhelming chorus of singing birds, as the first slanting rays of the sun struck the roof of our tent, just as you read it in early descriptions of the prairie. There was also no lack of reckless temperament in the weather. A thunder storm at night in a tent on the flat prairie is something one doesn't forget. The lightning flashed in such rapid succession, we almost had electric light in our tent, where we could see each other shivering, holding desperately to our tent poles. If we hadn't learned by experience to place the tent so that the car took most of the wind, we would simply have been blown and washed away. One night the lightning struck a pole one yard away from the tent. It happened to be taller than the tent pole, but the impact threw Ingri into the air and made me release for a moment my hold on the tent pole. In a second everything collapsed on top of us, and we found ourselves, together with a chicken we had just been frying, floating around in a pool of water. Fortunately we were dressed in nothing but bathing suits. But that night we had to crawl to the nearest house and ask for shelter. That was in Mattoon, halfway between Springfield and Vincennes, where Lincoln for the last time helped his father to build a farm and get settled before he started his own career.

Another night we pitched our tent in a lovely green spot at the brink of the Wabash River. Late in the evening an old ferry man came down to chat, and warned us that the river was expected to rise another four feet during the night. That would just have left us on the dry land, but somehow we got cold feet and moved on. Next morning we found that the river had risen not four but eight feet; the spot where we would have been sleeping was far out in the rushing river.

Our trip led us to one spot more interesting than the other. And all the way we met with people to whom we are extremely indebted, who went far out of their way to help us, and more than any place else in Springfield, where the doors to all the Lincoln treasures were opened wide to us even though we must have looked like gypsies. Here we found most of the material we used for our book, and, of course, in New Salem, where the whole village of Lincoln's store-keeping days stood as realities before us.

Ingri began her part of the speech by thanking you from us both. Let me end by thanking you, Mr. Melcher, Members of the Committee, and the American Library Association for the Caldecott Medal and also for your patience in listening to us here so long.

BIOGRAPHICAL PAPER

by *Bertha E. Mahony* and
Marguerite M. Mitchell

Ingri and Edgar Parin d'Aulaire

WEDDINGS in the Mortenson family were usually formal and rather splendid affairs. But Ingri Mortenson chose to marry Edgar Parin d'Aulaire simply and informally at her uncle's farm in the Norwegian country. Watching it all, a little niece asked, "Is Ingri getting just a little bit married?"

Ingri and Edgar thought that that was perhaps just what they were doing, for what loomed as most important then was that their marriage should not interfere with the ART of either. They had met in an art school in Munich not many months before. Now they wanted to paint and study in Paris. Ingri had arranged with her father to have, as increased allowance, the money which he might otherwise have spent on a grand wedding.

Ingri belonged to a large, gay Norwegian family, devoted to all the joys of outdoor life. Her father still led them on thirty-mile ski trips into the mountains when he was in his seventies. Edgar was the son of a well-known Italian painter and an American mother. His father and mother had separated when he was a boy of six. After that time he had lived now with one parent and then with the other. His first Christmas visit to the Mortenson family was a delight to him in spite of the rigors of his long first ski trip, and a revelation of what family life could be.

As Edgar had watched his father at work, he too decided very young to be a painter. Ingri, when she was a little girl, also secretly determined that she would be an artist. When she was fifteen, she had an opportunity to show her drawings to the great woman painter of Norway, Harriet Backer in Oslo. Harriet Backer gave Ingri great encouragement but warned her against marrying if she wanted to go far in her work.

Although both young people painted landscapes, each had a specialty. Edgar did murals and Ingri, portraits of children. Before coming to America Edgar had illustrated fifteen books published in Germany, and two published in Paris. He had exhibited in Paris, Berlin, Oslo and Tunis.

After their marriage, the d'Aulaires painted in France, Italy, Germany, Scandinavia, the Netherlands, Dalmatia, Greece and North Africa. They could always make themselves at home anywhere. For one thing, they are thoroughly experienced and ardent campers, and have camped with a tent all over Norway and in other countries as well, including America. Their ability to live in the open has played an important part in their work, as will be shown. For another thing, they speak fluently five languages — English, French, German, Italian and Norwegian — and, needless to say, they have the greatest zest for life and living.

It is as true of sport as of work, that one's return depends upon the effort one is willing to put into it. The d'Aulaires have never withheld effort from their work or their pleasures. The fjords of Norway are very deep, so fishing is done usually with nets, not with lines. One summer before they had come to America when money was lacking, Ingri and Edgar went to Norway, fished regularly and carried their fish over the mountains to sell, Ingri's burden, not light, being one-third of the load.

Married in 1925, Edgar first came to this country in the summer of 1929. Laughingly they explain that Edgar's way to America was paid by money received for damages from a not-too-serious bus accident in Paris. Edgar found work here and Ingri followed the next year.

When *The Magic Rug* appeared in the fall of 1931, we knew that this book represented something new in the art of children's books. The drawings had the effect of being originals. We did not know that this book probably marked a new chapter in the marriage of two gifted people. From this time on they were to cease any concern about the interference of their marriage with their work. Their work was to be completely fused in their children's books, however much each might continue to paint separately and individually.

The Magic Rug grew out of a visit to North Africa where they had made more than two thousand sketches and paintings. In the fall of 1932 came *Ola*, a story of a little boy in Norway's winter, a book which has so endeared itself to our children that Ola lives for them; and in recent tragic happenings, they have asked over and over again in the Children's Rooms of Public Libraries, " Is Ola all right? " " Do you know where Ola is now? Oh, I hope nothing has happened to him."

" Far up in the North the sun is afraid to show his pale face in winter. But the moon and the stars love the sparkling frost. They gleam fairy-like through the long night and the arctic lights leap across the sky in cold, silent flames. They glitter on the snow and the ice of a long, mountainous country down below. In their magic light the country looks like a huge silver spoon, thousands of miles long. This is Norway. And it is the strangest country in the world. It is so crowded with mountains, forests, huge trolls, red-capped gnomes, and alluring Hulder-maidens that only a few human people have room to live there. In this country there is a forest, in winter a very strange forest. For under the heavy burden of snow the trees turn into a crowd of solemn creatures. In the middle of the forest there was a small house. And in this house there lived a small boy. Ola was his name."

This is the way the story begins. The pictures reveal not only how Ola's house looks inside and out and Ola's good times, but also how the natural world looks to the children and how the folk and fairy tales grow directly out of this appearance.

Once children had had the story of Ola in winter, they must know what Ola was up to in summer. In 1933 came *Ola and Blakken*. And in this same year came another distinguished book from the d'Aulaires, *The Conquest of the Atlantic;* a book which to many of us symbolizes the ranging vision of this partnership. For this book the artists examined source material in the New

York Public Library and the Library of the University of Norway in Oslo; the Musée de la Marine of the Louvre in Paris gave them accurate ship models, apparatus and costumes of the different periods. It is a picture-story book of the piercing of mysteries and the annihilation of ocean distances down through the ages. Surely the speed with which the one-time mysterious Atlantic can now be crossed will eventually count for friendliness. At any rate, in times like these we must draw encouragement and balance from thoughts expressed in words like Lamartine's which the d'Aulaires use on the half-title page of their book: —

" Mankind is a weaver who from the wrong side works on the carpet of time. The day will come when he will see the right side and understand the grandeur of the pattern he with his own hands has woven through the centuries without anything but a tangle of strings."

In 1934 came *The Lord's Prayer*, a book about which there will always be differences of opinion. We wish the artists had not seen fit to make it. As a matter of fact, when the plan for the book was first presented to them they thought it impossible. Later Ingri remembered her own images for the words as a child and they felt that they could undertake the picture book. We believe that on subjects like this prayer, a child's imagination should be left free to the ever-changing vision which comes with the years.

Before their next book was published, Ingri and Edgar d'Aulaire were to take one of the trips which are so much a part of their life and work. From Hammerfest, the most northerly town of Europe, they were to take a small boat to Bossekopp and from there proceed on horseback to Gargia in Lapland. From Gargia they started out on sleds drawn by reindeer, driving their own sled — a new experience for them. In *The Horn Book* for September-October, 1935, they wrote about this trip: —

" Everything else ceased to exist; there was no mileage and no goal. Sometimes before night, we would reach a small cabin, and stay there over night. The next day we would be driving on again, the whole, glittering day, and this we did for weeks and weeks. Before we had got all the sketches and material we needed for our book, and had turned our noses towards civilization, we were able to race over the mountains with every Lapp that we met."

The book which grew out of this trip was *Children of the North-lights*. It follows a little Lapp brother and sister, Lise and Lasse, through a year of their life. It was published in September, 1935.

When examining the d'Aulaires' *George Washington* and *Abraham Lincoln*, grown-ups should remember two things — 1. That Edgar's mother was American. Her father had fought in the Civil War on the Northern side, although he had owned a plantation in the Southwest. Living in a foreign land, she had told the child Edgar stories of American heroes. Not only did Edgar have the bond of ancestry with America, but, as is characteristic of them, Edgar and Ingri walked over Virginia for their Washington material and camped for weeks with a car and tent in three states to gather their great portfolios of local color for the *Abraham Lincoln*. 2. That the d'Aulaires have made the drawings for these books from the standpoint of the children themselves. The horses do deliberately resemble rocking horses because the toy horse of childhood has been used as model. Toward the end of the book *George Washington*, turn to the picture of Washington taking command of his army in Cambridge. This is such a scene as a child might set up with his tin soldiers, toy buildings and trees. That is exactly what the artists had in mind as they drew.

Qualities which we feel in the two *Olas* and which some of us miss in the two American books have undoubtedly sprung from real roots of childhood wonder and joy cherished in long unconscious growth. Perhaps the American scene and material needed a longer period of assimilation. However we react to it, the work of artists always does something to strengthen and clarify our critical point of view. These are adult concerns. The children take no heed of them.

In 1938 came a book from the d'Aulaires which presents to all those interested in roots of creativeness what is perhaps the major wellspring of their work, namely *East of the Sun and West of the*

Moon, Twenty-One Norwegian Folk Tales. In their introduction the artists say: —

" . . . we have been imbued with the spirit and language of these tales since the time we learned to talk. . . . The most difficult work we had . . . was to pick out these twenty-one stories. It was as if parents had to pick out among their hundred children the ones they thought the most of, though, good and bad, they loved them all."

Through a whole year the artists lived on a little farm high up in the mountains of Norway while they worked over the translation of the stories and made their pictures. There is a gaiety and a sparkle to the English which, like the pictures, seem almost to have sprung from the lonely " light summer, the clear, sparkling fall, the dark winter when the light of the moon glittered on the snow."

Just how do these two people work together? Edgar says, "When you find something amusingly expressed in our books, then it has been said by Ingri." Ingri says, " The dramatic quality of the story comes from Edgar." They both would say that Ingri contributes the intimate knowledge of children. They both would say that Edgar directs the methods of their work, for these artists draw their color illustrations directly on the lithograph stone as early craftsmen did.

May Massee wrote of their work as follows:* " The finished books look so finished and sure that one might think that all the artists do is plan and draw — not so with the d'Aulaires, for they make their own lithographs, using the old technique of the artist lithographer who had to do all his work by hand, without the use of the camera. This means that first of all the color drawings have to be sketched on paper the exact size needed — and these sketches are complete color drawings, for they have to be copied exactly on stones.

" After a picture is complete on paper, Edgar makes the first drawing on the lithograph stone. He draws with crayon and his hand must be absolutely sure of every line, for there is no erasing

* From *Ingri and Edgar d'Aulaire; a Sketch* by May Massee in the September-October 1935 number of *The Horn Book.*

or going over lines on a stone or zinc. What is put down there is to stay and if a drawing has to be changed a whole new drawing has to be made.

" The first drawing is the black part of the finished picture. This means not only the lines, but all the shadows that need black and also some of the color spots that need a little black to deepen them. Only long practice and scientific accuracy (for the technique of an artist in his studio is as accurate as that of a scientist in his laboratory) have taught Edgar just how to make the key plate. And then the work of getting in the color begins.

" The lithographer makes four impressions of the key plate on a large stone that weighs about two hundred pounds. One of these impressions is left just as it is to show the black part of the picture. Then the artists must look at their color sketch and pick out all the red places for the red plate, the blues for the blue and the yellows for the yellow. This would be comparatively simple if the colors were just flat and clear, but most of the time they are mixed — for instance, the greens are always part blue and part yellow, and to know just how heavy to make the blue and how heavy to make the yellow requires not only skill but infinite patience. And each of these colors must have a separate drawing for itself, so that the finished stone has four drawings on it — one each for the black, the red, the blue, and the yellow.

" Now the lithographer must make the transfers and here, too, the artist must know what he wants and how to get it, for the wrong shade of color or the wrong etching of a plate may bring sea green on the meadows, and grass green on the sea, or tomato red on the faces, and easily spoil a picture. Multiply this process with the number of pictures in a book, and it is easy to see that any one of their picture books needs months of steady labor after the preliminary planning, the writing and sketching have all been done. "

For several years, when they have been in New York, the d'Aulaires have lived in a studio apartment at the top of one of the historic houses on lower Fifth Avenue close to Washington Square. During the past year the Ola of their picture books has come to life in a small Ola of their own. The pictures of the Ola of Norway might indeed be portrait drawings of Per Ola Parin d'Aulaire; and although the latter is less than two years old, he paid a visit to Norway when visiting was still possible and safe. He, too, is growing up as his father did, watching the drawing and painting of pictures.

Very soon the real little Ola will be turning the pages of these books and all unaware he will absorb the qualities of color, light and form that move before his eyes. His fingers will explore the patterns; he may even try to taste the luscious reds and yellows; he will walk around hugging one of the books close in his arms, instinctively the heir of all this magic. For a time he will ignore the text and feel no curiosity about the creators of his new kingdom. He will move about in his child world, recognizing little by little his own toys in the pictures; the paper doll quality of the flat drawings will seem realistic to him, and soon he will have a sense of companionship with the children and creatures and plants that adventure through these pages. He will find them as exciting and nourishing as his first taste of warm gingerbread.

Then in time the young Ola will come to realize that life has given him something very special; that all this magic came to him from a father and mother sufficiently gifted to do impressive murals or sophisticated abstractions complicated enough to shut out the child. But they preferred, instead, to share their riches with children, sensing perhaps unconsciously the dark days soon to fall upon the little people of so many countries, when they will need so desperately the help that can come only from an understanding heart. And then Ola will feel deeply proud that his parents were awarded an honor like the Caldecott Medal, so fitting and so timely.

They Were Strong and Good

illustrated by ROBERT LAWSON

written by THE ILLUSTRATOR

published by VIKING 1940

FORMAT

SIZE: 8¼″ x 10″, 72 pp. (unfolioed)

ARTIST'S MEDIUM: Brush

PRINTING PROCESS: Offset lithography

ILLUSTRATIONS: Front matter, full pages with some smaller drawings, black and white

TYPE: Goudy Modern

BOOK NOTE

THE story of the illustrator's forebears who are a pride to him not because of wealth or position but because of character. The book is a bit of social history out of a family album and presents the kind of family which " helped to make the United States the great nation it now is."

ACCEPTANCE PAPER

by *Robert Lawson*

Rising to Children's Levels

I HOPE that you will realize, without my saying much about it, how very deeply I appreciate the great honor of receiving this Caldecott Medal. I feel most proud to join the group of those who have held it before, and those who will hold it in future years. I hope it will give me confidence to regard my own work with a little less mistrust.

It gives quite a feeling of local pride, too, to know that another medal has come to our home town, for Jimmy Daugherty, who received the Newbery Award last year, lives just a few fields away from us in Connecticut.

It is pleasant, too, to know that the Newbery Medal this year has come to rest with Armstrong Sperry over in Silvermine, just a few miles away. In the old days this section of the country was mostly given over to the raising of onions, but now the chief crop seems to be medals. It just shows how civilization progresses and what versatility our thin Connecticut soil has. From onions to illustrators and authors — it's wonderful!

It gives even more of an Old Home Week feeling to know that this medal is to be given to one of May Massee's books. For it was May Massee who inveigled me into doing my first book for children — once she had gotten it through her head that I was not dead.

You see I had known May many years ago, just after the last war in fact, but we lost track of each other for six or eight years. During that period she had somehow formed the slightly errone-ous idea that I had died of the 'flu. It was probably the work of some jealous rival.

But in 1930, when Doubleday, Doran were planning to publish *The Wee Men of Ballywooden*, May was having a great deal of trouble in finding an illustrator who could satisfy Arthur Mason's idea of what the drawings should look like. Finally, in desperation, she said, " Now if Rob Lawson were only alive, he'd be just the person to do it."

The Wee Men immediately got to work and arranged things so that very Sunday she happened to see a drawing of mine in the *Herald Tribune Magazine*. She promptly called me on the telephone and found that I was not at all dead. In fact, I was a little hurt by the inquiry because at that time I felt very much alive and doing quite nicely.

So *The Wee Men of Ballywooden*, my first book, eventually got done, and after it came *From the Horn of the Moon*, also by Arthur Mason.

Since that time I have done many books for May Massee and we're still on speaking terms, which says a good deal for both of us, but every once in a while when I'm a couple of months behind with some drawings, she gets that old 'flu obsession and starts calling up on the telephone. So far I've always been able to convince her that I'm still alive — but you never can tell — sometime I may fool her.

I feel a tiny bit as though I were acting under false pretenses in accepting this Caldecott Medal.

For one thing I have never believed that awards should be given for any one particular work. It might be just a fluke, a flash in the pan. And in one particular year there might be half a dozen equally deserving works, while in another year the best that could be found might be far below the level of the ones which had to be passed over the year before.

I have always felt that awards might well be given for long and faithful service, as the army gives service stripes, or as our better penal institutions give their guests time off for good behavior. But perhaps it works out that way anyway. Certainly all the holders of the Newbery and Caldecott Medals whom I know have proven themselves by more than one particular book.

Another reason why I feel a little hesitant is that I really do not consider myself as strictly a " children's illustrator." There is something in that term " Children's Illustrator " that seems to me slightly condescending to children. I think that if we are to make any distinction, we should speak of illustrators who work exclusively for adults as " adult illustrators " and should say it with a slight curl of the lip.

If any one's work, whether it is illustration or writing, looks or sounds as though it were obviously intended for children, then it is talking down to children. It is talking baby-talk with illustration which is silly, and which children bitterly resent.

I have never seen in the work of any of the illustrators whom children have loved for generations the slightest indication that they were catering to limited tastes or limited understandings.

Personally I feel that children are much *less* limited in their tastes and understandings than adults are. For children are not limited by stupid second-hand notions of what they *ought* to like, or how they *ought* to think.

They have not read articles or heard lectures on what they should admire or how they should regard things. *They* have not heard anything about " trends " or " influences." They do not know that they ought to admire certain art because it is " naïve " or "spontaneous," or because it has a " vibrant line," or because it has been drawn with a kitchen spoon on a discarded shirt front.

Grownups may feel that certain books *must* be read or certain art *must* be admired because its creator lives entirely on cauliflower juice or sleeps standing up, or bathes only in the dark of the moon, but children are not impressed by this sort of thing.

They are too close to the everlasting truth from which they have sprung. They have not yet been educated or " guided " or " moulded " into the awful ruts of growupness. They are, for a pitifully few short years, honest and sincere, clear-eyed and open-minded. To give them anything less than the utmost that we possess of frankness, honesty and sincerity is, to my mind, the lowest possible crime.

I have worked for so-called adults for a good many years. It is only in the last few years that I have done much work for children, and I must say I can't see any difference except that working for children is a little harder, it is more fun, it pays much less in money, but much more in self-respect.

I have always found that trying to *rise* to the levels demanded by the clear ideals of children is a far more responsible task and a much more satisfying accomplishment than meeting the muddle-headed demands of their elders. Frequently some serious-minded soul says to me, about some drawing or bit of writing, " I don't think a ten-year-old child would understand that." When I was doing the drawings for *Ferdinand* an elderly aunt of mine looked over the complete sketches and the text and then said, " I just don't see any sense in this thing at all; I don't see why you're wasting your time on it. The idea of a bull smelling flowers; it just doesn't make sense." I tried halfheartedly to explain that it wasn't supposed to make sense, that it was supposed to make nonsense, but she refused to be impressed and finally she said, " Well, I guess I'm just not whimsical." If you knew my Aunt Emma you'd realize what an understatement *that* was.

Perhaps I have a retarded mentality that causes me to look up to the child of twelve and places grownups completely beyond my mental horizon, but I should hesitate a long, long time before pronouncing *anything* as above the head of a ten-year-old child.

If people with this point of view could only look back to their own childhoods and remember the amazing conglomeration of ideas, of excitements, of curiosity and longings that filled their heads at the age of ten, they would never *dare* say what should or should not be given to children.

I know that scientists now have all sorts of wonderful tests. With wooden cubes and gobs of mud and colored beads they can give mental ratings and prove whatever theory they happen to be intrigued with at the moment.

But any one who has ever been a child, and most of us have, knows that these things only skim the surface and that no one short of God can begin to plumb, to arrange or to classify the weird hodgepodge that forms the mind of a child. And the deeper, the more important certain thoughts and ideas are to them, the more jealously they cherish and shield them from the prying fingers of meddlesome grownups.

No one can possibly tell what tiny detail of a drawing or what seemingly trivial phrase in a story will be the spark that sets off a great flash in the mind of some child, a flash that will leave a glow there until the day he dies.

I have had many letters from children about books and drawings I have done and it is amazing to see what different things have given different children their greatest thrill. Nothing that you could possibly count on, nothing that could possibly be planned, a tiny detail in the corner of some drawing, a particular word or phrase, has opened a window for some child; it has given him a glimpse of something that will remain always.

When I was three or four years old my mother took me to France. Now I have not the faintest memory of that trip — nothing at all. In fact, the earliest memories that I have do not begin until a couple of years after our return.

Except for one thing. I can at this very moment remember the interior of Napoleon's Tomb more clearly than I can now picture our own studio. I can feel the chill of the railing that I pressed my chin on. I can see the slanting yellow sunlight. I can see the dusty, tattered battle-flags and the great shining, black sarcophagus with its incised gold lettering.

Why?

Would any learned planner of children's lives recommend a visit to the Tomb of Napoleon for a child of three? I don't think so. It would be way over his head. He couldn't possibly appreciate its grandeur or its significance. Much better to teach him French. Teach him the lovely little French nursery rhymes, and the charming little French songs.

They did that, too, and they're all gone with the wind, but Napoleon's Tomb remains clear and vivid.

Why should it? I don't know, and I don't think any one knows. But I do know this: that I am determined to cram into every drawing I do and every page I write for children, or any one else, every detail or thought that I can possibly squeeze into it, without reservation, and without any thought of "age groups" or "planned reading" or any set of rules or theories. I would like to give them everything I know or can think of and let them do the choosing. For I know that some little unconsidered phrase or detail is going to mean a lot to some child. Some seed is somewhere going to take root and flourish, and the more seeds we can plant the more chance there is that one will take hold.

I am sure that Poe was way over my head when I first read him (much of him still is), but he set bells ringing in my mind that still are ringing, and I could cheerfully cut the throat of any one who had forbidden him to me because I was " too young."

I am sure that Maurice Hewlett and Sterne and De Maupassant and Gautier and dozens of others were far beyond me when I read them as a child. I couldn't pronounce their names or half the words, but I would bitterly resent having been deprived of them at the time they came. *Now* I can see that some of them had certain lacks. I have grown up enough to pick at their feet and find flecks of clay. But then they were pure warmth and glory, romance and beauty.

Many things are, perhaps, above the heads of children, but so are the stars and the moon. Should we declare a blackout because a group or committee or trend has decreed that moonglow and starshine are suited only to the twelve-to-fourteen-year age group?

I have a terrible dread that we shall take our children's books too seriously and solemnly. That we shall consider them as a very special class apart from all other literature, all other art and all real life. Carefully designed, scientifically planned, grouped, classified and very precious. This bit of grousing does not apply to any particular group of people who really have to do with children's books. All the librarians, and editors, publishers and critics that I know are far too overworked with their own jobs to be messing around with the creative end of books, even if they were inclined to.

There are, of course, always a few people scattered around in the fringes of things, those natural uplifters and arrangers, who feel the call to plan and regulate everything in sight. If or when people of that type get their fingers into any creative field, we, who do the creating, might just as well kiss the boys — and girls — good-bye. For there is something about that type of mentality that paralyzes all imagination, that blights all fancy, that curdles all humor — from which joy flees, and beauty hides her face. It is this type of mentality; non-creative, insensitive and animated by a ruthless determination to do children good, if it kills them, that, I think, forms the greatest menace to children's books today. It is this type of mind that would like to decide what subjects are suitable for children, what phrases children can understand, what words are to be allowed or forbidden to children of certain ages. They would like to decide, for the children, what type of illustration they like best, what colors and techniques are most suitable. They would love to have a " planned economy " of ideas so that all books would put across whatever propaganda they happened to feel at the moment was most worthy. Hitler, of course, has done the same thing long ago, but at least he was efficient.

Creative genius just does not work that way. It springs up and blooms in unexpected out-of-the-way places, in new and strange and beautiful forms. It is like the little Johnny-Jump-Ups in our garden that come up everywhere and bloom and live happily in the most unlikely places. Just try to collect them in a nice, well-fertilized, orderly bed! They turn yellow and die or seek a more congenial location in some baked gravel walk, or among the iris, any place where they can be free and unimproved and flower their best.

No planned economy could ordain that a farmhand on some dusty Montana ranch would write gusty and rollicking tales of the sea, or that a sickly boy in a slum might produce jewel-like masterpieces of drawings, or that a staid Secretary of the Bank of England would pen one of the most delicately imaginative books of all time.

Our first line of defense against this sort of benevolent regimentation is the good sense, the good taste and the honesty of our editors, our critics and our librarians. But the final and deciding factor lies in the sturdy independence of the children themselves. For they *do* know what they want and what they like and we might just as well throw the rest out of the window.

We can make all the speeches and write all the articles we please. We can point out the beauties of this and the values of that and the uplifting power of the other and receive in return only a cold and fishy stare. If we do not give them, in books, *real* warmth and beauty, *really* living characters, *really* robust humor, thrilling and fantastic imagination, they can simply shrug and look for them elsewhere. And they can find them elsewhere. Children can stage a sit-down strike or a policy of non-coöperation or passive resistance that would make Gandhi look like a fumbling amateur.

Our very title pages are forbidding. The present trend is to make the title page of every children's book look as nearly as possible like a rare collector's item. Perfect, chaste typography, perfect taste, perfect spacing — perfectly deadly. They have all the warmth and interest, for children, of a nice new memorial stone in Willowbrook Cemetery.

I can remember, we can all remember, title pages that were filled with warmth and interest. Some of them had " rustic " lettering, made of tree branches and roots. Gnomes and mice and beetles crawled through them. They were highly inartistic, they were in very bad taste, they were Mid-Victorian, they would never get a nod from Fifty Books of the Year — but children happened to love them. They were really warm and filled with something to look at, they had definite personality.

We can all remember the beautiful, rich medieval intricacy of Howard Pyle's title pages. No one, even now, can question their artistic rightness, but they *did* take a lot of time and a lot of skill, and we haven't enough of either nowadays.

So the children go to the movies where they can find color and warmth, action and interest and thoroughly enjoy a little dose of bad taste. And then they have the newspaper strips to fall back on, and here again I can feel a great sympathy for Junior. At this point I would like to say a word in defense of the much misunderstood and maligned newspaper strip. Not that they need it, Heaven knows, they are doing very well for themselves. But at the risk of revealing myself as a moronic lowbrow I must confess that I have found a great deal of pleasure and interest in some of them, a great deal to admire and a great deal to envy.

Many people connected with children's books and many worried mothers have spoken to me of "those awful comic strips" as though they were a combination of leprosy and the opium habit. In every case I have asked if they have really looked at the newspaper strips in the last ten or fifteen years and in every case they have answered indignantly, "Of course not."

If they only would. If they would just study them for a while with the open eager mind of a child or a slightly childish adult. They would be very much surprised, very much relieved, and perhaps very much interested. They might even become, as I have, devoted admirers of that completely charming character "Joe Palooka." For things have changed since the days of Happy Hooligan and Mutt and Jeff. They are not comic strips or "funnies" any more. Only a very few of them make any pretense of being funny. They are mostly adventure serials.

They have *real* interest and suspense. Their characters have *real* and recognizable personality. They are highly moral. They cover fields that interest children. They deal with airplanes and tanks, ships, motor trucks and submarines. Their characters are cowboys and mountaineers, G men, international spies, office boys, ball players, prize fighters, soldiers and sailors. Their settings range from the Orient to the Arctic and to strange imaginative lands. Some of them are historical. There was one recently on highlights of American history and another on important inventions and the origins of great American industries. The research is thorough and correct, they were well drawn and well thought out. I do not know of any child's book that has presented American history half so absorbingly.

As for draughtsmanship, some of these features are amazing.

I do not know of any one working for children's books, or for anything else for that matter, who can surpass, and very few who can equal, some of these men in technical dexterity. I do not think we can look down our noses at the newspaper strips. I am sure we cannot afford to just sit back and bemoan the fact that thousands and thousands of children have the bad taste to prefer them to our nice children's books. But we can, by a thorough and open-minded study of them, learn a great deal, a great deal that would help make our books more vital.

All this may sound like decrying the great strides that have been made in recent years in the quality of children's books, but it is not. I know how fine and how beautiful children's books are now. I know many of the people who have been responsible for raising their level. I know how hard and how sincerely they have worked to do it, and I have untold admiration for them and for the results of their devotion, for it is true devotion to a fine ideal.

But my great fear is lest we improve them too far. Lest we refine them to a point where their real vitals become attenuated. That we raise their level to a layer of the stratosphere where children cannot breathe. That in our absorption in achieving perfection we lose all touch with children, who, after all, are pretty close to the earth and pretty real and pretty grubby. People have done this with plants, with religions, even with dogs. There was no animal in the world much finer than the old-fashioned, hard-working, intelligent collie dog. But earnest, sincere breeders have laboriously refined it and raised its level until it is now a most beautiful, streamlined, aristocratic, useless nit-wit.

We must not do that with children's books.

We must not use children as guinea pigs for theories or as excuses for beautiful and unsalable editions. I would rather see a hundred thousand children writhing with glee over a small, dog-eared, cheaply printed book, than to have a hand in producing the most perfect specimen of the publisher's art, with seventy-nine copies in circulation and four thousand in the warehouse. Those four thousand copies are not doing children any good;

they're not doing anybody any good, except perhaps the mice.

The future outlook for children is pretty grim. They have a pitifully few carefree years ahead and I think we owe it to them to cram into those years everything we possibly can of beauty and joy and fantasy and thrill, regardless of the binding.

We must not give them just a splendid or an intriguing Juvenile List. We must give them Books. Books that will become tattered and grimy from use, not books too handsome to grovel with. Books that will make them weep, books that will rack them with hearty laughter. Books that absorb them so that they have to be shaken loose from them. Books that they will put under their pillows at night. Books that give them gooseflesh and glimpses of glory.

We must give them not what we think they ought to have, but *everything* we have to give, without restraint, with absolute frankness, and honesty and sincerity. *They* will do their own choosing, *they* will do their own selecting, and what they choose will be honest and of good repute.

BIOGRAPHICAL PAPER

by *Helen Dean Fish*

Robert Lawson — Illustrator in the Great Tradition

. . . I DO not know of any artist possessing Robert Lawson's versatility of mood and medium who is also possessed of his perfect integrity in his work, and his ability to treat each task he accepts with an imagination that gives lesser text its fullest possible distinction, and meets the challenge of great text with matching greatness.

After his service in the first World War as camouflage artist in the A.E.F., Robert Lawson returned to New York to resume a career that had been interrupted almost at the very start. He found work for the next ten years making illustrations for posters, advertisements, magazine stories and greeting cards. During this period in commercial art, nothing was ever cheaply or obviously treated by him, and each job added something to his stature as an artist. Then, in 1930 came an invitation to illustrate a book.

When *The Wee Men of Ballywooden* appeared, its lovely black and white drawings of delicate humor and rich imagination instantly attracted children's-book lovers of all ages. Here was something new and lovely — an artist to be watched. Other manuscripts were, of course, brought to him. Those he accepted for illustrating were highly varied. After three books by Arthur Mason, there was Ella Young's *The Unicorn With Silver Shoes*, and Margery Bianco's *Hurdy-Gurdy Man;* Elizabeth Coatsworth's *Golden Horseshoe* and Munro Leaf's *Story of Ferdinand;* a book of old nursery rhymes, *Four and Twenty Blackbirds*, and Mark Twain's *Prince and the Pauper; Mr. Popper's Penguins, Wee Gillis* and Eleanor Farjeon's *One Foot in Fairyland*, to name only a few. Then he came to *Pilgrim's Progress* and then to the first book written and illustrated by himself — *Ben and Me,* the story of a mouse who lived in Benjamin Franklin's fur cap. What other artist could have produced in a single year two more completely contrasted and more individually delightful books!

In these varied books, Robert Lawson has varied his technique and his method. His first books — the Arthur Mason titles — were done in a very fine pen line. This was the technique which led him to take up etching a little later. In 1934 and 1935 came a transitional stage, necessitated by the limitations of reproduction, and shown by the work in W. W. Tarn's *Treasure of the Isle of Mist,* and Elizabeth Coatsworth's *The Golden Horseshoe.* This pen work was less delicate. Then began a brush and black tempera method that developed until it reached a very fine climax in *The Story of Ferdinand* in 1936. Robert Lawson had also developed a method of his own, a rubbed or brushed Woolf pencil technique on smooth Whatman drawing board. He described his discovery in an article in " Art Instruction ":

" I noticed at one time how much Woolf pencil rubbed and smeared when used as a pencil. Experimenting, I found that it could be rubbed with a brush to give a tone that is easily picked off with kneaded rubber for lights. A very sharp pointed pencil, used almost like a pen, gives definition and textures. The whole process consists of an endless series of drawing, brushing, picking out lights with the rubber, and then doing it over and over again, finally fixing and picking out the highlights with white tempera or by scraping with a knife."

It is this method that gives the lovely softness and richness to the illustrations of *Pilgrim's Progress.* Naturally, this medium requires reproduction by offset.

Robert Lawson is a native New Yorker, brought up in a New Jersey suburb, and has now become an enthusiastic country dweller in Connecticut. He has built a charming house near Westport which he calls Rabbit Hill, because it really is on a hill and there really are rabbits. The studio looks out over a field of them and sometimes he finds them in the hillside garden.

Marie Lawson shares her husband's studio, and a seven-foot shelf of volumes, illustrated individually by the two Lawsons, contains a goodly number of lovely books by her. She shares also her husband's high ideal of craftsmanship and beauty in children's books. Mrs. Lawson has written discerningly of her husband's work and, referring to his turning from the field of commercial art to the illustrating of children's books, says: " He has never regretted the hard training of the commercial field. The different mediums required developed a greater technical versatility; the limitations of space a finer sense of design; the insistence on accuracy a keener observation of detail, a surer draughtsmanship. But however much beauty can be brought by sheer skill of rendering to building materials, automobiles and cigarettes, these things were not, after all, his chosen world. His preference was always for a world not wholly of man's material making. The word ' wholly ' is deliberate, for he has no sympathy with the purely ephemeral world – that of gossamer fairies and meaningless abstractions. His special world is really this world of our own, amplified and enriched by a wider horizon. Within it, because of his singularly vivid awareness, the figures of history move not as ghosts, but as living men and women; field and forest are still peopled by those fantastic beings who never existed save in the imagination of man throughout the ages. Here the haunting melody of Pan's piping cannot be drowned by the roar of modern machinery, nor the faint footprints of Titania obliterated by new roads of progress."

Robert Lawson's book illustrating – especially his more delicate pen and ink work – led him in 1930 to experiment with another medium – etching. In 1931 he received the John Taylor Arms Prize, given annually by the Society of American Etchers, and that same year saw his first one-man show. A critic has said: "No definite story is ever told in one of Robert Lawson's etchings. There is no beginning and no end; but for the space of a breath a door swings ajar into another world and those who choose may enter in."

The drawings in *Pilgrim's Progress* attain more completely than those in any other of his books the artistic stature of the etchings. *Pilgrim's Progress* is a good book for children to learn early and to grow up with. Robert Lawson's pictures for it are good pictures for children to know, to visit again and again, to possess as a home treasure and to remember in later life. They are reassuring pictures of eternal things. Who knows, in this reign of war that has usurped the world, what a refuge for the spirit, even of a little child, may be Robert Lawson's picture of that blessed land where saints securely dwell?

(Robert Lawson died May 26, 1957.)

THE CALDECOTT AWARD 1942

Make Way for Ducklings

illustrated by ROBERT McCLOSKEY

written by THE ILLUSTRATOR

published by VIKING 1941

FORMAT

SIZE: 9″ x 12″, 68 pp. (unfolioed)

ARTIST'S MEDIUM: Lithographic crayon on stone

PRINTING PROCESS: Offset lithography

ILLUSTRATIONS: Front matter, full-page and double-page spreads, all in brown

TYPE: Goudy Modern

BOOK NOTE

THE pictures and brief text tell how Mrs. Mallard raised her family by the Charles River in Boston and when they were ready, led them through intervening streets to the pond in the Public Garden. At the busy traffic corner of Beacon and Charles Streets a police car with four policemen escorted the Mallard family safely across, an event founded on fact.

ACCEPTANCE PAPER

by *Robert McCloskey*

Ducklings at Home and Abroad

ALL the way out here on the train I've been wishing that I could draw pictures or play the harmonica instead of making a speech to show my appreciation in receiving the Caldecott Award. Thank you very much.

Besides not being a speech-maker, I'm not an authority on children's literature, or on graphic arts, or on children's illustration. In fact, I'm not a children's illustrator. I'm just an artist who, among other things, does children's books.

I didn't start life training with any burning desire to create little gems for the young or give my all for good old children's books. But like a musician who likes to have his music listened to, the architect who likes to build houses that are homes, I like to have my pictures looked at and enjoyed. I grew a bit tired of turning out water colors by the ream and having only one in four hundred ever find a useful spot on a wall, the others stored in portfolios in some gallery or with canvases in a dusty studio corner. Yes, I'm working on children's illustration. I'm proud of that. But I'm still for hire — to paint, sculp, whittle, or blast if it's on some job that will bring pleasure and be used, whether it be in a bank, post office, or chicken coop.

I've got this all figured out now to my own satisfaction. It's a " find your market early scheme " and closely related to the plan of selling little shavers a safety razor for practically nothing with the coming of the first fuzz. *Then* sell them razor blades for the rest of their shaving lives.

My plan is for young artists to do children's books and find a public whose average age is about six. Fifteen years later, when that public becomes of age, there ought to be an excellent market for pictures in a right price field. A point might be brought out in an early book that no newly married couple should be without a work of art. In another fifteen years, when the artist is in his prime, the law of averages should have it that one out of every so many of his public should have become an executive, a head librarian, a banker, or a postmaster — people with lots of influence and plenty of money and wall space to dispose of. You've guessed it — in steps our artist and sells off enough murals to retire to Provincetown and spend the rest of his days in peace and quiet, painting an occasional boat or dish of fish.

Of course something may not work in this plan, just as some unscrupulous members of the " razor plan " grow beards or purchase electric razors. Instead of selling that first picture to the newlyweds, our artist may find that he has become purveyor of children's picture books to a second generation. But that, I'm sure you will agree, would be a happy ending, and I'm sure the artist would be happy, and relieved about the whole business, too.

The thing which I can talk about which might be of interest to librarians is how the duck book was constructed and put together.

Most of my friends think it happened something like this: One day I was sitting on a park bench in Boston reading the want ads of the *Transcript* when I just happened to notice all the birds in the park. I thought to myself, " Why not write a children's book about pigeons?" So I started writing a book about pigeons, only pigeons were too hard to draw, so I changed the pigeons into ducks. . . .

Now it wasn't quite like that but oddly enough this story *did* start in Boston. While living on Beacon Hill I walked through the Public Garden every day on my way to art school in the Back Bay section. I noticed the ducks in those days but no ideas in that direction ever entered my head. I was studying to be an artist, and I was hell-bent on creating *art*. My mind in those days was filled with odd bits of Greek mythology, with accent on Pegasus, Spanish galleons, Oriental dragons, and all the stuff that really and truly great art is made of. I liked those ducks, and I enjoyed feeding them peanuts, all good relaxation. I thought, for a mind heavy-laden with great art thoughts. It never would have occurred to me to *draw* those things or to *paint* them unless they were in a deep forest pool with a nude, perhaps, and a droopy tree and a gazelle or two, just to improve the composition. That gives you a vague idea of the way things stood. But I don't regard the time and thought as wasted. I certainly got rid of a lot of ham ideas at an early age.

It was at this time that I made my first visit to New York. I came with a list as long as my arm of things to do and see — the decorations at Radio City, the Hispanic, Metropolitan, Modern, Science and Industry, and Natural History Museums, and Grand Central Galleries, too, of course. I did it up brown, mind ticking all the time. Today there are two things from that trip I remember. I went to call on an editor of children's books. I came into her office with my folio under my arm and sat on the edge of my chair. She looked at the examples of great art I had brought along (they were woodcuts, fraught with black drama). I don't remember *just* the words she used to tell me to get wise to myself and shelve the dragons, Pegasus, limpid pool business, and learn how and what to " art " with. I think we talked mostly of Ohio.

The other thing I remember is that she took me out to dinner. The food was Long Island duckling.

I went back to Boston a very puzzled art student. It was about this time that I started to draw and paint everything and anything. I lost my facility for making up droopy trees and the anatomy of non-existent dragons and gazelles. Why, I even drew ducks.

When a job took me back to Boston a few years later the idea of the book took shape. And by the time I had returned to New York it was on paper, in a very rough draft which I took to my publisher.

When I started making the final sketches for this book, I found that in spite of my various observations of mallard duck anatomy and habits, I really knew very little about them. I went first to the Natural History Museum in New York, where I took careful notice of the two stuffed mallards that were in the cases. Then

I went to the Musem Library and found a top view of a duck's cranium, with minute measurements and a rough estimate of how many years ago ducks were fish. But hidden somewhere I found valuable information on the molting and mating habits of mallards.

At this time I had the good fortune to meet an ornithologist, George Sutton, and with his kind help I found out a great deal about mallards, studying markings on skins and making notes on wings. At last I had knowledge that I could use, but not enough. I needed models.

Time and finances would not allow such a simple solution as going where there were wild mallard ducks. I had to acquire them, so I went early one cold New York morning to Washington Market and found a poultry dealer. " I would like to acquire some mallard ducks," I said, and I was promptly shown a very noisy shipment that had just come in from the South. I looked in the cages and tried to pick out a pair that were not adulterated with puddle duck. I pointed to a duck and the dealer promptly made a grab in the cage, coming out with a squawking bird held tight around the neck. This process was repeated four times before the two of my choice were caught. Each time a bird was yanked out by the neck. I could not bear to see those two mistakes tossed back into the cage so I bought all four, a neat little duck cage about 3 x 5 feet in area and just high enough, and a half-bushel of mash, all for under two dollars.

With pride I took my purchases home to the studio and displayed them to Marc Simont, my roommate at that time. (Marc is another artist who does children's illustrations once in a while.) He didn't even bat an eye when he found that all six of us were going to live together. The ducks had plenty to say — especially in the early morning.

I spent the next weeks on my hands and knees, armed with a box of Kleenex and a sketch book, following ducks around the studio and observing them in the bath tub.

If you ever see an artist draw a horse, or a lion, or a duck, the lines flowing from his brush or crayon in just the right place so that all of the horse's feet touch the ground, the lion couldn't be mistaken for a pin cushion, and the duck *is* a duck, and you think " My, how easily and quickly he does that, it must be a talent he was born with," — well, *think* it if you must but don't *say* it! Little you realize what might be going into that drawing — day after day of following horses in a meadow with hot sun, prickles, and flies, or coming home from the Zoo exhausted at night with the people in the car looking about and trying to place that distinctive smell, or what splashing and housemaid's knee is behind each nonchalant stroke of that duck's wing!

The next step was a trip back to Boston to make sketches for my backgrounds — parks, bridges, fences, streets, stores, and book shops. Returning to New York, I brought a half-dozen ducklings home and filled more sketch books — with happy ducklings, sad ducklings, inquisitive ducklings, bored ducklings, running, walking, standing, sitting, stretching, swimming, scratching, sleeping ducklings.

All this sounds like a three-ring circus, but it shows that no effort is too great to find out as much as possible about the things you are drawing. It's a good feeling to be able to put down a line and know that it is right.

From then on the making of the book was technical — the combining of ducks and ducklings with backgrounds, problems in scale and duck's-eye view and finally making lithographic drawings on zinc plates. Bookmakers were untiring in their efforts to find the right ink, type, paper, printing, binding, and to handle all of those minute details, any one of which, if neglected, could ruin a book.

When we first heard about this Medal, Mrs. Mallard said *she* should be allowed to wear it around her neck because she raised the ducklings, and Mr. Mallard thought *he* should wear it because he was the head of the family, and Jack, Kack, Lack, Mack, Nack, Ouack, Pack, and Quack all thought that they should take turns wearing it. But we finally compromised and pasted it on the book jacket, and we all are *very* pleased, and we all thank the A. L. A. *very* much.

BIOGRAPHICAL PAPER

by *Margaret McCloskey*

Robert McCloskey, Illustrator and Author

ROBERT McCLOSKEY was born in Hamilton, Ohio, on September 15, 1914. He went to the public schools there and remembers that from the first, art was a major interest, closely followed by music, dismantling clocks and inventing things. This combination of talent led to an after-school job at the YMCA, during high school years, teaching hobbies. He taught other boys how to play the harmonica, and shepherded them to concerts at churches, grange meetings, lodge meetings and such. These experiences contributed to the creation of *Lentil, Homer Price*, and *Centerburg Tales*. Besides the harmonica, he worked with a group of boys making model airplanes, and taught another to do soap carving. They met in the shower room once a week and the chips fell unhindered.

In high school, he played oboe in the orchestra, made drawings and wood engravings for the school paper and yearbook. During his senior year, he won one of the nation-wide Scholastic Awards, choosing a scholarship to the Vesper George School of Art in Boston. After three winters of study in Boston and three summers of counselling in a boys' camp near Hamilton, he moved to New York and called on May Massee, editor of Junior books at the Viking Press, to show samples of his work. She told him to go back for more training and really learn to draw.

For two years he studied at the National Academy in New York, with summers of painting in Provincetown on Cape Cod. Again he went to Miss Massee, this time with the story and drawings for his first book, *Lentil*, which she accepted and published in 1940. In addition to doing the book, McCloskey had worked on two mural commissions, one of which was in Boston. During his second stay there, he came across the story of the peripatetic ducks and from that came the Caldecott winner, *Make Way for Ducklings* (Viking, 1941). In the previous year, he had married Margaret Durand, daughter of Ruth Sawyer, well-known writer and storyteller. World War II had just begun, but before he went into the army, he wanted to finish another book. It was *Homer Price* (1943) and it was written for older children than the picture books he had done before.

His next three years were spent making visual aids for the infantry at Fort McClellan, Alabama. Of this experience he says, "My greatest contribution to the war effort was inventing a machine to enable short second lieutenants to flip over large training charts in a high breeze." With army discharge in hand, the McCloskeys headed for Maine. They were now three, counting Sally who was born in 1945. They have been in Maine off and on for ten years, leading an amphibious life on an island in Penobscot Bay. The island and the sea around and the villages and farms on the coast have provided background for several books. *Blueberries for Sal* was published in the fall of 1948. Second daughter Jane was born in 1948, too, just in time for the family to sail for a year in Italy where McCloskey had a studio at the American Academy in Rome. Primarily, he studied the making of mosaics.

Centerburg Tales, or the Further Adventures of Homer, was published in 1951, and *One Morning in Maine,* came out in 1952. The last few years have been spent in illustrating *Journey Cake Ho!* by Ruth Sawyer, and *Junket* by Anne White. In preparation is *Time of Wonder* to be published in the fall of 1957.

The Little House

illustrated by VIRGINIA LEE BURTON

written by THE ILLUSTRATOR

published by HOUGHTON MIFFLIN 1942

FORMAT

SIZE: 9¾″ x 9″, 40 pp.

ARTIST'S MEDIUM: Watercolor

PRINTING PROCESS: Offset lithography

ILLUSTRATIONS: Front matter, full pages and small decorations in four colors

TYPE: 18 pt. Garamont

BOOK NOTE

THE pictures tell the story of a little house with the city growing up around it in changing seasons and changing periods. Children play around it and people and vehicles pass by in a colorful pageant until at last the little house is moved out of the city to a new life in the green and sunny countryside, where the stars shine over it at night.

ACCEPTANCE PAPER

by *Virginia Lee Burton*

Making Picture Books

In the first speech I ever made I told the sad story of my first book, an effort upon which the blessing of printer's ink never fell. I wrote and drew that book with all the ardor of an aspiring novice. My friends and I thought that it was very good and very clever, but thirteen juvenile editors disagreed with us. When the manuscript finally came back to me for the last time I discovered the reason for its editorial unpopularity. For then I read it to my son Aris, who was about four years old, and he was so bored that he went to sleep before I could finish the reading. That was the best criticism I have ever received, and by its principle I have been guided ever since.

Children's books are for children. That, of course, is a truism, bald and obvious, but just because it is obvious it is too often ignored or forgotten. Children live in a world of their own, different in many ways from our adult world, and books for children must deal with the things of their world. What we may imagine interests them often leaves them perfectly cold, and, on the other hand, what we dismiss as being of no interest may be fascinating to them. Naturally, then, they are the best of all critics of the books they are to read. I am fortunate in having two boys, two alert little critics for whom and with whom I write and draw all my books. And my boys, like most children, are both frank and keen in their criticism, and they tell me exactly what is right and what is wrong in my illustrations and in my manuscripts.

I have often been asked how I create my books. Actually I make them in collaboration with my children and their friends. I show them the pictures I have drawn, and I tell them the story that explains the pictures. I watch their fluctuations of interest, and I let them be my guides. When their interest lags, I know that I must delete whatever it is that bores them; when I hold their attention I know that I am on the right track; and when their interest is fixed but unsatisfied I know that I must elaborate my point, or make it more vivid.

In this creative collaboration with children I have learned several things. First, one must never " write down " to children. They sense adult condescension in an instant, and they turn away from it. Moreover, their perception is clear and sharp, perhaps more so than ours. Little things interest them. No detail escapes them. In the crowd scenes in *The Little House* there were so many people and cars and trucks it was difficult to keep track of heads and feet and wheels. Michael, my youngest son's job was to see that they were all on. Purposely, in the end papers, I put a flat tire on a car. He immediately spotted it. Indeed, every detail, no matter how small or unimportant, must possess intrinsic interest and significance and must, at the same time, fit into the big design of the book.

Second, the text and the pictures must be perfectly correlated, and it is vastly preferable to have them on the same page, or on facing pages of the book. Any one who has experienced the ordeal of reading aloud to a child a book with illustrations on a different page from the text will appreciate this point. A hundred times the continuity of the story is broken by the child's demand to see the picture on " the other page," and long before one reaches the end of the book its meaning and its pleasure have been lost in the fluttering pages. In all but one of my books, a case where circumstances dictated otherwise, I have not only placed text and illustrations on the same page, I have also worked the typography of the text into the pattern of the page. Many times I have sacrificed the length of the text or added to it to make it fit the design.

Third, children have an avid appetite for knowledge. They like to learn, provided that the subject matter is presented to them in an entertaining manner. The extent of this desire to learn was something of a revelation to me. In *Mike Mulligan*, for example, the diagram of the steam shovel, with each part carefully labeled, which I put on the end papers because I thought it too complicated and too detailed for the body of the book, aroused intense interest in the children. Or again, in *The Little House*, the border pattern, on the end papers, representing the history of transportation, proved to be one of the most appealing features of the book.

But if the children learn something from my books, I, too, learn in making these books, for they entail not a little research work, to say nothing of a variety of experiences. For instance, on one occasion I drove some three hundred miles over icy roads to attend a New England town meeting, which ultimately found no place in the book I was writing. Other experiences, such as examining steam shovels, snow plows, hydraulic bull dozers and a dozen other mechanical monsters of our time, were more fruitful. Especially memorable is the day that my son Aris and I rode in a grimy, greasy engine cab, with a battery of levers and gauges in front of us and an " awful noise " of escaping steam all around us — an experience which, I confess, I enjoyed more than Aris did.

To return, however, to the essential qualities of children's picture books, one must strive to give children what they like and want, and I am convinced that they like and want the best qualities. Among these qualities are clarity, well-defined detail, imagination and fantasy in the pictures; rhythm, simplicity and significance in the text — and in both there must be humor, from subtle (for, contrary to much adult belief, children are fully capable of appreciating subtlety) to blatantly obvious. To cite only one instance from my own work, my children never look at the bowed legs of Stewy Slinker without smiling. In brief, children's books must contain the same human and æsthetic elements that appeal to adults, but these elements must be selected from the children's world.

Perhaps I should say from the children's *worlds*, for there are different worlds for children of different ages. Thus one must pattern one's books for definite age groups. *Choo Choo*, my first published book, was written for my son Aris, who was then four years old. It was the story of a run-away locomotive, a rampant adventure of the sort which Aris often produced in miniature in his toy play. This was something which he could and did understand and which held his interest because it was to him a super-dramatization of one of his daily diversions. My second book, *Mike Mulligan and His Steam Shovel,* was for my second son, Mike, when he had reached the age of four; and again, it was a story of things with which he was familiar in his play, about which he wanted to know more, and which he liked to see dramatized. When I wrote my next book Aris was nine years old, and he had fallen prey to the dime comic books. Hoping to counteract the not too elevated taste induced by this variety of literature, I did *Calico, the Wonder Horse.* At this time it was my good fortune to meet Grace Allen Hogarth, the new juvenile editor of Houghton Mifflin Company. *Calico* was a new thing in the way of children's books, an experiment, as it were, and as such a risk for any publisher. Despite all this, Grace Hogarth encouraged me, gave me a free hand, and in a sense fostered this book into existence.

In *The Little House,* next in the sequence of my publications, I dared to make another departure from the usual in books for children. This time I was writing for the age span of from four to eight. The heroine of my story was the little house, but unlike most central characters the little house is stationary until the end of the book while its surroundings change. And the changing surroundings represent the sweep of social history, or to make a very bad pun " her-story." My problem was to convey the idea of historical perspective, or the passage of time, in terms comprehensible to a child. At the outset, the rising and setting of the sun signify the passing of the hours of the day; the waxing and waning of the moon, the succession of the days of the month; and the rotations of the seasons, the evanescence of the year. Once this rhythm is established, the child grasps the idea of change and perspective, and conceives the century of a city's growth, with the development of transportation, of paved streets, of reinforced concrete buildings, and the general idea of urbanization. A nocturnal scene every four or five pages spaces the bright colors and accentuates the sense of the flow of time. Many people have said that *The Little House* has a message, that the further away we get from nature and the simple way of life the less happy we are. For my part, I am quite willing to let this be its message.

But apart from the significance of any one book, it seems to me that books for children are among the most powerful influences in shaping their lives and tastes. In this sense these books are important means of advancing to a better world, for the future lies to some extent in the hands of the children of today. Tomorrow their ideas and their tastes will be the ones that count. Books created primarily for entertainment can do much to form the norms of future thought and action. Educational books can perhaps do still more. The drawings in educational books now used in the schools are not often of the best quality, and yet they have had more influence on the æsthetic and intellectual standards of the country than most of us realize. In recent years these standards may have been raised somewhat, but there is still ample room for improvement. Few of our best illustrators have gone into educational work, and the consequence is that most school-books are not as well illustrated as they might be. Remember that taste begins with first impressions. Remember, too, that children are taught reading by seeing, that is, by associating a picture with a word. If the picture is well drawn and finely designed they learn more than a literal definition. They acquire a sense of good design, they learn to appreciate beauty, and they take the first step in the development of good taste. Primitive man thought in pictures, not in words, and this visual conception of the outside world is much more natural and far more fundamental than its sophisticated translation into verbal modes of thought. The basic things are always the most important, and good art, certainly a basic thing, impressed on young minds through the medium of children's books is without doubt one of the best possible ways of giving children a true conception of the world they live in.

BIOGRAPHICAL PAPER

by *Grace Allen Hogarth*

Virginia Lee Burton, Creative Artist

OUR work, editors' work, is perhaps, first of all, to discover and to encourage the half-formed ideas and inarticulate beginnings of an author's or artist's creative expression. To most of us who are editors of children's books this is most satisfying and rewarding — so much so that we are apt unwittingly to come to consider the creative work our own and to speak of " my books " as easily and naturally as the authors and artists themselves. We often lose sight of the fact that we are masters in our profession only when we have helped our creative artists to the point where they no longer need us except as windowpanes through which the largest possible audience can see their books exactly as they were created. I was fortunate in never having had to outgrow any overweaning of Virginia Lee Burton.

Whatever help she needed at first had been given her by Houghton Mifflin before I joined the staff. I know, since she confesses it, that her first book was turned down by thirteen publishers, including Houghton Mifflin. Finally, her oldest boy, Aris, had grown up enough to be critical. He was bored — so bored that he fully confirmed the opinions of the offending publishers and put the new author-artist on the right track. And so it was that my first introduction to Virginia Lee Burton was through her first two published books, *Choo Choo* and *Mike Mulligan and His Steam Shovel*. Long before I met their creator, all steam shovels had become Mike Mulligans and all engines not choo-choo*s*, but " Choo Choo " to my children.

And then, one day, I happened into Lovell Thompson's office

when he was talking to a young girl. " Jinnee and I," he said,
" are trying to compete with the comics. Have you any ideas on
the subject? " I wouldn't have needed any further introduction,
even if I hadn't known that Virginia Lee Burton was considering a " comic book." This person looked the way the author of
Mike Mulligan and *Choo Choo* should look. I have tried since to
decide what it is about Jinnee that makes every one think of her
as sixteen. She is slight and not too tall; attractive with the attractiveness of good health and good spirits. Her head and features seemed vaguely familiar to me, but it was some time before
I realized that in every detail — jaw line, set of eyes, even hair-do,
she might have been a Fourth Century B. C. Aphrodite. I suppose
this is what is known as " classical New England beauty." Actually, Jinnee is only a little over thirty, but her work and her approach to her work are extremely mature. Now that I know her,
it is hard to remember that I ever thought her a child.

The result of the conference about comics plus the help of
Virginia Lee Burton's two boys, Aris and Michael, and the neighborhood children, was *Calico the Wonder Horse* or the Saga of
Stewy Slinker. Calico and the villain, who was originally Stewy
Stinker, were created at great cost in time and effort. I think I
am right in saying that Virginia Lee Burton worked longer and
harder on this book than any she has ever done. The rhythm of
the many designs that carry Stewy along to the climax of his tale
required hours of thought and planning and hard work.

This " competition for the comics " was Jinnee's only book in
1941, although she also illustrated Leigh Peck's *Don Coyote*, which
she found " relaxation." It is something of a miracle that she can
produce books at all since all her writing and drawing and painting
are managed in the hours left over from cooking, housekeeping,
entertaining, consoling, encouraging, and disciplining — the work
of being wife and mother. These working hours, she confesses,
are often from 6.00 A.M. to time to get breakfast and get the boys
off to school, and then between breakfast dishes and getting lunch.
The afternoon is harder because the boys' practicing, always a
struggle, goes on in the room where she works in the winter when

the barn studio is too cold, and, anyway, the later the hour, the less easy creative work becomes. And yet she has always made her deadlines! Due credit should be given to George Demetrios, her husband, who as well as being a sculptor and teacher of the first rank, manages to help with the boys, the garden and the cooking, too, when things are complicated or the publishers press too hard.

In 1942, Virginia Lee Burton in her " free " time produced the illustrations for *The Fast Sooner Hound* by Arna Bontemps and Jack Conroy, and her own story, *The Little House*. Mr. Bontemps begged for this illustrator for his railroad yarn because he had been happy with her pictures for *Sad-Faced Boy*, an earlier book. In *The Fast Sooner Hound* Jinnee proves her ability to draw animals and humans equally well, an achievement that is rare in an artist. *The Little House* is so completely Virginia Lee Burton's own that the business of turning it into a book was as routine and frictionless as any publishing adventure I have ever had. The idea had been in her mind for some time, and it seemed to me *right* from the moment when she first told me the story. As the work progressed, World War II also progressed and there was one moment when Jinnee began to have doubts about her work — stirrings of conscience over her war effort. I felt then, as I do now, that if *The Little House* does nothing more than re-affirm the realities, the peace and security of a little child's world, it is building for a future in which these realities may be unquestioned.

Most editors have learned the odd fact that when nature bestows creative gifts, she is apt to lavish them all at once. The painter is so often something of a musician. The illustrator, often under protest, discovers that he is also a writer. That Virginia Lee Burton is both, is at once evident. But it is a surprise to most people to learn that she never intended to be either one, but a dancer. Her sister has succeeded in this art and, as a child, Jinnee never thought of anything else. She was born in Newton Centre, near Boston, and lived there while her father was Dean of Massachusetts Institute of Technology and her mother, as Lena Dalkeith, wrote stories and plays. When Jinnee was seven, the family moved to California where they lived, first in San Diego, then in Carmel, and later in Berkeley. It wasn't until she entered the Sonora Union High School in the foothills of the Sierras that Jinnee got her first push toward art. She won one of three scholarships given in the state, for the California School of Fine Arts. It was in this high school, too, that she added the "Lee" to Virginia Burton at the suggestion of the principal, a very good one indeed, Jinnee says, and she still sends him each new book. After graduating from high school, the scholarship took her to Berkeley again where she worked for a year and a summer, both at art and at dancing. Practice on a bar in the living room filled in any spare time and helped to turn Jinnee into a near professional dancer and to get a stage job for her sister.

Virginia Lee Burton returned to Massachusetts with her father in 1928. The first winter here, she went to art school three nights a week, but worked so hard at dancing that she was soon offered a contract. However, it was at this moment that her father (unfortunately for him, but fortunately for children's books) broke his leg and Jinnee was the logical one to stay at home and look after him. She canceled her dancing contract and turned back to drawing and painting, getting a job with the *Boston Transcript* in 1929. She worked under, and was something of a *protégée* of, the great H. T. P., the dramatic critic who terrorized even the visiting New York producers. After each performance, Jinnee sketched the actors from memory, working all night to produce her work for the next day's edition of the paper — good training for deadlines, she says. The album of her *Transcript* drawings is amazing. They have the same vitality and humor, but they are faltering and unsure. Not all artists can improve in drawing. They often develop mannerisms to hide their weaknesses. The ability to see faults and correct them makes for greatness.

After two winters with *The Transcript*, winters that were also full of teaching and odd jobs, and two summers of being swimming and art director at camps, Jinnee worked for *The Bostonian*, which tried to be a Boston *New Yorker* (and failed) and went to the

Saturday morning classes at The Museum School. It was here that she met and was taught by George Demetrios whom she married on March 28, 1931. After a year of living near Boston, they moved to Folly Cove, Gloucester, where they have lived ever since.

It takes more than one visit to Folly Cove to discover all that Jinnee has done since her marriage. She has produced Aris, now eleven, and Michael, now seven. She has worked, with George's help, at drawing and painting. She has done murals and has exhibited in Boston. She says that picture books started after Michael was born and when Aris was just old enough to want them. Four years ago, she organized, with the help of fellow artists and friends, the Folly Cove Designers. The group started with nearly a hundred per cent Finnish potential talent. They design and cut linoleum blocks and print linens, dresses, curtains, bedspreads, etc., so effectively, in fact, that they now are a going concern with markets in New York, Boston, and other cities. It is a temptation even to an editor to interfere with her own deadlines by too frequent visits to Folly Cove where the food and talk are good and the real things in life matter.

All these things show in the work of Virginia Lee Burton. Its strength lies in the joy she brings to it. Its success lies in its nearness to the world of children. She says, " My last book, *The Little House*, is dedicated to Dorgie, which is what the children call my husband. The idea for that book came from actually seeing our own house being moved from the side of the main road back into a hill amongst some old apple trees. A lot of the detail is taken from our immediate surroundings and much of the content is the experience of our own house." The Caldecott Medal for 1942 has been awarded to *The Little House*. The story may be of Jinnee, George, Aris, and Michael's house, but it is also the story of any real house. And what is more, it was tested, as Jinnee says, by her " best critics " — her children and their friends.

Many Moons

illustrated by LOUIS SLOBODKIN

written by JAMES THURBER

published by HARCOURT 1943

FORMAT

SIZE: 8⅜" x 9¾", 48 pp. (unfolioed)

ARTIST'S MEDIUM: Color separations for line and halftone reproduction

PRINTING PROCESS: Offset lithography

ILLUSTRATIONS: Front matter, full pages and half pages in three and four colors

TYPE: Estienne

BOOK NOTE

A story about an imperious princess, aged ten, who wanted the moon, and the excitement this demand caused in the court. The Lord High Chamberlain, the Royal Wizard, the Royal Mathematician were all called upon in vain, and at last it was the Royal Jester who helped the Princess satisfy her troublesome desire.

ACCEPTANCE PAPER

by *Louis Slobodkin*

A Sculptor 'Makes Moffats'

BUT for a certain bend in the road, the little princess, if I were destined to do her in some art form, might have been created in polished brass and perched on top of some memorial flag pole, or perpetually blowing a trumpet from a limestone church corbel, or reposing benignly carved in marble and tucked securely into the corner of a pediment of some building. The bend in the road which brought the Caldecott Medal and me together in Cleveland on May 11, 1944, began some six years ago.

I had taken my family up to Cape Ann where we usually summer, and there we met two nice young people, sunning themselves on an old stone wall. They were the Estes, Eleanor and Rice, and the strangest thing about them was — they were librarians. Now I don't know why that should have seemed strange, but I have had the same reaction when I met my first anthropologists and again when I met my first professional wrestlers. Come to think of it, maybe sculptors seem strange to people, too, these fellows who stand hacking away at stone or building a lump of clay for a long, long time. Anyway, I met the Estes, and since then I've met so many librarians and they're all such nice people.

By the next summer or the summer after that, Eleanor Estes had written her first manuscript, and it had been accepted. Since these were long summer afternoons, we all sat around and talked. We talked of books, of type, of the principles of illustration. Eleanor had definite ideas on how she wanted her book to look, and I, with the wisdom of an armchair strategist, talked with great authority on the relation of line to type, etc. If the talk had shifted to toe dancing, I would have talked with equal easy assurance on *pas de deux* or something else I knew little about.

Later that fall when Eleanor asked if I would illustrate her book, *The Moffats*, I said yes, indeed, but frankly I was not as brave as I sounded. I was told to make a few drawings, ink ones, and take them up to Mrs. Elisabeth B. Hamilton, juvenile editor at Harcourt, Brace, to make sure they could be reproduced. I studied the manuscript, made my drawings, and took them up. I was told to go ahead. I did and returned some time later with about 130 ink drawings and 20 or 30 pencil drawings I wanted to finish for that book. Then I discovered there were limitations to book-making. After many consultations between Eleanor and me, we eliminated drawings by the democratic procedure of voting them in or out by a show of hands and left about 100 line cuts in that book.

And so I was launched, a little late in life, along this new road towards a new form of expression, and into a completely new world, where, to paraphrase Mr. Melcher's excellent *P. W.*, you meet such interesting people, authors, publishers, librarians, print-ers, pressmen. And I learned a new language: picas, overlays, slash vignette strip-ins, print and turn, and print and tumble. To one who has spent his life with flying buttresses, bull points and cabbage modelers, that sounded like a bit of *Finnegan's Wake* and, although I was hardened to dying plaster and feather-edged gran-ite, I was a little shocked to hear of a bleeding page and that a book has a spine.

That first book was not as easy as it sounds. Having devoted my life to sculpture, I needed to establish a new æsthetic logic on how to approach this problem of doing a book. It was not so much the difference of the scale of the work because all sculpture of any importance, I might venture, all major architectural works and monuments, usually start by being pencil-sketched on the back of some old envelope from somebody's pocket. The idea is jotted down in scale and usually preserved carefully through the enlarged sketches to the full-sized work. No, it's the demands that books make on the mental processes which were the points of departure.

When you start a sculpture composition, you develop one main thought; all sketches and primary indications tend towards developing that idea with all its ramifications. Say it's a colossal figure or composition of a couple of sculpture units. After your primary sketches and mechanical preparations are complete, you settle down to work, five months, seven months, a year or more, on one shape, one movement, and one thought. Of course, you develop and clarify and carry through essential *nuances* of good sculpture. But a change in the composition, a deviation from this one idea, the mere movement of a ponderous clay arm, a few inches in any direction, is a major operation, an engineering feat. There's the readjustment of the weight, the sawing through of the armature, the risk of destroying all the work you've done in the past six months and throwing that much of your life into the clay bin. You don't often change from your first idea: you compromise. And that's true, too, of changes in a stone carving.

Now, moving from this one-composition and one-idea way of a sculptor's life, to the crackle of thinking of hundreds of compositions within a short space of time was the main difficulty. For each drawing was a complete composition in itself. Every Moffat was an individual sculpture unit. Then there was another element, space, and the shape of space, limited by the requirements of the book. Sculpture makes its own space. It pushes its way into existence.

Movement, and there is plenty of that in the Moffats, was no problem. Sculpture has movement, subtle and restrained. The problem of the " yellow house " suggested a theory that might be the solution.

This drawing for books might be another variation of architectural sculpture. A manuscript may be considered a blueprint. The author was the architect. There was this house with a number of rooms in it, a front yard, and a back yard, a little landscaping there, set on half-moon shaped New Dollar Street, the railroad tracks at one end and a trolley line at the other. That's city planning on a small scale.

I consulted with Eleanor and actually drew floor plans and elevations of the yellow house and of all the other houses around and the brick lot, the street, and the surrounding territories that had something to do with the action of the story. It was so clear in my mind that sometime later, after the book had been printed, when a train I was traveling on one summer afternoon stopped on a trestle outside of New Haven, I looked down at a small town which was strangely familiar. It was the actual town of Cranbury out of that book!

Of course, this architect had done a very unusual thing. She had not only laid out a house and street, in her manuscript, she provided the tenants. That's something blueprint architects wish they could guarantee. I didn't know whether to consider the Moffats and their friends and enemy (that was the Frost boy, you know) tenants or mobile units of sculpture. But, in short, this architectural theory worked, for books, or seemed to.

I went back to my sculpture and, of course, there was a flurry on the publication day of this first book — thousands of reproductions of my mistakes — and then, along came *The Middle Moffat*. I worked *The Middle Moffat* at the same time that I was carrying through three large sandstone panels in their final stage in my studio. What with stone dust in my inkpots and ink spots on my stone — then finding as I smashed a fine chisel with my stone mallet it had become a quill pen and ripping my paper with the lost stone chisel found again in the ink — I don't remember the æsthetic theories involved.

The system I used was a very simple one. I read and reread the manuscript. I kept making notes and notes of the pictures I'd like to do, indicating them roughly on the typewritten sheets transferred to my dummy, and then taking one chapter at a time I did the drawings. I drew a good deal at home in the evening and late into the night, and it was only natural that our boy, Michael, who was just beginning to talk — that's putting it mildly, getting quite loquacious — would be shushed by his mama or his big brother Larry, " Papa's making Moffats." Since through all that period of his articulate life this went on, drawing in our house was not drawing, it was making moffats.

Some of the chapters in *The Middle Moffat* struck me so funny as I read them on subway trains instead of a newspaper, I'd guffaw out loud and people would gather themselves together for a quick exit, in case anything else developed. The Three Bears, and that basketball game when Janey took up sports. Not only the chapter itself but the situation was really this. Janey knew nothing about basketball, neither did that sports expert, Eleanor Estes, and I knew less than either of them. I was never any good at anything like that — basketball, baseball, or any sport. I used to box and wrestle a little. There was a time I swam long distances — very slowly — so when we all got together, Janey, Eleanor, and I, over a bit of basketball, what happened happened. I had remembered vague things about basketball courts, baskets, and girls in bloomers, but I never felt those drawings were really adequate. From the couple of hundred drawings made, 130 line cuts got into that book. It might be a little crowded. Anyway, I finished it, and I finished and installed my sandstone panels at about the same time, and that theory about the relation of architectural sculpture to books, what with the activity of Janey in *The Middle Moffat*, and all those other goings on, that theory wasn't finished, but it had received an awful kick in the cornice.

Now, speaking of theories, recently I've had a curious thought, not a theory, that designing and illustrating a book is something like cooking. I might enlarge on some of the principles of how to cook a book.

First, there is the author's manuscript. It is to be prepared for public consumption. A mimeographed copy of the typewritten pages would be pretty raw and perhaps indigestible. You carefully study the main motive of this manuscript, pinch, sniff, and sample it a bit. Whenever I receive one (always a cold blue carbon copy) I quickly ask: May I make some penciled notes as I read? I scribble over every page just a little; that's just to thaw it out and get rid of the ice-box chill. By that time, I've sensed whether this manuscript is meat, fish, or fowl, and have come to some conclusion as to how it might be handled.

Now, how and what to do, to enhance sympathetically, enrich, and bring out the maximum flavor, texture, color, and quality is the problem. Seasonings and embellishments must be in character with the main motive. Whipped cream on roast beef is no more foolish than flippant drawings on a solid bit of writing or *vice versa*; a heavy curried gravy on custard — maybe that's good! What herbs, relishes, garnish, and side dishes will be used to complement the flavor of the meat, fish, or fowl manuscript is now decided. You think of the potentialities and taste of the manuscript. Is it rich, mild, subtle, dry, sweet, or like veal that's too young, and certain river fish so bland in flavor that it must depend on a clever, overpowering sauce and decoration to hide its shortcomings?

I hold no brief for cooks or book designers who drown all their work in the same kind of sauce and ruin the natural flavor of any manuscript with the tiresome monotony of commercial capers and whirligigs. You must consider the limitations, production, and capabilities of the oven (the printing press). Then your budget. You can't use truffles, sherry, or heavy cream — or five or six colors, special type, trick margins, and costly board covers on work that is expected to sell for a small sum and in a limited market. You might have to confine yourself entirely to black pepper, salt, a bit of garlic — just a few line cuts — and it's not to be scoffed at if it's properly done. Garlic is called *la fleur de cuisine* by the *cordons bleus*.

So after you've seasoned, stuffed, dressed, and tied your roast neatly with the type, drawings, colors, and, of course, allowed for shrinkage by keeping your color high-keyed and your drawings so they will reproduce, you pop it into the oven or the press, and pray everything blends together nicely, and that there's some gravy.

Then — there is hash — and stewing a book and not to mention just unadulterated pot-boiling. . . .

This can go on and on, but before I leave this dissertation on how to cook a book, I'd like to register my indignation as a father and a taxpayer concerning one form of our American cuisine and bookmaking. There is the chilled lime gelatine, garnished with brilliant little bits of pimiento — nestling in a few leaves of lettuce and tenderly resting on nothing — school of cooking and bookmaking. These literary feasts, tasteless, dainty, precious, and unnutritious, are being served up to our healthy little girls and boys, served up, rammed down their throats as pure literature, beauty and art. But getting back to the main road after this culinary digression:

We just began to swing into *The Sun and the Wind and Mr. Todd*. It was a nice contrast from the hundreds of pen drawings I had done. Eleanor and I had talked now and again about this book. The manuscript had a swirly spaciousness and I liked the thought of working with my elbows free in sanguine again. That is the usual medium I used around the studio, and the type of drawing gallery and museum people expected from me, in their invited shows. Pen drawing, no matter how free the technique, still demands precision, and there is a lot of nervous tension. The book was to be something grandiose with a counterpoint sort of meek and mild—a tongue in the cheek symphony of deep bass— interposed with the timid piping of a piccolo — a gentle victim of an Olympic battle. Of course, Mr. Todd was really a grown-up Moffat, and I delighted in the idea of working him against the great baroque hulks of the Sun and the Wind, particularly that boasting windbag, the Wind. Those drawings were finished up on Cape Ann. That summer I shocked all my painter friends by working right through. I had expected to take it easy the last week of the season, but it turned cold, or perhaps the momentum of the Sun and the Wind was still with me, and I spent that last week dashing about wildly, splashing huge water colors all over the place. We returned to New York with porfolios jammed with the results of that water color binge, and the drawings and data for *The Sun and the Wind and Mr. Todd*.

So it was only natural, after watching the drawings through the offset process which was a new experience for me, that when Elisabeth Hamilton offered me Mr. Thurber's manuscript for *Many Moons*, to get started all over again. It was to be printed in offset lithography, in color, and I was to do my own color separation and have complete liberty. Now, I knew absolutely nothing about color separation. That didn't bother me. I could find out. What I did not know was — what do young people think about color? I mean people about ten. I had had definite reactions about their thoughts on drawing.

It is my conviction that people of ten and younger have a keener sense of appreciation of those qualities that make good drawing than any of us beyond that age. Drawing is the most lyric of all the plastic arts, the most closely related to poetry. A well-indicated line should, like a line of poetry, suggest things, stir the imagination, and start a fount of ideas. With their keen imagination, children react quickly to the emotional intention of a line. They see as much, and more, than you can suggest in your drawing. And by drawing I don't merely mean dexterity in the sense of that story that's told about Giotto in response to someone who had questioned his ability: — he silently picked up a long pencil and, with a simple turn of the wrist, he drew a perfect circle on a sheet of paper. That was a good trick, but I believe the story was untrue. I am certain Giotto was too great an artist to waste his time on a circle that meant nothing. And by drawing I don't mean mere factual representation, and there's a story equally false that might illustrate that too, of Raphael, who, being in the customary condition of an artist, broke, drew a perfect coin on the table in a tavern after he'd finished his meal and thus fooled the tavern keeper.

Our brilliant young under-ten-ers have little concern with mere dexterity or factual drawing, and I believe not at all with photographs. We would all have spent more time with the family album instead of with *St. Nicholas Magazine* and the Katzenjammer Kids, when we were young, if that were true. Any kind of drawing attracts their attention. They disregard it if it's bad, and return to it if it is good.

Now about sculpture — I know they have a delightful indifference to sculpture, yet a fine appreciation for the elements that make good sculpture — a plastic consciousness. You must all know little boys and girls who treasure beautifully shaped pebbles and stones, or curiously formed pieces of wood, or collections of sea-shells. These are the purest forms of sculpture without laurel leaves or buttons — abstract shapes which influence our best sculptors.

But, the only articulate expression I've ever heard from those under ten years old about color was the very audible " Ah " that is heard on a Fourth of July night when glorious purple, green, gold, and red rockets burst in the darkened skies. And, too, their admiration for the primitive clashing colors they dress up in on Hallowe'en and similar occasions. I thought of colors like that as I worked.

Well, the technique and the theories for *Many Moons* were all set.

Since I had no contact with the author and worked only from the manuscript, I then had to conclude and interpret my characters, background, etc. The manuscript was short, there were no descriptions of the main personalities or the settings.

Take our princess — she was little, and ate too many raspberry tarts and went to bed, stayed there except once when she went out to play in the garden. Overeating and such indolence might suggest a fat little glutton — or an only child, imperious — nothing less than the moon would suit her, and she kept a number of grown-ups racing about to satisfy her whim. One might draw a nasty little brat.

But then she might be just a little girl (incidentally a princess) who ate just a little too much, say half a tart. A little girl, a little stomach, a little spoiled, and timidly being just a little difficult — because she already knew the answers — with the traditional golden tresses of a princess (blondes seem to get green around the gills quicker than others due to overindulgence). I felt that, since she was our heroine and heroines should arouse sympathy, it was best to present her so.

Then there was the problem of movement. There were two main sets: the princess's bedroom, and she sat there; and the throne room, and the king sat there. There had to be some movement. We couldn't have people just sitting around, or keep repeating the jester going up and down the stairs. I hoped with strongly contrasting colors turning a page of blue and purple to the next of bright yellow and so on, and in handling the subjects of conversation as animated things and a little free interpretation of the script, I could suggest an illusion of movement in the book.

Then when I finally got down to doing my drawing and water colors, I had to get some actual ideas on structure and some convincing data on palaces, etc. I raked my memory for palaces and all things royal. I remembered the palaces I'd seen in Europe. They would never do. It seemed to me that no child would accept any of these huge ornate warehouses I recalled that real kings and princesses lived in, as a real palace. That's true, too, of the thrones, throne rooms, royal bedrooms, and other regal paraphernalia one saw on a sight-seeing tour in Europe, in the old days, for a few francs here or a couple of pfennigs there.

So I tried to imagine a palace, a princess's bedroom, a throne, and all that, as they would look had I never been contaminated by actually seeing them; in other words, trying to see them as children might, with their vivid and rich imagination, in the brilliant colors, the all silk, and satin, velvet and gold, and luminous marble they seem to feel is part of the everyday life of a princess.

And as I've indicated in my drawings and water colors in *Many Moons*, the king, come what may, always wears full court regalia and is never seen in his shirt-sleeves, and a little princess always wears a golden crown, even to bed, just a little one.

So, with a few more technical this and thats, the drawings were made, the separations finished, the book was printed — and *this Award* happened. I feel it my duty to tell you in what direction I am going, bearing very proudly this Caldecott Medal which you have so generously awarded me.

After some years of working at sculpture, theory and procedure become simplified. If someone were to catch me unawares and ask quickly what I am trying to do with architectural sculpture, I might unwittingly shout, incidentalism. I'd like to do my sculpture on buildings or in a setting so that when one sees the building one realizes, incidentally, there's a piece of sculpture there, that it relates so well to the wall and its surroundings, it looks as if it belonged there, and functions as a horizon or focal point to the eye. It serves best that way.

If I were questioned about sculpture for exhibitions, museums, etc., I'd say quickly, if I were off-guard, apples and a good tree trunk, for I'm trying to get the strong, plastic life of apple shapes, and the growth and supple movement of a tree trunk.

Now about books — and I'm very grateful to you for having let me talk about them.

Among my friends, there are some who collect books and when they show their treasures, their most sacred possessions are not always the beautifully bound, finely printed volumes, but often some lesser book by a lesser author, a first edition which on page 177 has a misprint. The presses were stopped, corrections made, and there are only a few of these books extant.

Somehow, a mistake happened, and a bit of human frailty got through the rolls of the press, and this bit of warm humanity has become a precious book exhibited by the Grolier Society.

If someone were to ask me, now that I've worked just a few years on books for children, what am I trying to do, what is my ambition, I might say "humanism" and explain that I'm trying to get as much humanity through the rollers of a press, with all its mistakes and frailties, that I can, deliberately and intentionally. It may clog the presses, but it's worth trying.

Eleven years ago last night, there was a big bonfire started by a tyrant who had wanted to be an artist but could only become an assistant paperhanger. That fire was fed by books. Those books were burned for many reasons. One of the main reasons was that they were concerned with humanity and human relations — of course, those books weren't lost. They were printed on indestructible truths, with the fireproof blood from the heart. My ambition is to do work that will have that much reason to exist.

BIOGRAPHICAL PAPER

by *Eleanor Estes*

Louis Slobodkin

A Sculptor Enters the Book World

POETS, children, and artists are the people who see things fresh and clear, and it is to them that most of us turn our eyes for a new vision of life. George Bellows said of one of his contemporaries, "He had the essential requisite of an artist — that of perpetual youth." Louis Slobodkin has this quality to an amazing degree. He has retained the fresh perception of youth and combined it with his great gifts as an artist. This quality of freshness is present in all his work, in his drawing or his sculpture, as anyone who has lived with his pictures or a piece of his sculpture can testify. And the drawings in his books are as fresh to the eye the hundredth time one looks at them as the first.

The world of books is vitally enriched when an artist with the abundant resources and the high accomplishment of a Louis Slobodkin enters the field, adding his own individual mark and mature interpretation of life to our fine store of beautiful production. Louis delights in drawing and designing the kind of book that children will really love and hug close to them. *Many Moons* is just such a book and it is good to know that his brilliant water colors in this book have won for him the Caldecott Medal for 1944. The sensitivity of his line and the fine craftsmanship of his work make him a logical choice for this prized award.

This artist has an extraordinary gift of intuition and he is able to sense and convey a wide range of feeling — how small boys and small girls feel, how a horse, dogs and new-born kittens feel, and how a little princess who has eaten too many tarts feels. We follow his fragile, piquant little princess gravely through the book as though we were walking in a dream through a strange enchanted land of ethereal light and moon pools.

Louis' pictures overflow with warmth and humanity and it would not matter what language the text they complemented was written in, for they read for themselves and have a completely universal appeal. Indeed, when Anne Parrish and Josiah Titzell first found *The Moffats* in a bookstore, Anne Parrish felt impelled to write the publisher, " Louis Slobodkin's illustrations would have made me buy the book if it had been in a language I could not read. I would have had to buy it if there had been nothing in it but the drawing of the Two Wild Roses."

No matter what medium Louis employs, his style is vigorous and original. It is, of course, his wide background as a sculptor that gives his drawing its roundness and shape. One very small boy who could not yet read was absorbed by his lusty drawings of the Sun and the Wind and kept cupping his hands around their strong shoulders as though he expected he could lift them out of the pictures. This reminded me of another small boy I once knew, who, when he was shown Picasso's picture of the boy with the horse, reached his hand behind the print to feel the horse's back.

No one who meets Louis can fail to feel the impact of his engaging personality and charm. The same qualities that exist in his work are very much a part of him as a person. He has a tremendous vitality and exuberance, a great capacity for generosity and friendliness, an abundance of warmth, humor, and wit, a bright and optimistic outlook. He is an original thinker and to hear him express his aesthetic ideas is an education in itself for the lucky listener. It is said of some people who write and then start painting that they should stick to writing; or of a painter who becomes a sculptor that he should stick to painting. But this noted sculptor, who has only recently added book illustration to his artistic accomplishments, shows himself equally at home in the world of books as in the world of sculpture. But then Louis has been drawing all his life.

His life began in Albany, New York, on February 19, 1903.

However, Louis is sure that the records are wrong and that he was really born on Lincoln's birthday. His interest in Lincoln is deep, and all through his life he has made many drawings and statues of him, culminating in the great monumental one which stands in the Department of the Interior Building in Washington. This eight-foot bronze statue, resting on a block of black Virginia granite, was cast from the working model of a sixteen-foot statue designed and executed for the New York World's Fair.

Louis' childhood was spent in Albany. One of his earliest memories is of his mother humming a certain repetitious Russian song as she sat sewing. Now when Louis has a particularly tedious stretch of work to do of a somewhat technical nature, either in relation to sculpture or drawing, he finds himself humming this same monotonous but soothing melody. But art is not all technique and the inventiveness essential to an artist Louis probably inherited from his father who is an inventor, the creator of many interesting gadgets. Louis' early years were dotted by a number of significant happenings which affected strongly his future development as an artist. He likes to tell the story of the only lesson in drawing he ever received. This unique lesson he picked up for himself when he was just a little boy of five from a big boy he did not know. Louis was running across the brick pavement of the school yard late one afternoon when he saw a boy drawing a large head on the wall in white chalk. Louis stopped short to watch. The boy drew a three-quarter view of a head and then so indicated the nose that the head took on form and dimension. The face came right out at Louis, who was literally overcome at this revelation unfolded before his eyes. He had been drawing flat patterns right along, but now he saw that the illusion of the third dimension could be indicated in drawing as well.

When he was about ten years old something happened to him which proved of equal importance to the lesson on the wall. His older brother brought him some red and green modeling wax. Until then he had known he would become an artist, but now his keen pleasure in this new medium led him to the conclusion that he would become a sculptor. Thereafter he spent most of his time drawing or modeling, and as the years went on, school became more and more irksome to him, for he longed to get to work as an artist.

Sometimes this compulsion to draw had its touchingly amusing side. One year at Christmas time the teacher was having the blackboard decorated with colored chalk drawings. Louis had in mind a particularly fat and jolly Santa Claus, such as formerly adorned the Christmas cover of the *St. Nicholas Magazine.* He wanted desperately to draw his Santa Claus on the blackboard, but his teacher said, " No." A boy named Baldy was to do the decorating. Louis' anguish grew as he saw blackboard after blackboard covered by Baldy's drawings, while his Santa Claus remained imprisoned in his head. He had to draw it! So after school hours were over and the classrooms practically deserted, Louis ran in and out of them looking for an empty blackboard. Finally in his old Fourth Grade Room he did see a narrow board with nothing on it. Might he draw a Santa Claus on this? he anxiously asked his former teacher. After an interminable line of small delinquents had been dealt with, she replied, " Yes." So there with tremendous relief Louis drew his Santa Claus, a magnificent one in red and white chalk.

In spite of drawing and day dreaming his way through school, Louis did learn some things and what he learned he knows very well. Let any one try to trip him on " attribute complements," or anything he learned by heart! It is true that to this day Louis' spelling is glowingly original, as a careful scrutiny of any of his pictures in which spelling occurs will confirm. But his vocabulary is prodigious and, although he has little formal knowledge of most foreign tongues, he could easily and happily make himself understood all around the world by his sure and astonishing instinct for accent, inflection, and the right lift on an eyebrow. In fact, not the least startling of Louis' own " attribute complements " is his talent for singing songs in what he claims to be the Arabic, the Hindustani, and other lesser known Asiatic tongues, all in all an amazing but completely convincing performance.

At fifteen he came to New York and enrolled in the Beaux

Arts. The date of his arrival in the city was Armistice Day. Louis had always heard of the wonders and joy and gaiety of New York City. But this was something beyond anything he had dreamed. He literally floated over the city on ticker tape and he says that New York has always seemed somewhat of a let-down to him ever since that momentous day.

During Louis' years at the Beaux Arts he studied sculpture all day long and earned his way by running elevators at night. He speaks fondly of his nights in the elevator, for he did an extraordinary amount of reading in them, riding up and down, up and down, ranging through the philosophers, the great poets, and Buckle's *History of Civilization*. He thoroughly absorbed the reading he did at this time and Plato, Aquinas, Kant, and Goethe, among others, were thoughtfully assimilated. Louis claims that an elevator is a particularly sympathetic type of room in which to read, small and tight and intimate. He resented passengers when he was in the midst of a good book and liked the elevator to get stuck between floors so he would be shut up with his book without interruption for a time. That an elevator shaft has marvelous acoustics he also discovered. A great deal of the fine music he heard during these student years he sang up and down the elevator shaft in his own symphonic renditions. Meanwhile for his work at the Beaux Arts he was winning medal after medal.

Louis is an extraordinary *raconteur* and many of his most lively stories center around his trip to the Argentine. His terra cotta and bronze sailors keep cropping out from time to time, plastic evidence of that voyage. But some of these stories cannot be translated into sculpture and they should be in a book. Perhaps some day when he gets out his portfolio of drawings and water colors of sailors made on that trip, he'll take his pen in hand instead of his mallet and give us a book about that journey instead of a piece of sculpture.

Next came some years of study in Paris, which he loved and where he tried to overcome his linguistic lack by raising a beard, and then Louis, back in his own studio in New York, entered into a particularly productive period. He took his inspiration from

Biblical sources rather than the more traditional Greek for many of his pieces. Especially exciting are the magnificent and monumental Shulamite, the Bathsheba with its harmonious flow of line and shape, and King David, carved out of a lovely pink Colorado stone. A great deal of his work has been placed in public buildings in various parts of the nation. The Lincoln is probably the most noted, but a very fine Hawaiian postman cast in aluminum stands in the Postmaster-General's office in Washington, and the cast iron bas-reliefs on the new Madison Square Post Office in New York show some of his architectural sculpture at its best. Louis takes an exceptionally keen pleasure in architectural sculpture, because, as he says, it is nice to know that your work is going to be anchored to earth rather than wandering homelessly from museum to museum.

The broad sweep and heroic concept of his work make it all the more startling to contemplate the ease with which he turns from a piece of sculpture of epic proportion to the drawing of pictures for children's books, and gives proof of his truly amazing versatility. However, he often says, "You have no idea how frightened I was to tackle those first Moffat drawings."

It is perhaps this tender approach that accounts for much of their charm and profound simplicity. It would be impossible to mention favorites among the delicate line drawings for these books because they are all favorites. It was a very rich joy and pleasure to watch them come into existence, from the first swift impressionable pencil sketches to the finished pen and ink drawings. My husband and I laughed and glowed over each funny, poignant, endearing picture as he drew it, from the delightful suspense of the dancing-school class in Moose Hall to the mistiness of the desolate amusement park.

Many of Louis' pen and ink drawings appear as casual and easy as if his hand carelessly roamed across the page trailing a sensitive line behind. Sometimes I daresay this does happen. But often I have seen him erase and erase and scratch out, even sandpaper the surface of the paper and then redraw until he attains exactly the right lift to an arm, a mouth, or an eye, an eye which may be reproduced as small as a dot. Infinite pains and care are taken to create what he knows he wants to say.

Louis and his wife, Florence, whose poetry sometimes breaks into print, live near Central Park with their two sons, Larry, who is fifteen and already off to college, and four-year-old Michael. Life with Michael has not been without its effect upon Louis and the first book of his own, *Magic Michael*, will be published in the fall. This book is a beautiful, rollicking, rambunctious surprise, and it would be unforgivable to detract from its wonderment by speaking more about it now.

Many of the prominent artist groups absorb much of Louis' active interest. He is the Vice-President of An American Group, and a vital force in the Sculptors' Guild. His bright, friendly face is a familiar one all over New York. He is an indefatigable worker. He works in his studio on a three-legged table balanced on his knee and surrounded and embanked on all sides by his sculpture. And he works on buses and subways, making notes, at meetings of artists, and at home with Michael climbing up his back. And if he comes to call, " Well, here I am with my busy work," he says, and spreads out his latest dummy and gets to work.

Indeed Louis is a dynamo of energy. He gives the impression that, for him, subways, buses, and trains move faster than for anyone else. He certainly gets around the city more swiftly and covers more territory than anyone we know. Maybe it is because his grandfather was a Ukrainian cowboy and the wide wind of the steppes is in his blood.

THE CALDECOTT AWARD 1945

Prayer for a Child

illustrated by ELIZABETH ORTON JONES

written by RACHEL FIELD

published by MACMILLAN 1944

FORMAT

SIZE: 6⅞″ x 8½″, 32 pp. (unfolioed)

ARTIST'S MEDIUM: Watercolor

PRINTING PROCESS: Offset lithography

ILLUSTRATIONS: Front matter, full pages in four and two colors, decorative initials

TYPE: 24 pt. Deepdene

BOOK NOTE

THIS childlike prayer, written for Hannah, Rachel Field's little daughter, has been printed before but not illustrated as a book by itself. A realistic picture on each page makes the meaning of the phrases clear to little children and close to their daily life.

by *Elizabeth Orton Jones*

Every Child and His Hilltop

THERE was once a little girl who found it very puzzling to say "thank you." The words were too small for the feeling, the feeling too big for the words. She would slip away — crawl under the piano or under the dining room table and sit there in silence, with the big feeling inside her . . . Oh, to crawl under a table right now! The feeling is *very* big — *thank you!*

Much of the big feeling is that I am in no wise worthy. The Caldecott Medal — *full-sized* — for *me?* Surely it should be in miniature, for me! I do not consider myself an artist. Not *yet.* The very word "artist," to me, carries with it a little vision of the state of *having arrived.* I think of being an artist as an achievement I may work toward my whole life and even then not arrive. Though I should like to be able to say, right out loud to myself, on the morning of my 99th birthday, "Old girl, you are an artist!" The same applies to the word "author." And as for "author-artist" . . . ! Whenever I am asked, point blank, what my profession is, I carefully avoid those words and answer, "I draw pictures. I write stories."

I suppose I *could* answer, "I make books — for children." But would the person to whom I was giving the answer understand that that little statement works both ways, that the *reverse* of it completes the truth? I make books — for children. That's only half the truth. For as soon as a book I have made is in children's hands, they shoot back into my hands the makings of another book. It's very like a game of "catch" — a magical, never-ending game of "catch." I make books — for children: children make books — for me. There's the complete truth.

In a sense, I am standing before children at this moment as surely as I'm standing before you. In another sense, I am talking to children through you. What do they think of all this? Is it with their consent that I receive the Caldecott Medal, full-sized, and the full-sized honor that goes with it?

It would be difficult to talk directly to them about the honor. The meaning of honor is singularly lacking in their particular way of looking at things. And, for the most part, the extent of their knowledge of reward is finding it *in the doing*. As for the medal itself, if I were to pass it around among them, they would be interested, of course. *Very* interested. They would look at it, feel of it, turn it upside down and rightside up. They would say, " It's pretty! " And then they would say, " What's it for? " It would be difficult to talk to children about the *use* of the medal. In fact, it is difficult to talk to children — period! — unless what you say has something to do with something they know about. Has the Caldecott Medal something to do with something they know about? Of course it has. Drawing.

It is *not* difficult to talk to children about drawing, for they are fellow-indulgers, all. To them, drawing is as natural a part of everyday life as eating or sleeping or washing your neck — far *more* natural, usually, than the latter. To them, drawing is not tied and bound to talent, nor to theory, nor to technique, nor even to subject matter. To them, the possibilities of drawing are by no means limited to things visible. To them, it is no more unusual to sit down and draw a picture of God than it is to sit down and draw a picture of a potato. To them, drawing a picture of how happiness feels on a bright sunny morning doesn't present any more of a problem than drawing a picture of Daddy's blue overalls hanging on the line.

When the manuscript of Rachel Field's *Prayer for a Child* came to me in the mail, one bright sunny morning, with Doris Patee's suggestion that I draw pictures to go with it, I knew at once that I should like to *try*.

I sat down with the little prayer. It was not new to me. I had already read it in the Memorial *Horn Book* for Rachel Field. I already loved it. There is a difference, though, between reading something to take into yourself to keep and reading something to take in and then give out again through your own interpretation.

I remembered, the first time I read it, how it seemed to breathe — as things written for a particular child often do. Rachel Field wrote the prayer for her little girl, Hannah. It was Hannah who had caused it to breathe.

I wondered. Who was I to make pictures for Hannah's prayer? I didn't know Hannah. I had never met Rachel Field *actually* — only through her books. What kind of pictures did she see when she first read the prayer to Hannah? What kind of pictures did Hannah see as she listened? What kind of pictures was I going to draw for Hannah and other children to look at?

For a long time I sat with Hannah's prayer.

"*Bless this milk and bless this bread.*" — I thought of my old silver cup and how it used to feel to my hand, heavy with milk and cool and shiny.

"*Bless this soft and waiting bed . . .*" — I thought of the blue and white patchwork quilt made by Mamie, with pictures from Mother Goose and from Æsop on it. I got my old silver cup out of the cupboard and polished it. I got the blue and white patchwork quilt down from the shelf and unfolded it.

"*Through the darkness, through the night, let no danger come to fright my sleep . . .*" — I ran to the window seat and knelt there, to feel again how it used to feel looking out into the dark sky.

I had no little girl. The little girl closest to me was the little-girl-I-used-to-be.

"*Bless the toys whose shapes I know;*" — I got out the toys I had kept and put away in cardboard boxes.

I'd have to pretend. I'd pretend that I and the little-girl-I-used-to-be were two separate people. I'd pretend we both lived in my studio. She would go to sleep and wake up, get dressed and undressed, think thoughts and dream dreams in my studio. While I drew.

"*Bless the lamplight, bless the fire . . .*" — I would try to draw the quiet, comfortable happiness a child feels at bedtime. I would try to draw the change of thought that comes softly as a change of breeze at the end of a day — when everything in the outside world begins to fade, and everything that means home, especially what is a child's very own, begins to shine with nearness and dearness and familiarity.

"*Bless the hands that never tire in their loving care of me.*" — I would try to draw security.

"*Bless my friends and family.*" — I would try to draw companionship.

"*Bless my father and my mother . . .*" — I would try to draw love.

"*Bless other children far and near, and keep them safe and free from fear.*" — I would try to draw the feeling of fellowship that exists, without the necessity for a San Francisco Conference, among all children.

"*So let me sleep and let me wake in peace and health, for Jesus' sake . . . Amen.*" — I would try to draw the confidence a child feels in being sure of the presence of God.

All this I would *try* to draw.

I couldn't actually see all this, of course. Not with my eyes. I couldn't actually see the little-girl-I-used-to-be. So a real little girl came to pose for me. Her job was to pretend *she* lived in my studio. She pretended very well. There was no milk in the cup; the piece of bread was a pad of paper; she had to get undressed and go to bed at eleven o'clock in the morning. But such things are not at all puzzling when there's a reason. And pretending is as good a reason as any.

I found that the toys whose shapes the little-girl-I-used-to-be knew were simply too worn out to pose. So I put them back in their cardboard boxes and administered anæsthetic in the shape of more moth balls, to insure their well-earned rest. I went uptown and looked around in the stores. But I couldn't buy what I was looking for; not for any amount of money. Only after a long life of being much-slept-with does the real character of toys begin to show. I gave voice to my need one day while taking tea with a friend. The children of the house happened to be present, but seemingly paying no attention. After a while, however, the little boy who lay on his stomach on the floor, drawing, left his picture and ran upstairs. His sister followed. In a very few minutes they were down again, and my lap was filled with what I had been looking for. Their most cherished toys — the ones always taken on long trips — the ones always slept with — were hereby offered me to take home to keep as long as I needed them. I got up in the night, that night, I remember, and went into the studio and lit the lamp. There were the toys, patiently waiting out the first night they had ever been separated from their owners. Prowlie, the teddy bear, had his arm around Abigail, the rag doll, in whose lap sat Salisbury, the rabbit. Gentle patience and utterly selfless loyalty showed, if anything ever showed, in Prowlie's shoebutton eyes, in the smudge which was Abigail's nose, in the patch which covered Salisbury's whole behind. Prowlie seemed to be saying, " Of course they're all right, Abigail. Don't worry! Whatever this is, we're doing it because they want us to, remember. Whatever is expected of us, we must do it well." With a feeling of truly humble respect, I went back to bed.

Drawing is very like a prayer. Drawing is a reaching for something away beyond you. As you sit down to work in the morning, you feel as if you were on top of a hill. And it is as if you were seeing for the first time. You take your pencil in hand. You'd like to draw what you see. And so you begin. You try.

The result depends on a good many things. On how much you know about drawing, for one. If you don't know much, the picture isn't very good. Good or bad, however, it is never what you tried to draw. The picture is *never* what you saw from the top of your hill. Never. But if somebody — a grownup or a child, a little old beggarwoman or a king — anybody! — can, by looking at your picture, catch a glimpse of what you saw . . . if somebody — anybody! — can in that way understand what you tried to draw, then — likening drawing to a prayer again — your prayer has been answered.

I have a picture — or, rather, a postcard print of a picture — at which I am very fond of looking. It is a picture of a whole countryside of little hills, with a wide blue sky above. And on top of each little hill sits a child, singing. I like to look at that picture and think: Every child in the world has a hill, with a top to it. *Every* child — black, white, rich, poor, handicapped, unhandicapped. And singing is what the top of each hill is for. Singing — drawing — thinking — dreaming — sitting in silence . . . saying a prayer.

I should like every child in the world to *know* that he has a hill, that that hill is his no matter what happens, his and his only, for ever. I should like every child in the world to know that what he can see from the top of his hill, when he looks down and around, is different from what can be seen from the top of anybody else's hill — that what he can see when he looks straight up is exactly what everybody else, looking straight up, can see, too.

I should like, if you don't mind, to accept the Caldecott Medal, and the honor that goes with it, as a trust. I should like to try to express my gratitude for that trust on every page of every book I'm ever to make — for children.

BIOGRAPHICAL PAPER

by *Annis Duff*

"Our Miss Jones"

ONE afternoon, a year ago last February, Elizabeth Jones came to tea. It was quite an occasion, for although we had known her incarnate, so to speak, for a comparatively short time, we were very much at home with her because of our long and intimate friendship with *Ragman of Paris*[1], *Maminka's Children*[2] and *Twig*[3]. Deirdre's first pet-names for Steven came from Elizabeth Jones: "My sweet raisin, my little mouse, my rather small beetle." And Steven had felt such an immediate kinship with Elizabeth that he spoke of her as "our Miss Jones," and behaved with her as if she were his own age.

On this particular afternoon she told us she was having a little difficulty in finding the right models to sit for the drawings of "Toys whose shapes I know" in Rachel Field's *Prayer For A Child*[4]. She knew precisely what she wanted: toys that though loved by some child, were not so worn that they'd lost their shape and color. She needed one woolly one, a good friend for sleeping with; one small one, the right size to fit into a child's hands; one toy of wood or paper; and one "good old soul of a doll."

Deirdre and Steven went upstairs, and if we'd been noticing particularly we might have thought they'd grown tired of our party. Presently they came down again, and with them came Prowlie, the second-generation teddy bear; Teddy Wear-wee, his inseparable companion; Salisbury, the small gray rabbit from England; the big Swedish wooden spoon known as the "tuvebon," Steven's favorite plaything from the time he could almost have been picked up in it; and Abigail, the Brown County pioneer doll handed on to Deirdre years ago by someone who had loved

---

[1] Oxford. [2] Macmillan. [3] Ibid. [4] Ibid.

her dearly, and now Steven's cherished friend and confidante. All of these were piled into Elizabeth's lap. Elizabeth examined them gravely, asked a few questions about their ancestry (this out of understanding of their owners' pride, not from concern with their social fitness), and then said, " Of course! " So they all went home for a long visit with " our Miss Jones."

The next week the Duff children came down with measles, and the companions of the nursery began to be missed rather badly through the tedious feverish nights. There was much talk of how the toys were faring, whether Miss Jones remembered to put them to bed comfortably, and if they were homesick at all. But before the expected appeal came to have them brought home, there arrived a most enchanting letter with a beautiful colored picture of the toys sitting in Miss Jones' studio chair, and a long account of the trip to Highland Park, of being tucked in for the night under warm blankets, and of Miss Jones' pussy, Piley, who " makes a noise like a little washing-machine."

After that, until the spots were all gone and the two Duffs restored to a state of unrelenting vigor, we talked endlessly about the book Miss Jones was making, wondering if all the pictures would be as lovely as the one she'd made of the toys, and growing more and more excited at the prospect of seeing a finished product in which we'd had a little share.

Well, we did see all the pictures before they went off to the printer, and found them so full of " innocent beauty and child-like truth " that it seemed almost impertinent to try to put our feeling about them into words. Then, just at Thanksgiving, the book itself arrived, with Hannah's sweet little kneeling figure on the jacket and inside on the fly-leaf this inscription:

For Deirdre and Steven Duff — bless them. And bless their dear Prowlie, their dear Abigail, their dear wee Salisbury, their dear Teddy Wear-wee, and their dear spoon — who so graciously consented to be in this book, and who were such a help and such a comfort.

With love and with thankfulness,

ELIZABETH ORTON JONES

Thanksgiving Day, 1944.

Prayer For A Child was not, for our children, so much a beautiful new book as a beautiful new experience, a visible linking up of the Unseeable with the seen and felt and known. Their own deep sense of thankfulness for the comfortable, everyday simplicities of food and sleep, companionship and security, was expressed for them in the words of Rachel Field's prayer and made infinitely alive and intimate by Elizabeth Jones' pictures. It gives us much happiness to know that " other children far and near " have felt the same response, and that their elders have recognized the value and beauty of the pictures in *Prayer For A Child* by awarding to the creator the Caldecott Medal.

Years ago, when Deirdre Duff first read *Maminka's Children*, she hazarded the opinion that " Miss Jones must be a very special kind of person to make such a wonderful book." Miss Jones *is* a very special kind of person, so special that you'd never single her out from a crowd as having the unmistakable aura of the artist. She is a *person.*

The first time I ever saw her to know who she was, I recognized her right off because in the first place I was looking for her — it was at a performance of Gladys Adshead's *Brownies, Hush!* for which Elizabeth had done the pictures; and in the second place she was so unmistakably the same kind of Jones I'd known in her brother and sister, who had been students in my husband's classes some years before. Only, whereas Tom and Annette are strikingly dark as to eyes and hair, this Jones has the lovely russet-brown look of her mother, very attractive with her small, delicately modeled features — the straight nose, chin square and firm without being aggressive, and a mouth that never smiles by itself but helps with the lighting up of her whole face when she is amused or pleased. It isn't easy to describe the appearance of someone who has such mobility of expression; talking or listening, laughing or serious, she has always an animation that is never tiresome because it is so honest and spontaneous. A quite unpretentious person, this Miss Jones, who nevertheless is a positive presence when she's there, and always leaves behind her a sort of sparkle.

To say that she is at her best with children might seem to

suggest that she withholds something from her grown-up friends, and this is not so. She is a thoroughly satisfactory companion, informed and responsive, full of lively imaginativeness, stimulating ideas and penetrating common sense. But in her relationship with a child there is a subjective understanding, a subtle sympathy that creates an immediate at-homeness. I am inclined to think that this accounts for a good deal of her success at making books for children because it comes from her ability to identity herself with the child she once was and has never lost.

One of my pleasantest occasions with Elizabeth Jones was an evening when we sat by the fire drinking coffee and wandering from one subject to another with fine disconnectedness until she began to tell me about herself as a little girl. Several times since, I've thought about some episode or another that she described, and have wondered, " Now what book had that in it? " — only to remember that it was part of the Autobiography of Elizabeth Jones as told to Annis Duff in the dead of night.

There was small Elizabeth, living in a little house — " oh, a very *little* house " — by the side of a deep ravine. A narrow bridge led across to where the road was, and the grand piano had to be carried over by several staggering men. She had no companions of her own generation until she was nearly six, but Pantzy and Mamie, the Bohemian girls of the household, gave her their love and care and companionship then, and for many years after Tom and Annette joined the family circle. She lived in the kitchen, she says, listening to their colorful tales, hearing their songs, watching them dance, and seeing them cook the wonderful Bohemian food.

Elizabeth glows with a sort of wondering delight as she tells about their radiant and untiring happiness in devising pleasures for a responsive child: the tiny doll's dress, begun at suppertime, and brought for her to see in all its embroidered beauty by a blink of lamplight long after midnight, and left for her to find like a dream come true in the morning; the miraculous appearance in the kitchen one evening (when Pantzy had mysteriously disappeared upstairs) of an old Bohemian beggarman who with complete rightness proved to have known Mamie's family in the Old Country, and told fine tales of their life and times; and — what later became one of the most delightful episodes in *Maminka's Children* — the making of the Christmas bread, which is traditional in the Jones family to this day, though Pantzy and Mamie long ago carried their gift of happiness to other spheres.

When Elizabeth was about five, her family moved to a more spacious house, and she was given a beautiful walnut bed with a broad polished headboard, so that she might learn to enjoy and respect beautiful things. She had at this time a rather glamorous night-life of her own devising. Partly from loneliness, and partly from imagination clamoring for an outlet, she created a setting in which her home was an orphanage presided over by one Miss Brown. Every bedroom was a dormitory with rows of beds down each side, each bed having a headboard perfect for use as a blackboard. Each night when she'd been left alone to go to sleep, Elizabeth played with her equally orphaned companions. Night was the time for lessons: arithmetic, reading, grammar, spelling, and finally, and best of all, drawing. For this Elizabeth took a piece of chalk to bed, and just before she went to sleep she would draw a picture on the sleek headboard, and first thing in the morning she would rub it out. One morning her mother, coming in to close the window, found the chalky adornment still there. A mild reproof, combined with practical instruction as to the relative merits of chalk and olive-oil in the care of fine furniture, provided Elizabeth with a new kind of situation for her nocturnal adventures, and her prestige was greatly heightened among her shadowy companions.

Like many children gifted with imagination, Elizabeth thought herself " different," and had no means of discovering whether or not her school friends felt as she did about books, or made response to the beauty all around. So she was all bottled up and lived in a state of bewilderment, badly needing a like-minded companion, but not quite knowing how to reveal her need.

When her brother and sister were of an age to be away from home, the three spent their summers in a little house built for them on their uncle's plantation in Virginia. Here, free to pursue her own pleasures in congenial company, Elizabeth found a satisfying outlet for imaginative energy. A beagle-hound was their favorite playmate, and the Jones children talked a private jargon known as Beagle Language. Elizabeth at this period made a practice of setting difficult tasks for herself — reading the Bible all through, staying up all night, or making a dictionary of Beagle Language. She usually accomplished what she set out to do, and if the immediate results were not always essentially practical, the strengthening of her determination and ability to carry through an appointed task doubtless served her well in the fulfillment of her intention to develop skill and understanding as an artist.

"When did you find you wanted to be an artist? " I asked her — a silly question, now I come to think about it. She naturally couldn't answer with any definiteness, but supposed she must have settled on drawing as the most satisfactory of her gifts when she realized that in spite of having had much music at home all her life — her father and mother are both gifted musicians — she didn't want it as a career. When, after completing her work at the University of Chicago, she studied first at the Art Institute of Chicago and later at the School of Fine Arts at Fontainebleau, she discovered that there were people who felt and thought and *saw* as she did. "They talked about beauty right out loud! It was wonderful! "

Then she went to Paris, to study with Camille Liausu. "And when," I asked, "did you begin to draw children? " She said that she was working in the studio one day, fearfully tense and serious, when M. Liausu told her to get her coat and go out into the park. "Don't take pencils or paper. Don't do anything. Just watch the children playing and then come back and see if you can get some movement into your drawing." She watched one child; she watched two children; she watched groups of children. And then she went back and drew something of what she had seen, and it was good.

She spent other and more days watching children and getting them down on paper. She came home to the United States and had a one-man show of color etchings of children at the Smithsonian Institution. And she wrote and made pictures for a little book called *Ragman of Paris*. I remember reading the closing chapter of it, reprinted in the May-June *Horn Book* in 1937, and thinking what a jolly book it would be for my six-year-old son — if I had a six-year-old son. It all came back to me the other day as I watched Steven crouching down to talk to a prowling pussy in the woodlot, and later heard him explaining that he was looking for the pussy's green whisker.

Maminka came along before our son did, and when I think of Deirdre's shouts of laughter as we read the chapter about the big noodle, I can scarcely wait until Steven is ready for it, too. Then there was *Twig*, funny and wistful and very spacious in its understanding of a child's strength in imagination; and *Small Rain*, to me the most perfect of all books of Bible literature for children because of the quality of sheer joyousness that shines in all its pages. This quality is a reflection of Elizabeth herself, whose own " joyous inner wisdom" sees the eternal verities as a perennial source of happy well-being, and knows that children should have them so.

With every new book, Elizabeth Jones shows a greater sureness of technique, a finer, freer, lovelier expression of her delight in " clear-eyed, soft-faced, happy-hearted childhood, and the coy reticences, the simplicities and small solemnities of little people." When first we used to read *Prayer For A Child* and look at the pictures, every time we came to " Bless the hands that never tire," Steven would add, " Bless the hands of our Miss Jones." So say all of us. Hands that can bring into concrete form the vision and beauty and humor of Elizabeth Jones' particular kind of seeing from the top of her own particular hill have a great gift to bestow on the children of this world.

THE CALDECOTT AWARD 1946

The Rooster Crows,

A Book of American Rhymes and Jingles

illustrated by MAUD AND MISKA PETERSHAM

published by MACMILLAN 1945

FORMAT

SIZE: 8″ x 10¼″, 64 pp. (unfolioed)
ARTISTS' MEDIUM: Lithograph pencil with color separations on acetate
PRINTING PROCESS: Offset lithography
ILLUSTRATIONS: Front matter, full-page illustrations and many smaller ones in four colors and two colors
TYPE: 18 pt. Memphis Bold

BOOK NOTE

COUNTING-OUT and rope-skipping rhymes selected by the illustrators bring up visions of generations of American children in the playground and the street; familiar finger-plays and folk-jingles recall the nursery and the home. The book overflows with chanting and playing children.

ACCEPTANCE PAPER

by *Maud* and *Miska Petersham*

A Short Tale

of the Depressions and the Peaks That Occur in the Making of the Little Pretty Picture Book

FOR us the idea of preparing a speech was difficult but the making of a book comparatively simple, so today, instead of a speech, we have made for you a book. We found on our bookshelves a beautifully bound dummy dating from those days when publishers handed them out by the dozen for the artists to play with. This dummy is not made from the grayish, half-transparent, fifty-pound war-paper with printing on the back of a page showing through in strange smudges. This book has thick beautiful pages — and pure white paper is always an inspiration. There is no time more thrilling than when, complete with bright ideas, you sit down at your desk with a pencil and a piece of untouched white paper in front of you. It is a rare moment, for at that point the paper has the possibility of turning into a masterpiece. Unfortunately, you always run into troubles and snags and the finished drawing is far from the one you anticipated. Sketches are fun but we often get over-conscientious and tight with finished drawings.

This book is but a sketch. . . . — First come the end papers. We have always felt that in good bookmaking the end paper designs should be decorations and not pictures. Here we have made a design of many bright intermingling colors. To us, this represents our studio in Woodstock, pine trees, a garden and sunshine, a wren building near one window, a tree-toad chirping, much family, and people we like about us. Golf clubs, stamps and stamp albums, clay ready for modeling and some cooking pots and pans are all mixed up together in this decoration.

A little above the middle of the page we have left a bright circle and in here we shall add a picture of the Caldecott Medal, which is the reason today for making these end papers so gay and happy and for leaving out all grays and shadows.

Next comes the title page and it reads:

*A SHORT TALE OF THE
DEPRESSIONS AND THE PEAKS
THAT OCCUR IN THE MAKING OF THE
LITTLE PRETTY PICTURE BOOK
WRITTEN AND ILLUSTRATED BY*
MAUD AND MISKA PETERSHAM
BUFFALO, 1946

The next page is the Contents and here there are three chapters.

Chapter I. MAUD's chapter
Chapter II. MISKA's chapter
Chapter III. MAUD AND MISKA's chapter

On page four comes the Dedication. As a rule we don't believe in dedications in a book, for they seem too personal, but this particular book needs one. Only once before have we used a dedication in any of our books and that was in *The Christ Child*. After three months of travel in Palestine, we settled down to finish up illustrations for the book. We were living in a strange city and we were a little homesick. A baby boy was born in the apartment house where we were staying and we often left our desks and wandered into the garden to watch him sleeping there. Then we would go back to our drawings for *The Christ Child*. It was only when we left that we discovered the baby's name was " Christian Emmanuel." And so we dedicated that book to him.

There are three dedications in this book of ours today.

The first pays tribute to those understanding persons who, to the artist, play the rôle of Counselor, Judge, Policeman and Nurse; who at times must wear wings and a halo, who lift the artist out of deep ruts of no ideas and calm him down when ideas are rampant, who recognize a book when it is only a few scratches on paper and a light in the eye, and who, above this, is a Friend.

So on this page Miska and I affectionately place a dedication to the " Editors of Children's Books " with whom we have worked.

As a second tribute we proudly write in large letters "To the Librarians." There is no way of knowing the countless boys and girls who are happier and richer, whose lives have even been transformed because of books thoughtfully and lovingly handed to them by the librarians in the many children's libraries through-out our country. We appreciate the many new friends they have found for us and our books.

When we first started to make children's books, we naïvely and innocently believed that the toil and labor was over when we handed in our last finished drawing. We sat back proudly and expectantly. Now we know differently. When our work is finished, no matter how carefully the drawings have been made, and the text written, they are still not a book. It is the printer who takes up where we leave off and who turns our work into something tangible, something which can be held in the hands of each child. Here we pay tribute to "those Two" who through so many years have toiled so faithfully to reproduce our work.

Chapter I

ONCE upon a time, long, long ago, after we respectively said good-bye to the advertising studio where we were both working, Miska and I started making children's books together. Miska solemnly told me that a picture wasn't worth making unless you were willing to suffer over it. At the time that seemed to me a strange and dreary statement. Now I understand, although I must say it has been on the whole " pleasant suffering." But it does mean that we have put our hearts and all our efforts into the pictures and books we have made. We always try to tell a story in our pictures and often we put a little unimportant story within a story. We have the satisfaction of believing that some children discover these — which are not for everyone, but something between us and certain children.

We have committed some grave offenses in our work. Once

we proudly sent off some animal drawings. These were some of the first we had ever made. The editor slipped. The drawings went through and when the books were published, letters from children poured in. Why had we given the big bear, the middle-sized bear and the little bear, hands instead of paws? Why did the wicked, still-hungry wolf in Grandmother's nightcap and nightdress reach out a hand to Red Ridinghood?

I suddenly realized that while we were making the drawings we were thinking of the animals as behaving like people (perhaps Miska even posed for that big bear). We made them smile, we made them frown like people (even making faces ourselves as we were drawing) and so — we just gave them hands.

Again and again we are justly called to account by children. In our *Story of Trains* it passed unnoticed for a couple of years that we had drawn a locomotive gaily pulling a string of cars that were not even coupled to it. It took a small boy to find that.

A biology professor was once greatly upset because we placed the wrong number of legs on a wee little butterfly in the corner of some drawing.

And now in *The Rooster Crows* again we have gone wrong. In the "Bye Baby Bunting" picture, Father's gone a-hunting, Mother's gone to milk a cow — but alas our critic tells us Mother is sitting on the wrong side of the cow and at the wrong end of her anatomy. I can't claim to having ever achieved the art of milking, but I have seen cows — and something, I admit, *is* wrong with that picture.

We learn many things from the children who write us. I am continually surprised how much color means to them, for they speak of it so often. They are always very definite in their ideas. One child gave us a hard question to answer when he wrote that he had definitely decided to become an author and would we please give him all the facts on how to be one. We were put in our place by another child, who told us that he liked our books very much but he had a bike and he loved that best because that had a speedometer. I should like to know the little girl who wrote that she had just read our *Bible Stories* and the *Story of Ruth*.

She said, "I forgot to tell you that I thought Ruth was very loyal not to leave Naomi. I would have done the same. Thank you very much."

I wish all critics were as truthful as children, even if indirect. A long letter from a western boy ended by telling us that he liked the *Story of Joseph* and the *Story of Moses* very much indeed but would we *please* write a book about boys and girls having fun. The happiest compliment we ever had was from a little pig-tailed girl who was very disappointed when she met us and said, "Oh! I didn't know you were just real people. I always believed you were magic."

There was a sad time a few years ago when, for the first time, working on children's books brought us no pleasure. In fact it seemed almost impossible. Half-heartedly we tried this and that and a book failed to materialize. (We also have books turned down, you know.) Red Cross work, a garden, standing on the post watching for planes that never appeared, even listening to the news, all seemed far more important. There were plenty of good books for children, so why waste our time trying to make another?

Then just at that lowest moment it was the simple, happy things we had known and felt as children that seemed the only truths worth hanging on to. I realized that books for children were still important and that any truth or beauty, which even in a small way we could give a child, could be a vital influence. One night at that time, while trying to forget the eleven o'clock news which we had just heard, and while trying to put away the worry that so many weeks had passed since we had heard from our child, I played a childish game with myself. Instead of counting sheep I tried to recall the foolish little rhymes and jingles I had not thought of for so many years. In the morning I went to my desk and wrote them down and then naturally they had to have illustrations. It was purely an escape move on our part but while we were working on those pictures we found we could live in a little world which was decidedly more sane than the real world was at that moment.

We worried our friends and their friends for different versions of the jingles and they grew and grew in number. When we decided to put them into a book the task of selection was difficult. It was surprising how many of the jingles involved problems and prejudices. Here are a few and you will understand that they could not be included.

"Eenie, Meenie, Minie, Mo." I know we would have been in trouble with parents and teachers if we had given the next two lines. Another we didn't use was this: —

> Republican Rat take off your hat
> And make way for the Democrat.

From the father of a friend in the Deep South came a rhyme that when a small boy he and other children of the town had shouted.

> Jeff. Davis rode the big white horse
> Lincoln rode the mule
> Jeff. Davis was our President
> Lincoln was a fool.

From a woman who lives in the West Virginia mountains came this rhyme.

> George Washington was our first President,
> And he wore purple socks;
> He rode upon an old gray horse
> And got the chicken pox;
> He chased an old blind woman
> And had to run for fair
> And that is how, as history says,
> He crossed the Delaware.

You can see we had to make a selection and there were many jingles we found which we did not include in *The Rooster Crows*.

Now I turn this book over to Miska and to his chapter.

CHAPTER II

I LEFT Hungary in 1911 soon after I finished art school. When I arrived in England, the customs official asked me if I had anything to declare. I answered in French that I was a painter, meaning that no painter would have any luxury articles. The customs man looked at me, marked my strange assortment of luggage "free" and asked no further questions and I was in England where I had long wanted to be.

With a name which no Englishman could pronounce, and knowing but a few words of the language, I found myself in a difficult situation. For a time I wandered about with my paintbox and was happy discovering the countryside and watching the people. After the little money I had brought with me had vanished, I found earning a living was a tough proposition. A few book covers and a few odd jobs of lettering hardly paid for my scanty and often far-between meals of fish and chips. At rare times only did I have tea with sugar.

Then a rich friend of mine turned up in London. I knew he must be rich, for although he had left Hungary for America but a few years before, here he was with two months vacation, traveling and visiting back home, and now seeing London. One day he asked me what success I had had in England and I told him that success was not remotely possible. Then he asked why I didn't go to America. I was very much surprised, for I couldn't understand who there could be in America who would appreciate art. I could see no opportunity for an artist in a land inhabited by Indians and cowboys.

As a boy I had read eagerly stories by Fenimore Cooper and books about America by the German writer with a fanciful mind, Karl May, who, although he had never been in America, outdid any American author with his exciting tales of Indians and palefaces. In Europe we thought him a marvel, as he himself was the hero of all the tales he wrote. My friend then told me that he would pay my passage back to England if in America, within six months, I could not make a living. In five minutes I had made my decision.

In a short time I was on a boat coming into New York harbor. No one had told me that I needed money to enter the United States of America and all but a few dollars of the little I had left after paying for my ticket had been spent on the boat. I had had a wonderful trip but had practically no money left. There were three friends with me and we pooled our money. It made about seventy-five American dollars which we put in a roll with the larger denominations on the outside carefully held in place with a rubber band. One of my friends, who had been in America before, stood first in line. Supposedly slipping the money back in his pocket after he had shown it to the official, he passed it to me. When called upon, I produced a roll of money, loose and considerable looking, with no rubber band, and this I in turn passed back to the friend following me.

This little incident over successfully, we felt quite happy but we were not in America yet, as we had to pass the doctor's inspection and that is very frightening to any foreigner, for if the doctor said "no" we knew there was no chance of entry. But to my surprise the doctor looked at me with a nice big smile on his face and asked if I spoke English and what my profession was. I told him my English was not very good but that I was hoping to improve it in America and was also hoping to make my living with art. Then he patted me on the back and assured me that in America I would have no trouble in earning my living with art, although it might take a little time to get acquainted with the new country. He shook hands and wished me good luck and happy days in America. And that was my entrance into this country.

This friendly, open country was amazing and unbelievable to me. The language was to my liking. If I could not make myself understood right away, people would listen and help and in many cases "yes" or "no" was enough without any frills. My friend was right. In six months I was working. I had an apartment with another friend. I owned a new suit of clothes from Wanamaker's and a pair of American-made shoes that all Europeans longed for, and I had extra money in my pocket for a glass of beer with which I was presented a roast-beef sandwich. I had misjudged America and no doubt about it.

But it was a little disappointing about the Indians; and then one day I saw them. They were on Madison Avenue — feathers, war paint and all — just as they had been in the stories I had read.

I followed them only to find they were part of a circus opening that day at the Hippodrome.

I knew there were many Hungarians in America, but I was greatly surprised at something that happened. A friend of mine was coming from Europe and I had given him directions in a letter, written in Hungarian, of how to find my apartment if I should miss him at the boat. When he arrived he decided it was all so simple he would not bother me but would come to the apartment by himself. He took the wrong subway and landed in the Bronx — 180th Street, but not the right place. Trying to retrace his steps and start over again he was completely lost. Finally at a subway station which was not busy he approached the ticket-chopper, a big colored boy who sat half reclining, reading a newspaper and with his feet comfortably placed on top of the machine. My friend spoke a little English but with a terrific accent. The boy listened, then reached for the letter to see for himself the address for which my friend was asking. He turned the letter over and continued reading to the end, laughing and apparently enjoying it. Amazed, my friend asked where he had learned the Hungarian language and the boy answered, " Why, I come from Pittsburgh."

I found here a country that I had dreamed of, but never thought could really exist; I found ideals and principles that I had always believed in. I don't think any American-born can appreciate this country as I do.

In the books we make I am happy when we can picture some of those wonderful things which American children can claim as their heritage. Working on *An American ABC* book meant a great deal to me aside from the making of the pictures. In *The Rooster Crows* we have tried to put into the hands of children little snatches of story that are rightfully theirs. And now we are working on a book of United States postage stamps, those small squares of paper commemorating events of which American children can be so proud. We are trying to put before the children of this country those things which are theirs for the taking.

Now comes the last chapter, our chapter, Maud's and mine.

CHAPTER III

THE climax of this tale is short but exciting. Today, June 18, 1946, we have received the Caldecott Award. We are proud and happy because it comes to us as an assurance that the love, the hard work, and any skill we may possess, which we have put into our work, have been considered worthy. If we have given any child real joy or have made him a little more appreciative of the beautiful in this world, we are satisfied.

Although dawn is the proper hour for the Cock to crow, with us it is tonight that the "Rooster is Crowing."

BIOGRAPHICAL PAPER

by *Irene Smith Green*

Maud and Miska Petersham

FOR two full decades the name (rather than names) of Maud and Miska Petersham has been known constantly to all whose experience with children's books goes back to the 1920's. This old and rich acquaintance is deeply rooted in our picture book literature. It is interwoven with the growth of better illustration in books for the young. It stands the test of years because it is planted in the bedrock of good work, work that is sound, informed, and enduring.

Therefore when we hail the Petershams today as the year's winners of our highest award to children's artists, we give them more than a passing salutation. Linked to the season's celebration of *The Rooster Crows,* which has just received the Caldecott Medal, is this long-time association with all their books. Here then is no calculated honor, but one to express spontaneous and grateful affection.

When *Miki* was published by Doubleday in 1929, a wave of fresh air breezed through the current picture book modes. At once we knew that our immediate borders included far-off Hungary, stretched there by a book that was honest and gaily childlike. That year we saw how the children loved it. *Miki* has never faltered in their regard. It is still asked for, slept with, worn to tatters in growing families, and replaced continually in public library children's rooms. About two years ago, at the height of the war, the seven-year-old nephew of one of my friends was playing a bombing game with some other children. When it was his turn to play, the city happened to be Budapest. "Oh," she heard him say, "I wouldn't want to bomb Budapest! That's where Miki lives."

The origin of *Miki* is of course well known. It pictures the life in Hungary that Miska Petersham knew as a boy, and it was named for the artists' small son. In story sequence came next a picture book almost equally beloved, *Auntie and Celia Jane and Miki* (Doubleday, 1932). "Auntie" thereupon joined Miki as a favorite picture book character. Like him she was real, the half-sister of Maud Petersham's mother; and a central figure in the family till the end of her life. Her book is a story about two generations. When Auntie was a young school teacher, Celia Jane chose to stay with her, rather than go back home with her mother and father and sisters, at the end of summer. In the second part of the book Celia Jane (Maud of course) is a grown-up woman with a little boy of her own named Miki.

Celia Jane had always felt that there was something very special about Auntie. Now Miki was sure of this. Auntie could tell the best stories. She could bake the funniest cookie-men. She could make stretchy candy and cake with maple-sugar frosting. . . . When Miki was sick and cross, Auntie always had time to read to him. They liked the same stories and books. . . . About the only things they really could not agree upon were turtles and snakes. So the days went by, and Miki and Auntie were always the best of friends, and the older Auntie grew, the more special she became.

One more Miki book was published in 1934, *Miki and Mary: Their Search for Treasures* (Viking). Mary, too, is real — a cousin, then small; still a close member of the family, oftener called Mitzi. *Get-a-way and Háry János* was among the early excitements of the brand-new Viking Junior Books. May Massee, who as Children's Editor at Doubleday, Doran had published the preceding picture books, brought it out in 1933. Háry János is a "wooden soldier doll from Hungary, faded and one-armed, but still proud and boastful." Get-a-way is an old, worn toy horse whom Háry met on a junk heap. This story tells of their rejuvenation and eventful lives in the magic land where old toys become new. The distinguished lithographs gave full scope to the Petershams' enthusiasm for old toys, which they had collected or sketched in their journeys all over America, Europe, Egypt, and Turkey.

Their lovely illustrations for *The Christ Child* (Doubleday,

1931) were inspired during three months which Maud and Miska Petersham spent in Palestine. There they made the sketches, then completed the drawings in Leipzig. Today, as fifteen years ago, it is the Bible picture book which children and their elders cherish first. Sharing in the same reverent picturization is *Jesus' Story, A Little New Testament* (Macmillan, 1942), or *The Story of Jesus,* for Catholic children. Their others from Biblical sources are *Stories From the Old Testament: Joseph, Moses, Ruth, David* (Winston, 1938), and *The Ark of Father Noah and Mother Noah* (Doubleday, 1930).

During these busy years the Petershams not only produced their own books, text and pictures, but illustrated many others besides. Sandburg's *Rootabaga Stories* (Harcourt) and Lamb's *Tales From Shakespeare* (Macmillan), both about 1923, were the introduction to their work now best remembered. A variety of storybooks and collections had preceded these. However, their very earliest drawing for children appeared in schoolbooks published by Macmillan. They illustrated many lively tales, but the most characteristic is *The Poppy Seed Cakes* by Margery Clark (Doubleday), whose excellent design, brightness, and animation have delighted its legions of readers since 1924.

Between 1933 and 1939, Maud and Miska Petersham were occupied with the famous Story Books for the John C. Winston Company. Their colorful pictures and interesting texts furnished exactly the information children wanted, on a great variety of subjects: clothes, food, houses, transportation *(Story Book of Things We Use)*; gold, coal, oil, iron and steel *(Story Book of Earth's Treasures); Story Book of Wheels, Ships, Trains, Aircraft;* corn, rice, sugar, wheat *(Story Book of Foods From the Field)*; wool, cotton, silk, rayon *(Story Book of Things We Wear).* Our library shelves never dared thenceforth to run low on these indispensable subject books for the younger readers. I can remember a little girl on Christmas Day in 1939 running about the house, neglecting toys and picture books, hugging *The Story Book of Rayon* and caroling to her parents' astonishment, " Goody for good old rayon! "

In 1941 we were all more aware of America than we had been since 1917, and we welcomed *An American ABC* (Macmillan) with its spirited interpretations of The Liberty Bell, The Declaration of Independence, The Mayflower, Yankee Doodle, and other symbols of our national life. The artists offered it as an expression of their own vital creed. Which brings us to *The Rooster Crows, A Book of American Rhymes and Jingles*, published by Macmillan in 1945 and winner of the Caldecott Award. Designed as companion to *An American ABC*, this is Americana highly appealing to the young. The beautiful pictures in soft, airy colors are full of humorous, homely details which confirm the rhymes' origins in American soil. These seventy-seven jingles, finger games, and rhymes for skipping rope and counting out are a part of our language: " Bushels of wheat ...", " This little pig . . .", " Roses are red . . .", " The bear went over the mountain. . . ."

Maud and Miska Petersham work together on the same pictures. Theirs has been called " a perfect collaboration." Miska is right-handed, Maud left; surely a partnership by destiny. Their texts come off the same way, from both, although Maud does most of the actual writing. They tell about Willy Pogány being responsible for their start along the road they have happily followed, through many years of bookmaking for children. Mr. Pogány had more work ahead than he could finish and turned over a children's book to the Petershams. This happened after they were married. In the illustrating of books they have been faithful to the children's field, and have never worked separately.

Nothing about this perfect collaboration is more amazing than the fact that it began. The fortunes that brought together this boy from Hungary and girl from New York State designed a stirring true-life romance. It began just before World War I. When, in May, 1946, I heard Maud and Miska Petersham reminiscing, the years rolled away. Against the backdrop of more recent history their story grows with meaning, pure commentary on old Europe and a new land.

Miska Petersham was born Petrezselyem Mihaly, a Magyar, in

a small Hungarian town near Budapest in 1889. He has been self-supporting since he was twelve. By walking miles each day to the art school in Budapest he learned to paint; paying for it with drawing jobs of any sort to be had, such as making slides for doctors at about seven cents each. The professors at the art school unanimously conferred upon him graduation honors not won by a student in many years. They offered him a three-year scholarship for study anywhere in Europe, but it required his agreement to live in Hungary for fifteen years afterward, and the offer was refused. At twenty-one he would be forced to serve three years in the Hungarian army. Forseeing the ruin of his hands for his chosen future, the young artist escaped from the country secretly, and made his way to England. There he changed his name to Miska Petersham, which the English could pronounce, and began studying in a London art school at night.

England in 1911 was not an easy place for a struggling painter, foreign born. For his first Christmas he was without food three days. Then came a letter from an old friend, bringing the unsought gift of a gold piece. Occasional orders earned what money he lived on. Miska remembers one time when he had only a shilling left, and how carefully he planned what it must buy: a meal that night, and a loaf of bread to last many days. As he stood hungry and discouraged in an art gallery that afternoon, waiting for the inexpensive Fish and Chips to open, two girls came in collecting funds for victims of the *Titanic* disaster. Miska offered his shilling, meaning to ask for half back in change. But they did not understand his limited English and took it all. That night he went to the house of a fellow painter in a distant part of London. The usual four-hour walk took him six, because he was weak. The friend's cupboard, too, was bare. They pawned Miska's watch for one and a half shillings, bought tea, condensed milk, bread, and from a pushcart as a final bargain a big bunch of scallions. Miska remembers how they played chess all night, made sketches in the park in the early morning light, finished off the bread and scallions, and how he returned to his lodging while his power lasted.

This big, broad-shouldered boy from the Hungarian plains had a strong physique. Else he might not have survived times of such hardship, until a few paying jobs eased the struggle. But living was very hard. A friend urged Miska to go to America with him and two others who were sailing in a day or so. Hastily Miska collected salary due him and bought a ticket. A newcomer to our shores was then required to show possession of sixty dollars, and Miska had about six. How the four boys used in turn their combined capital of eighty dollars, Miska himself relates in these pages.

We can guess that this youthful European artist had a look about him which won friends. He received kindness and help from people who simply liked him. Commercial art jobs at various advertising agencies shaped his early career in America. Although his first place paid only eight dollars a week, others soon paid more. But Miska was interested in ends beyond the pay-check. When he amassed a hundred dollars it was his habit to quit the current job and take a trip. He saw many parts of the country that way. There were always more jobs.

In the course of things he worked for the International Art Service in the old Aeolian Hall, where his talents were highly rated. There he met Maud Fuller.

The Fullers had lived in Kingston, New York, when Maud was born, and subsequently in South Dakota, Pennsylvania, and back to the Hudson Valley, according to the assignments of her father, a Baptist minister. The four little girls were trained for parsonage decorum. Maud says her earliest memory is of being made to behave in church. The family moved west, but she still loved most the summers in New York State with her Quaker grandfather and with Auntie. Late one summer when her parents and sisters were leaving, Maud hid until their train left. That time she lived with Auntie for four years.

Maud's parents, both college graduates, wanted their girls to be trained for careers. Maud had won a high school art award that took her to New York City for a year before Vassar. Her mother had especially progressive ideas, befitting a member of Mount Holyoke's third graduating class, back in days when college education for women was uncommon. Maud graduated from Vassar in 1912, then went on to the New York School of Fine and Applied Arts. Like career girls today, she had fun in New York. Her first job was at the International Art Service, where as a beginner she had to get through some drudgery, such as cleaning up other people's drawings. At the time the agency's most skilled commissions were being reserved for a rising young commercial artist with a foreign accent, Miska Petersham.

This Petersham offered to look over her drawings and to criticize them professionally. He came early in the mornings and cut short his lunch hours to help Maud Fuller improve her work. Soon he was worrying because Maud was "wasting her time." He persuaded her to go home (then Newburgh) and draw. He would come up weekends to view her progress. Perhaps he did come as art critic, not suitor; anyhow his displeasure frightened Auntie. Miska explained to her that he could not afford the train fare unless Maud worked seriously! He said she must be free from the interruptions and demands of a large family, and spend a definite number of hours each day at her drawing board. Once understanding the problem, Auntie became Miska's ally for all time. He might have seemed out of place in the Fuller family (for he was a Catholic, a foreigner, and an impecunious artist); but Auntie understood and loved him. Also, she took over some of Maud's household chores.

Now Maud's very real ability began to prove itself. She returned to New York ready for worth-while commissions. By this time Miska Petersham and Willy Pogány were working together. Miska continued to tutor Maud. Naturally they got married. Their first apartment was in Greenwich Village, gaily furnished on one hundred dollars. They lived in New York for many years.

Miki was born in 1923. Soon afterwards they built their home at Woodstock, New York, a famous art colony. On a sunny afternoon this past May we sat on their terrace, the Petershams, Doris Patee of Macmillan's, and I. The curving Catskill uplands stood green above the valley. Tall old pines, fruit trees, and flowerbeds surrounded the house, "built of stone so it could be left." That it had been left was fully proved by the hospitable interior, full of treasures from many corners of earth. For when they need to see a thing they must draw, they go in search of it, whether into the next county, to Mexico, or farther. But their summers are always spent in Woodstock, and there Miki grew up. Auntie, too, was there until her recent death when she was ninety-eight. Miki is still very young, but he is married, and is a veteran of a year in the Pacific as navigator on a B-24.

The Petershams are working just as hard as ever in their Woodstock studio, making pictures together. Each has also another engrossing hobby: for Maud the shaping of beautiful ceramics; for Miska, his marvelous stamp collection. Today she is a tall, lithe, vivacious woman, fleet-footed as in Vassar days. He is still powerfully built, with the kindest eyes, and a gentle manner of speaking.

They thank their son for serving not only as a frequent model, but also as touchstone. They learned wisdom in reaching children's tastes by watching Miki's reactions to their drawings. As long as he remained unmoved they worked to find the missing spark. Their approach therefore is always lifelike and vigorous. They tackle their stories *pictorially:* places for the pictures first, the text to be adjusted.

These artists came in when our present picture-book era was young. *Miki* set a standard. They took their responsibility seriously, in a period when too often children's illustration was, for lesser workmen, no more than a casual interlude. From the start they made complete layout dummies, worked closely with their engraver, guarded each step toward the book. With infinite painstaking, free from hurry and from avarice, Maud and Miska Petersham have cared only to give their best. In this they have had their true reward.

THE CALDECOTT AWARD 1947

The Little Island

illustrated by LEONARD WEISGARD

written by GOLDEN MACDONALD*

published by DOUBLEDAY 1946

FORMAT

SIZE: 10″ x 8″, 40 pp. (unfolioed)

ARTST'S MEDIUM: Gouache

PRINTING PROCESS: Offset lithography

ILLUSTRATIONS: Front matter and 5-color, full-page illustrations on every other page, alternating with 2-color duotone

TYPE: Bulmer

BOOK NOTE

THE pictures show the changes the seasons bring to a little island out in the ocean. The story tells of a kitten who learns from a talkative fish about the island and how " all land is one land under the sea." Birds, flowers, and sea creatures decorate the pages.

*pseud. of Margaret Wise Brown.

ACCEPTANCE PAPER

by *Leonard Weisgard*

The Language
of Color and Form

WHEN news of the Caldecott Award for *The Little Island* first arrived, life couldn't have been brighter or more exciting.

But when I was told a speech had to be prepared for it, life became gloomier and gloomier.

Speeches terrify me; right here and now I expect to melt into a puddle of fear, wetness and bewilderment.

Pearl Primus, the dancer, was once a guest of a school in Harlem. She came and danced her message to the beat of drums and in a very exciting costume.

A week later I was the guest of the same school. The children couldn't have been more disappointed. There I was in a business suit and hiding behind large sheets of drawing paper. But then I was able to draw what I had to say rather than speak, as I now have to.

With mere words, no large sheets of drawing paper, how can I properly tell you how grateful I am to children and to librarians everywhere, and to thank you for the Medal? I remember, as a child, always being told, children should be seen and not heard. This advice now seems especially right for an illustrator.

It seems to me that through the years all the things that should be said and felt about books and children have been said; sometimes with the impressiveness of thunder, and sometimes with the eloquence of silence.

Perhaps too much has already been said, maybe not enough.

Perhaps this is the time to say "Thank you," to quickly retire, try to do better and say no more.

Or perhaps now is the time to say these things over again, as simply and directly as any of us can.

I wonder if I should try to amuse you with adventure and romance that would make you and myself wonder what next?

Should we think of the world as we would like to make it? Should we wish it were better, so that we could all sit back, marvel at it and at little children looking at us, all safe and secure?

I wonder if I should tell you about a childhood that wasn't always filled with strawberries and cream, and that would make you remember your own laughter and pain of growing up?

We were all of us incredible creatures when we were little. We could see and hear and feel and smell and with easy concentration create things that never were and things that were yet to come.

We can all remember when we originally saw and felt things not yet inhibited by manners or sentiment. Then we were lower to the ground and nearer to detail; then we could create a piece of silver out of some tinfoil down below in a drain, spot a robin on a water tower which could become a chimney pot wearing a red hat, make a brown cow out of an old glove, build a city in the folds of a bed sheet, or even transform a doting aunt into a witch!

Do you remember when words and sounds and images had particularly curious meaning for you? When with a clothespin pinching your nose snuffly noises would become a foreign language? Or a foreign language itself became music making pictures or fantasy?

Do you remember books that made you angry, books that made you happy, some books that stayed with you always?

There was a collection of English nursery rhymes in my childhood that always made me angry. It was all so quiet and polite, the children and the world in it were so pale and washed out.

The old Peter Newell books were always full of fun and calamity that wasn't too disastrous.

And I might as well confess those Fairy Tales that had *no* pictures always meant that I could create my own.

Books at school were upsetting to me. Those frightening black and blue worlds, where everything was outlined in black and indiscriminately filled in with one color. There were blue cows and blue people beneath a sky filled with blue sunshine on blue grass. On the next page the world would suddenly have turned orange. An orange child carrying an orange bucket filled with orange juice under an orange sky.

Fortunately children looking at books, drawing, singing, watching or just listening, seem to catch instinctively those details which are most important to them.

They focus without being hampered by superficialities. And with this faculty of perception children are closer to the primitive and nearer to significant detail. Children are never as disturbed as grownups by contemporary arts, a streamlined plane, or a gallery of modern painting. They see an image with real meaning and vitality and sometimes with incongruous humor making a sharper reality.

I remember an ugly old Victorian sofa, covered with faded green plush. It would become for me when I was a child the country fields with the sunlight lighting up the dust particles, and warming the grass upon the seat. Even now I cannot see a patch of grass in sunlight without seeing that old sofa.

I remember the sharpness of small pain, of infinite curiosity which would inevitably end in small joy or great disaster, of hiding things in my nose or cutting the Brussels lace dining room curtains, because the pattern was so disturbing and the starch so stiff. I was obsessed with the darkness of drawers, and wanted to create my own expressions with the hands of the clock, paint permanent shadows behind furniture and people. I remember the crazy pleasure of standing in puddles, and that great desire to animate all dead things. I remember in the summer heat blowing on flies and expecting them to believe winter had returned. I remember that disturbing feeling, believing grownups could see my thoughts. These first experiences, which we all felt intensely, sometimes had real meaning, which was almost always too deep to explain. This was our magic.

As we grow older and taller we seem to forget this magic and some of our original truths. Yet most creation that endures beyond the destruction of time has the simplicity of this childlike magic.

Ways of life, religions, myths, folk art, poetry, music, farmers' tools, chairs and tables and what's on them, all these and children wherever they are on earth, have a strong primitive relationship for me.

Our adult reality is a world of precarious balance. Some of us enjoy all the ingenious complexity of today's machinery, while some of us are still carrying burdens, even use our fingers instead of forks and knives. Men have split the atom and released stores of energy, but there are still people who wait for rabbit's foot luck or the misfortune that is sure to rain from umbrellas that are opened in the house.

Some are bound to the primitive and some to the modern. Some of us moderns yearn for the basic truth of the primitive.

But those original realists, the children to whom primitive mysteries are plain and natural, are for me the most exciting examples of the curious balance that swings the world. They are simple. We are self-conscious and complex. Yet they apprehend more directly than we do the machinery of a watch, the parts of a flower, all of architecture and design, even the love and hate of man. Children have not yet suffered the overdevelopment of the various machines of the mind. Drawings on cave walls in the childhood of time caught the simple reality of primeval life because of an intense closeness to nature.

The first stories of man over all the world were seen and heard and felt with the simple intensity of children. Children haven't changed, but what about the illustrator and his world?

There are times in illustrating when the artist of today must rub his nose against the surface of things to try to catch with the honesty of a child a yellow sun like a pat of butter in the sky, with clouds of cottage cheese and the smoke of boats flying in all directions, with no concern for north or east. Houses with windows gaping and people like raisins on the street, a fire engine tearing off the page and a policeman stopping everything.

We experimented with color for sound and shapes for emotion, letting the child bring his own magic of movement in a series of noisy books.

A radiator was drawn in a shape suggested by the hissing noise it makes. The circular rhythm of a clock ticking, even a square clock, set the clock on a circular background.

However, this is one method and there are others. One of the most impressive examples, for me, of a more formal approach, is Audubon's. In his picture of a White Bellied Booby, somewhat resembling a penguin, the bird sits on a stump with a view of his natural habitat telescoped beneath his legs. In the slight distortion of detail, there is a sense of drama making this picture more effective illustrative art, while the booby still has every feather in place.

To what degree illustration should be sheer realism, sheer fantasy or an ambiguity between is perhaps a matter of age level and the kind of writing to be illustrated.

A good rule for an illustrator is an old one: " The success of an illustration lies in the instinctive transference of an idea from one medium to another. And so the more spontaneous it be and the less labored in application, the better."

Now this is no place for me to start reciting the history of illustration nor to tell you how printing methods and the economies of the times have influenced illustration. I could talk for a long time about the children's books of the past and the precursors of Superman which also caught a directness of action and a luridness of detail. Instead I had better try to tell you what my own work with books has taught me. Of course some things are hard to tell, especially for a man whose language is color and form — not words.

How can I explain that I don't see black separated from the realm of color? Nor objects in terms of outlines? How can I tell what I feel about the shades of night?

If I could speak in the language of the fish from *The Little Island*, I would say that all the land is one land under the sea.

Then, I might try to explain how pictures for *The Little Island* and Golden MacDonald's text grew right up out of the water. This is a real little island off the coast of Maine belonging to a group of other little islands, called Vinalhaven.

I saw this island grow tall or squat as the tides rose and fell. I've watched the mists blow in and hide the little island, sometimes leaving only the pine tree tops exposed hanging in space. I rowed to and from the little island with the seals swimming just below the surface of the water; I've seen the sun rise and make a golden island for just five seconds in an early morning sea.

Everything is fast and fleeting around the little island, the sea is never still, the clouds fly quickly into different shapes, the colors change from sunlight to mistlight, the trees are always moving and the birds are always flying and screaming. This active little island was an elusive subject. The easy thing for me as an illustrator was to put as much of it as possible into wherever it is we store such things. I took it home to Connecticut, and remembered it in my own way.

I've tried to tell you how elusive, really as elusive as that little island, it is for me to talk of illustrating and bookmaking. Who dares explain the poetry of living and dying, or the minds of little children?

Yet in a way you already know it. You know it in your own lives. You know it in what you see and hear and feel with children all around you.

BIOGRAPHICAL PAPER

by *Clement Hurd* and *Edith Thacher Hurd*

Leonard Weisgard

IT was not the night one would have chosen to go to the country for dinner. The rain and sleet slanted across the train windows. The wind blew in those angry little gusts that only early March can produce. The old engine puffed through the wintry Connecticut countryside and chugged into Danbury at last.

There was Leonard waiting for us on the station platform. He was wearing his favorite brown corduroy jacket and greeted each one of us with a warm smile of welcome.

In the first place, one must get the setting for this party and now with the award of the Caldecott Medal to Leonard, I realize what an important party it was. It was being given by Leonard in honor of *The Little Island* which he had just finished illustrating, and included Margaret Wise Brown as author (doubling for Golden MacDonald), Peggy Lesser of Doubleday's as publisher, Alvin Tresselt, with whom Leonard has collaborated on several books, and the Hurds just to enjoy themselves.

After driving through the town of Danbury, we bounced over a muddy country road to the little Victorian house. Set back from the road, it looked down through tall maple trees to the lake beyond. At least that is all we could see through the early March darkness.

But this darkness was gone in a second, when Leonard opened his front door to us. Inside there was light. It was a warm, welcoming light coming from electric lights, kerosene lamps, candles and best of all a fire crackling happily in the open fireplace. All these combined to give a feeling of cheerfulness and gaiety — a party feeling indeed.

Without a word, each one of us started on our own trip of

exploration. We found ourselves in a veritable treasure house. But these were not the dead kind of fancy antiques one finds in a museum or in a rich man's house. These were alive and what's even better, they were used and personal to Leonard, who had picked them up during several years of foraging in the antique and junk shops of Connecticut.

An old, hand-painted, German clock ticked on the wall. White ironstone china gleamed from the sideboard and every once in a while Leonard would smile to himself as someone questioned him about some bit of painted furniture or glass, for he had painted it himself. It was impossible to tell the old from the new! Everywhere there were things of great beauty, things with humor and just comfortable things but nothing dull.

During these inspections we were constantly being sniffed and then at last passed as friends, by Finigan and Suzie, two eager black poodles. Anyone who knows Leonard's books at all, knows what an important part these two have played as Muffin, in *The Noisy Books*, and "the Poodle," in *The Poodle and the Sheep*, as well as many other books. There were also, of course, the cats. They sat staring at us coldly from the corners of the sofa or curled up on the warm hearth.

All this time there kept coming from the huge and completely modern kitchen, the most delicious smells of mysteriously good things being taken out of the gleaming white stove.

I have heard the expression of "a groaning board," but never have I seen one that groaned louder than this one. The table itself was round and showed the results of many hours of scraping and polishing to attain the soft glow of rubbed pine. There was comfortable room for all of us around the edge and in the center was an enormous Lazy Susan. It was made as part of the table and that night it twirled as good a dinner as I have ever eaten. There was a steaming turkey stuffed with chestnuts and covered with roasted oranges. There were sweet potatoes soaked in sherry wine. There was a huge wooden salad bowl and there was a pie to finish off with. It was only after the third degree, administered by the ladies, that Leonard confessed to " just a little help on the turkey and the pie from a lady down the road," otherwise he had been chef.

At last when none of us could possibly have tucked away another bite, the great moment arrived for which the party was planned. Leonard led the way to his little studio behind the kitchen and there it seemed another feast was waiting for us. This time, however, it was a feast for the eyes. All the pictures for *The Little Island* were arranged along the wall, some scarcely yet dry.

Suddenly, every one of us was taken out of the wintry Connecticut and transported to that little island off the coast of Maine. We had visited Margaret Brown on her island, so we knew well the rocks and flowers that Leonard showed us that night. It was all there in Leonard's pictures; even the way it must be on that little island in the silence of winter and with its earliest spring flowers in bloom.

At Leonard's party for *The Little Island* that night, I felt for the first time that I understood many other sides of his creative quality. Of course I had known his books for many years and I had known him in that New York way of seeing him from time to time at luncheon or at a cocktail party. But as is usually the case with one as retiring as Leonard, one needs more space and repose than New York offers, to round out the connection between the creative personality and the work.

Leonard was born in New Haven, Connecticut, on December 13, 1916. His father happened to be running a store at the time and Leonard insists that in order to keep from misplacing his young son, his father often kept him in a cracker barrel! During most of his childhood both his mother and father were in business of various kinds, so that Leonard was left a great deal with his step-grandmother, to whom he was devoted. When he was eight years old, the family moved to England, his father's birthplace, for a year. Leonard has already described this year in *Young Wings* and has done it better than I could, so I will quote:

"Through pale English sunlight I mostly remember having to go to bed at an early hour, pots of tulips, custard, jujubes, coal dust, trams, a balloon blowing away over the roof tops of London, the smell of fish and chips, and learning to like a large English sheep dog. Then, too, there were wonderful aunts and cousins. But we always seemed unable to avoid train wrecks, ship wrecks, bicycle upsets and ferryboat capsizings, coming out of them with no more serious results than shaky knees and a great longing to return home to America.

"There were, however, three cheering experiences I can't forget about England — a copy of Mother Goose nursery rhymes, nicely illustrated in English fashion; *Alice in Wonderland* with Tenniel illustrations, which have that remarkable quality of withstanding time and much looking at; and a beautiful pantomime performance of the beloved *Jack and the Beanstalk*."

After returning from England, the Weisgards settled in New York City and Leonard went to school for the first time. He went through the Public Schools of New York and graduated from high school, but, as he says, received more education outside than inside the schools; "spending a good deal of time on the Brooklyn Bridge watching the boats, and riding up and down elevated trains, smelling the city and listening to its noises."

He studied illustration at Pratt Institute but left after two years "because he wanted to illustrate." He has also studied dancing and for a time viewed it as his future career. He studied under Doris Humphries, Charles Weidman and various other exponents of the Modern Dance, and even traveled around for a time with a dance troupe giving recitals before Labor Unions. However, at that time it was almost impossible to support oneself as a serious dancer and so he gave it up, even though he still feels that to him the creative satisfaction in dancing is greater than in any other art.

Since bringing out *Suki, the Siamese Pussy*, which he wrote and illustrated himself in 1937, Leonard has illustrated an impressive list of more than forty books for children of all ages.

In 1940, Louise Seaman Bechtel, writing an article for the *New York Times Book Review*, entitled *The Art of Illustrating Books for Young Readers*, picked Leonard out as one of the new artists who had stepped the farthest away from traditional styles and who, both in method and in imaginative approach, was speaking to children in a somewhat different new way. She predicted that his verve and simplicity would receive wide approval from children. It is interesting to me that not only has Mrs. Betchel's prophecy come true, but also a like verve and simplicity are widely practiced by others in the field today.

I do believe that Leonard has had as much influence on this trend as anyone, but that the most telling influence was from the whole group of the William R. Scott books from 1937 on; of these books Leonard did his share of illustrating and designing. The Scotts brought a breath of clean, vital fresh air into the field by consistently speaking directly to the children.

Leonard has spoken from time to time of the influence upon him of modern French and Russian bookmaking, and I think the influence was in the background to give him a certain freedom of treatment and brilliance of color not common in America when he started working.

When we look back over the familiar old favorites in children's illustration, such as Tenniel, Beatrix Potter, Kate Greenaway, Jean de Brunhoff — and let's not forget Mr. Caldecott himself with his genial, bald-pated John Gilpin — the universal quality we find is a radiation of enjoyment that is picked up by the people of any age. There is never any condescension to child level or a talking down to children; but rather the feeling of a nice, congenial friendship between an adult creative spirit and the children. All of which is rather a fancy preamble to saying that the quality running through almost all of Leonard's books is that intangible feeling of the enjoyment of picture making; of the creative satisfaction first and the result second. In any work of art it is not the tangible result that is of importance, but the creative spirit that comes through the tangible surface.

Another quality that runs through his books is that his style, although a very personal one, seldom runs away with the show. Leonard seems to be able to control it to fit into the book before him. An example of this is *The Water Carrier's Secret*, by Marcia Christina Chambers, which he illustrated in 1942. Here Leonard has drawn Mexico and Mexicans with such feeling and truth that many Mexicans, including the Mexican Consul in New York, have remarked on how well he must know Mexico. (Also a tribute to Leonard as a researcher. His only visit to Mexico was four years later in the summer of 1946!)

Leonard has a charm in his drawing and painting of animals that reveals a background of many years of loving attention. Never has a kitten been portrayed as so timid, or so bold, so fierce, or so scared, as he has portrayed Timothy in *Timid Timothy*, which he illustrated for Gweneira Williams in 1944. What child could resist this kitten even if he has to stay on the pages of a book?

Once more in *The Poodle and the Sheep*, by Margaret Wise Brown, Leonard gives the story a feeling of fresh, cheerful humor and pace. The poodle is not really bad, even though he was put in a dog jail for chasing sheep. The sheriff is not really fierce, although he pursued the offender over land and sea in a ferocious manner. The unity between the pictures and story should make this little book some sort of classic by now.

This leads us to a series of books that I really believe are on their way to being classics, the *Noisy Books*. These were written by Margaret Wise Brown and brought out each year by W. R. Scott for the successive five years starting in 1939. These books are important for various reasons aside from the illustrations, but one of their most outstanding qualities is the obvious collaboration between author, publisher and illustrator. In fact, it seems to be so close that it is hard to tell where one stops and the next begins. However, there are certain qualities for which the primary credit should go to the illustrator. One of these is the creativeness with which a small number of colors were so used to look like a great deal more. It is a very clever and unusual solution to the color layout. There is a variation to the successfulness of the colors used in the different books but those in the first, third and fourth seem to me particularly good. One secondary motif that runs through the books, and is very successful, is the adaptation of the shapes around the objects to conform to the noises they make. One is not actively conscious of this, but I am sure that it has an unconsciously integrating effect in the child's participation in the story, — such an important part of this series.

Leonard has illustrated several classics and it is interesting to see the way he combines a traditional feeling for the pictures, while actually treating them quite freely. One of his earliest books is *Cinderella*, that he illustrated in 1938. Here he already had that happy combination, although he hadn't then come into the really bold freedom of color that is so characteristic of his later books.

The *Punch and Judy* that he did in 1940 stands up today, in my opinion, as one of the most brilliant of all his books. He has combined the traditional humor and vitality of Mr. Punch, with a richness of color and a theatrical elegance that positively captures the essence of all puppet shows.

From here I shall have to jump over a great many extremely good books, such as *Red Light Green Light*, *Little Lost Lamb*, and *Rain Drop Splash*, and come up to the present outstanding two: *The Little Island* and *The Golden Egg Book*. The first of these needs little said about it by me, as it is the center of so much attention. However, after seeing the original pictures, it was a joy to find how truly close the reproductions came to them, so close indeed that if this were general in the reproduction of children's books, we illustrators would be a happier group than we usually are.

The Golden Egg Book, published this spring by Simon and Schuster, seems to have many publishers wondering how it could be sold for a dollar. I must say that it is astounding, but this merchandising feat should not be allowed to overshadow the real beauty of the book, with its freshness of life and lovely sense of nature-in-the-spring. What a lot of real work this represents! Leonard reports that he received a letter from a disappointed lady who thought she was buying a flower book. When she got home and looked at the book more closely, she found not a single flower was named. Leonard sat down and patiently went through the book, giving her the exact name of every flower he had included!

These two most recent books are outstanding works in the children's field, both beautiful pieces of illustration, splendidly reproduced. Undoubtedly they show Leonard at the top of his creative development as an artist so far. Nothing he does, however, can entirely win me personally away from some of his early, simple books, such as *Punch and Judy*, *The Noisy Books*, and even little *Timid Timothy*.

Despite the recognition and honors that are coming to him, Leonard Weisgard has a restlessness concerning his work and future. Perhaps it is the reaction of an unusually sensitive person to the sadness and unrest to be found all over the world today. All I can say for his future is that whatever he comes to do, it will be creative and it will be well done; whether it be in the children's field, in advertising, in the theatre or perhaps just returning to the making of new antiques for another old house.

THE CALDECOTT AWARD 1948

White Snow
Bright Snow

illustrated by ROGER DUVOISIN

written by ALVIN TRESSELT

published by LOTHROP 1947

FORMAT

SIZE: 8⅝" x 10¼", 32 pp.

ARTIST'S MEDIUM: Acetate color separations in black India ink

PRINTING PROCESS: Offset lithography

ILLUSTRATIONS: Full pages and doublespreads in three colors, with some smaller illustrations

TYPE: 18 pt. Spartan Black

BOOK NOTE

THE big storm comes and everything is buried in white snow, bright snow. The children greet it with feelings quite different from those of the postman, the farmer, the policeman, and the policeman's wife. When the sun comes out, there is general rejoicing for Spring is at hand with the first robin.

ACCEPTANCE PAPER

by *Roger Duvoisin*

Outwitting the Comics

IT is surprising that the pictures for *White Snow Bright Snow* have been so honored, for after such a winter everyone should be tired of snow, even in a children's book. Of course, there are many parts of the country where little or no snow has fallen, and it may well be that most of the approval has come from these places. Now that the award has been made, I can safely say what I have known all along, that the book brought the winter upon us. This conclusion has been arrived at by simply putting two and two together. It was the first time that I had the opportunity to illustrate a book about snow and it was also the first time that I ever saw so much snow in one winter. If I had announced this finding earlier no one could have felt any sympathy for the book.

This misery brought upon us all by that book! I was well punished though, and when for two days I worked with the shovel to clear our five-hundred-foot drive of White Snow Bright Snow, I bitterly regretted the days I had spent putting snow upon the white pages with the brush. Well punished, too, when snow and ice broke our electric lines and thus for almost two weeks deprived us of water, light, and heat. And what strange discoveries about snow did we make this last winter! Did you know, for instance, how many pails of White Snow Bright Snow it takes to make a pail of dirty drinking water? Did you know that when White Snow Bright Snow is gathered even far into the fields, where the snow is virgin, where not a lonely rabbit has left its tracks, it makes but a dirty sooty water? I did not call the Museum of Natural History to find the reason but there is the fact. And what of the discovery that our great and proud mechanized civilization can be crushed by an extra six inches of White Snow Bright

Snow? Our great cities can live on somehow with an eighteen-inch snowfall, but are completely upset, dislocated, brought to the brink of catastrophe by a twenty-four-inch fall.

The only good thing that the book brought this winter is the assurance that never again will our elders dare mention the Blizzard of Eighty-Eight! Ours was better.

But, if all that trouble did not prevent *White Snow Bright Snow* illustrations from winning a great honor, it is not only because they found enough good friends in the South and West who could easily dismiss the black side of white snow, nor even for their quality as illustrations, but also, I think, because the childhood love for snow, like all childhood memories, is strong enough in all of us to make us open our hearts to everything connected with snow.

When the snow begins to fall, a few timid flakes at first, and then the heavy whirling mass of white which buries everything, our pleasure in looking out the window is very complex. It is partly the pleasure of seeing fields and woods being transformed into a beautiful landscape of fairy tale, but in it, too, is the secret childhood urge to go out and feel the snow, to plunge our hands into it, to make snowballs and snowmen. Unfortunately, when we try, cold hands and snow in our neck soon disappoint us, force us to return to childhood only in thought, and to mere intellectual contemplation of the landscape and of the children at play.

How children love snow! Nothing in the world can be as completely satisfying to them as snow. Nothing can lend itself so well to the fancies of their imagination — not even sand on the beach, not even a muddy puddle after the rain. They can jump into snow from the porch railing, they can war upon each other with snowballs or break windows, close the driveway with that four-foot snowball, build forts, tunnels, snowmen — why, even sleigh and ski over it!

Last Christmas, my son Jack and two little daughters of a friend of ours who were spending the holidays with us began to fret near the door like puppies in front of the icebox. Their joy grew in direct relation to the news of mounting troubles which came over the radio. When the radio blared that trains were stopped dead in their tracks all over the surrounding states by the same fluffy White Snow Bright Snow that snowmen are made of, their enthusiasm was boundless. The mournful glances that the father of the two little girls gave the snow because it prevented his going home that night was answered by the joyous thumping of snowballs against the windowpanes.

No wonder then that a book about snow can win some affection, and no wonder that the illustrator's old love for snow will come out of him when he is asked to paint snow on the pages of a book. Besides, what looks more like snow than the white pages of a book? All the artist has to do is to let the white speak for itself. A red spot on the page and you have the feeling of a red brick house whose roof is confused with the snowy hills behind. In the snow landscape everything is guessed rather than clearly seen, and the white page will be the perfect snow landscape if hardly anything is added to it, if the spaces composed on it are suggested rather than actually drawn. It's like the solid black page which I remember having seen in a joke book somewhere, with the caption: " Chimney-sweep in a tunnel at midnight."

The illustrator, and also the writer of children's books, is thus lucky in his work because much of it consists of recalling the wonderful and charming impressions of his childhood so that he may pass them on to children of new generations; to re-create for them the world which made his own childhood happy. That is why many children's writers or artists start their career by doing a book for their own children. Publishers like to say this in their advertising, but it is generally true, at least when the children's book artist *has* children.

Children's writers and illustrators are like all other grownups. They are very sentimental about their childhood memories. They distort them unconsciously to fit their changing conception of life. These memories grow and evolve and go very, very far sometimes from the original thing, and when translated into a book, they sometimes meet the discouraging bored look of the child because they do not present to him a real child's world, but a child's world seen through grownups' eyes.

Parents commit the same mistake when they insist on giving children the toys and picture books which they loved when young, for children's tastes change as the things around them change. If we give a child a toy car in the shape of the old-fashioned automobiles which made us happy, he will be scornful. What he wants is a toy car in the shape of the modern streamlined automobile.

My father one day decided to buy me a bicycle, and of course I immediately pictured the beautiful wheels of that day. They were not yet streamlined, in the shape of an airplane, or a motorcycle, with all sorts of useless gadgets. . . . (There I go, trying to prove that the bikes of my time were better than those of today. . . .) Anyway, I wanted a bicycle with gearshift, electric lights, a real English one. But when my father came back from the merchant, how bitterly I was deceived. Proudly he brought along an old, old racing American bicycle of the 1890's, the kind you see in old photographs, ridden by mustached bicycle racers in tight-fitting, knitted sport suit with drawers that came down below the knees.

"There," said my father, "is a real bicycle, not these silly, heavy ones of today which weigh a hundred-fifty pounds. I had the very same one when I was young and *I* know how good it is."

We never learn, however, for one day when I became fed up with the cheap comics my son was so fond of, I recalled how much finer were the comics of my own time.

"Ah," I explained to my son, "these comics were charming, well-drawn and so much better written! Not that silly stuff which you like." Even though I went to an art school and was taught there a sense of criticism toward the things that surround us, I still delighted in remembering those old comics. I finally decided to ask a friend of mine abroad to send a bound book of these comics, many of which were still to be found in secondhand book shops.

Alas, my son reacted to these comics, as I did with my father's bike; I was also as disappointed as he for other reasons. I saw that they were badly drawn and dull. They had perhaps a little charm in their amateurish appearance, compared to the slick comics of today. The shooting in them was of a milder nature, and the villain was not so tough-looking — for we have grown tougher. But that was all. They told things my son could not care about, any more than I could care for the old-fashioned bike. He looked at them once and never opened the book again.

The *White Snow Bright Snow* book will have a luckier history, I hope, for industrial designers will never be able to streamline snowflakes, at least not in the foreseeable future.

Perhaps it is only illustrations for stories that are purely imaginative, like Tenniel's illustrations for *Alice in Wonderland*, which can live on for a long, long time, and never seem dull and outdated.

So the illustrator and the writer of children's books must find that compromise, that good balance, between what he wants to give out of his own memories and what he knows the children of today want and are interested in.

The illustrator of children's books has another disappointment sometimes. He can go on making every effort to do tasteful illustrations (in which endeavor he may or may not succeed, of course) and he will always be astounded to see what sort of things children may love. For taste, as educated grownups know it, is not a children's affair. They do not have good taste or bad taste; they simply are not conscious that there is such a thing. They will be fond of the most frightful illustrations just as they will love good ones. What they like is an illustration that suggests something which their imagination can grasp and build upon.

After working very hard all day to make a satisfying set of illustrations, I am often made thoughtful by the gleam of joy I see in my son's eyes when he comes home with a one-foot pile of comics which he has traded with a friend (the one source of comics parents cannot control). I have seldom seen a child open a good book with the same enthusiasm with which he plunges into a gorgeous pile of comics. Why is that? The reason is, it seems to me, that too often the writer and the illustrator, in their effort to give tasteful things to children, are too restrained, and do not go all the way with this abundance of imaginative situations which the children love.

I remember a talk I heard at the last annual children's book exhibition at the New York Library by Mr. Donald Adams, and with which I completely agree. He said that the books we remember and love best are the purely imaginative stories. And even history can be presented in an imaginative way like fiction, while keeping an eye on the accuracy of the statements.

Stories, short, up-to-date, and extraordinarily abundant — unfortunately also too often coarse, silly and tough — are what they find in comics. But it is possible to combine good taste with this abundance, and it is my dream to find the time and the talent to do some good books which can compete in a child's estimation with the comics.

I can find a good example in my own boyhood reading of how and why illustrated literature may be preferred to the best, and its effect. The classic struggle which takes place in many homes between children who try to smuggle in this literature and the parents who try to weed it out was going on in our own home between my father, my brother and me.

There was at that time a cheap little publication which caused the despair of parents with its popularity among children. It cost two cents and for that small sum we could plunge into the weekly illustrated paradise of shooting and extravagant rides, hair-raising murder and adventures, the hero of which was Texas Jack, the pitiless enemy of criminal cowboys and outlaws (pronounced in French *cove-boas* and *ootlavs*). It was the Heigh-Ho Silver of those days. It must have been written and illustrated by a Frenchman who had never come to America and his stories were all the more fanciful and unhampered by true facts. None of the lessons of history about America which we had in school could affect our extraordinary and over-romantic conception of the land of perpetual and gorgeous adventures.

If Texas Jack always got his man, my father, who was after

his skin to burn it in the living room tile stove, never got him. Texas Jack always won gloriously. All the tricks that my father concocted to track him down failed. One favorite and safe place to read Texas Jack was in the century-old branches of a cedar tree which served as the headquarters of the neighborhood boys. As a matter of fact, the West is vaguely associated in my mind with the old cedar tree — or we would read it in bed when my father seemed safely asleep. When he found that out and arranged to control our bedroom lights from his own bedroom, I discovered an easy solution! There was a light which my father could never control. That was the moonlight. My bed being near the window, I discovered that a moderately large moon could well light the pulp pages, if the sky was clear enough. And it was the very same moon, I thought with delight, which would a few hours later light the mysterious prairie home of Texas Jack. It's due, no doubt, partly to these pleasant nights by the window that I owe the present need for eyeglasses.

Well, we never missed an issue of Texas Jack. And as I said, all our history lessons never stamped out completely our Texas-Jack conception of America, because history was presented to us as a dead thing. Texas Jack, cheaply written as the story was, was alive. When I came to America a few years later, it was not in the land of Washington, Jefferson, and Lincoln that I landed — it was in the land of Texas Jack. And to this day, since I have never been to the Southwest, my idea of that country is colored by Texas Jack, right or wrong. As a matter of fact, I think that that conception would even survive a visit to the West, so deeply have these wild fictions taken root in my memory.

I remember that when I first visited the Adirondacks, I expected to find something similar to the image I had formed in my mind when reading Fenimore Cooper who was, after Texas Jack, one of my favorite authors about America. Even though the descriptions of Cooper were fine and accurate, the illustrations of the book were not, as I remember them; the illustrator had never seen America, I am sure. His forests were more like the mysterious forests of Tom Thumb or other fairy tale illustrations, than those of the Adirondacks, and I was vaguely disappointed when I went there to find something quite different, even though I was impressed by the beauty of the country.

And I am sure that American children have also just as wrong a conception of the rest of the world if they read too much about it in cheap, inaccurate fiction which does not combine imagination with accuracy.

And so the juvenile book artist should have the tact to guide the child while giving him what he likes and wants, should fully satisfy his hungry imagination without distorting his conception of the world about him. It is only by giving children all that their imagination will take that he can get to see in their eye this gleam of joy which shows their complete response to a picture or a book.

Another influence picture books must have, it seems to me, is counterbalancing the too great love that children have for mechanical things in opposition to things of nature. I think that we shall never put in the hands of children enough picture books about nature, and we must take the trouble to control the number of books they read about gadgets just as we must take the trouble to see that they do not read too much cheap literature. Of course, this is a quite personal opinion which is based on my own observation. In spite of all we hear about them, machines are dead things. They are but toys, even the ones that grownups love. Things of nature are live things, like people, animals, flowers, mountains. To study nature, to learn how to know it well, makes a child mature more rapidly. An animal is not a mechanical toy to play with. It is a creature which has its own personality, and its reactions, habits, likes and dislikes must be taken into consideration. To study it requires an intellectual effort from the child which he does not make in reading about mechanical things or playing with them. To read about nature is to learn about life. A man who knows about life is more mature than a man who knows only about machines. Only books, illustrated books about life, can counteract the ever-present mania of most children for mechanical things — a childish mania which too many of them carry into their later life. Unfortunately, just as children will too often discard a good book for a silly one, they will too often drop the good book to concentrate on a catalog for a new model motor-car. This must be fought not by forbidding the mechanical toys or automobile catalog, but by surrounding children with pictures and books which give them a sense of nature, a sense of their own relation to it.

I think that in all these things we must be grateful to librarians who know children so well, and who do so much to give them the books that will develop them properly. Librarians can afford to, and do indeed, consider a book only for its true purpose — not to make money with it, but to educate and amuse children the right way.

And every artist and illustrator, and children too, must also be grateful to Mr. Frederic Melcher, who has for so many years worked hard and in such a disinterested way to encourage better and better bookmaking for children, and has made parents conscious of the importance of good books for their children.

And so personally I thank both the librarians and Mr. Melcher for the wonderful encouragement which they have given me. I will not let them down.

I do not want to end without saying that Mr. Alvin Tresselt must have his share of the honor conferred upon *White Snow Bright Snow*. It is his story after all, and a charming and well-done story it is. When an illustrator is given a *good* story to illustrate, his job is made pleasant and easier. The story is to a picture book what the silk is to a textile pattern. You can cover up poor material with a flashy pattern only to a certain extent. It will fool no one very long.

by *Dorothy Waugh*

Roger Duvoisin
as Illustrator for Children

ONE of the most important attributes of an artist is the ability to enter into a mood; to absorb, mature, and completely comprehend it; then to give it expression: perhaps musical expression; or graphic, physical, dramatic, or literary expression.

To be a good artist requires the expression of no more than one mood. Some artists express a single mood over and over, through varying subject matter or varying arrangements of the same material. Some express a wide range of moods, either through one or many types of subject matter.

The capable illustrator must, of course, have artistic mood-sensitiveness, and must be able to mature and express what he feels. If he is to do versatile types of work he must be able to plumb a variety of emotions. Besides, he must be able to take his initial impulse from an author, accepting the tone which the author has set, subjecting himself to it, expressing and interpreting it with a new fullness which brings added meaning to the author's statement — but always in the author's key.

We are all familiar with the illustrator who reads a script, looks up the outward paraphernalia appropriate to the subject matter, and then makes drawings of superficial scenes described by the author, without adding any amplification of warmth, grace, humor, mystery, terror, or delicacy — whatever the appropriate feeling may be.

With the inept, inadequate illustrator it is as if the author walked down a road and the illustrator followed; the author said, " This is a large tree, green and full of shade "; and the illustrator echoed, " Tree; shade "; the author said, " It is dusk. A bent woman passes "; the illustrator echoed, "A woman. Here I have drawn her. I've put on her the kind of dress the encyclopedia calls for; I looked it up."

The illustrator who can rightly claim the title of artist follows the author in a much more sensitive mood; or accompanies him. The author says, " This is a large tree, green and full of shade "; the artist responds, " Largeness and shade, the calmness and cool-ness of shade; a largeness in breadth and height and depth, and in spiritual qualities; a largeness which makes details seem small and the wholeness great."

The author says, " It is dusk. A bent woman passes." The artist amplifies, in his own terms of expression. " A woman. She moves with a heavy heart. She is bending under the weight of some spiritual burden. She is a woman lost in the preponderance of nature, yet the center of all; the nucleus in incipient turmoil. I must express all that in my drawing."

I am trying to give a sense of difference — because so many indications show that few people in the children's book world are conscious of the difference — between the hack, who concerns himself with drawing physical objects, and the artist, who presents a pervading mood. There is a temptation to paraphrase the remark to Samuel, saying, " The hack looketh on the outward appearance, but the artist looketh on the heart."

To study Roger Duvoisin's illustrations with an eye for what he has added in atmosphere to the books he has illustrated — spirit-ual or emotional atmosphere, or mood — is a good exercise in the appreciation of art in contrast to hack work. His unusual versa-tility in mood-evaluation and mood-expression renders the con-tribution which he makes to an author's text particularly evident.

To appreciate this, select some three or four of his books which present moods of wide variety.

Take *Tales of the Pampas* as a telling artistic expression of the weird, the vast, the brooding, the tensely dramatic, and as a graphic expression of impending doom. Through the drawings the per-vading atmosphere of the tales is foreshadowed for the reader, to set him in a receptive mood.

Illustrations
from the Caldecott Medal Books
1938-1957

Illustration by

DOROTHY P. LATHROP

From *Animals of the Bible*

Selected by HELEN DEAN FISH from the King James Bible

Published in 1937 by FREDERICK A. STOKES & Co.
Now published by J. B. LIPPINCOTT COMPANY

One-third reduction

Illustration by

THOMAS HANDFORTH

From *Mei Li* by Thomas Handforth

Published in 1938 by Doubleday, Doran & Company, Inc.

Three-eighths reduction

The circus girl lifted her high in the air.

Mei Li balanced all right, but her legs wobbled a little.

Illustration by

INGRI & EDGAR PARIN D'AULAIRE

From *Abraham Lincoln* by the D'AULAIRES

Published in 1939 by DOUBLEDAY, DORAN & COMPANY, INC.

One-third reduction

Illustration by

ROBERT LAWSON

From *They Were Strong and Good* by ROBERT LAWSON

Published in 1940 by THE VIKING PRESS

One-third reduction

Illustration by

ROBERT McCLOSKEY

From *Make Way for Ducklings* by Robert McCloskey

Published in 1941 by The Viking Press

Three-eighths reduction

Illustration by

VIRGINIA LEE BURTON

From *The Little House* by Virginia Lee Burton

Published in 1942 by Houghton Mifflin Company

Seven-sixteenths reduction

Illustration by

LOUIS SLOBODKIN

From *Many Moons* by James Thurber

Published in 1943 by Harcourt, Brace and Company

Three-eighths reduction

Illustration by

ELIZABETH ORTON JONES

From *Prayer for a Child* by RACHEL FIELD

Published in 1944 by THE MACMILLAN COMPANY

One-quarter reduction

Illustration by

MAUD AND MISKA PETERSHAM

From *The Rooster Crows,*

A Book of American Rhymes and Jingles

Published in 1945 by THE MACMILLAN COMPANY

One-third reduction

How much wood would a woodchuck chuck
If a woodchuck could chuck wood?
A woodchuck would chuck as much as he would chuck
If a woodchuck could chuck wood.

Illustration by

LEONARD WEISGARD

From *The Little Island* by Golden MacDonald
(Margaret Wise Brown)

Published in 1946 by Doubleday & Company, Inc.

Seven-sixteenths reduction

Illustration by

ROGER DUVOISIN

From *White Snow Bright Snow* by ALVIN TRESSELT

Published in 1947 by LOTHROP, LEE & SHEPARD CO.

One-third reduction

Illustration by

BERTA AND ELMER HADER

From *The Big Snow* by BERTA AND ELMER HADER

Published in 1948 by THE MACMILLAN COMPANY

Three-eighths reduction

The pretty white-footed wood mouse flicked his long tail as he looked at the geese flying high in the sky. He knew that winter was coming, but he had worked hard and had a good supply of seeds stored away in his underground nest. He wouldn't be hungry in the months to come.

Illustration by

LEO POLITI

From *Song of the Swallows* by Leo Politi

Published in 1949 by Charles Scribner's Sons

One-third reduction

Illustration by

KATHERINE MILHOUS

From *The Egg Tree* by KATHERINE MILHOUS

Published in 1950 by CHARLES SCRIBNER'S SONS

One-quarter reduction

"An Egg Tree!" they said. "We've never seen a
tree that grows eggs on its branches!"

The children went home and told their fathers and
mothers about it. The fathers and mothers all came to
see the wonderful tree in the little red house.

Illustration by

NICOLAS MORDVINOFF

From *Finders Keepers* by WILL LIPKIND and NICOLAS MORDVINOFF

Published in 1951 by HARCOURT, BRACE AND COMPANY

Three-eighths reduction

Winkle jumped at the big dog's head, Nap at
his tail.

Illustration by

LYND WARD

From *The Biggest Bear* by L<small>YND</small> W<small>ARD</small>

Published in 1952 by H<small>OUGHTON</small> M<small>IFFLIN</small> Co.

One-quarter reduction

Illustration by

LUDWIG BEMELMANS

From *Madeline's Rescue* by Ludwig Bemelmans

Published in 1953 by The Viking Press

Three-eighths reduction

They went looking high

Illustration by

MARCIA BROWN

From *Cinderella* freely translated from Perrault
by Marcia Brown

Published in 1954 by Charles Scribner's Sons

One-third reduction

Cinderella went to sit near her step-sisters and paid them a thousand courtesies. She shared with them some oranges and lemons which the young prince had given her. The sisters were completely astonished. They did not recognize her at all.

Illustration by

FEODOR ROJANKOVSKY

From *Frog Went A-Courtin'* retold by JOHN LANGSTAFF

Published in 1955 by HARCOURT, BRACE AND COMPANY

One-third reduction

He rode right up to mouse's hall,
Where he most tenderly did call:

Illustration by

MARC SIMONT

From *A Tree Is Nice* by Janice May Udry

Published in 1956 by Harper & Brothers

Five-ninths reduction

Cats get away from dogs by going up the tree.
Birds build nests in trees and live there.
Sticks come off the trees too.
We draw in the sand with the sticks.

Take the Heritage Club Benét-Duvoisin *Mother Goose*, or the Merrill *Language Arts for Modern Youth* for gay, rollicking abandon.

Take *Riema, And There Was America, Robinson Crusoe*, or *Bhimsa, the Dancing Bear* for warm human insight coupled with intellectually poised observation.

And take *A Child's Garden of Verses, Jumpy, the Kangaroo*, or *The Christmas Whale* for friendly, childlike, casual imaginativeness, half reality, half fantasy.

From a study of these one will not only appreciate that in each case the author's mood has been sensed, and then presented from a new, highly appropriate graphic viewpoint; one will realize also that the important thing in the illustrations is the mood, not isolated pieces of subject matter. Not objects, or facts. Rather, the gaiety or the tenseness, the warm friendliness or the humor or the abandon which is created by means of the atmosphere of the drawings.

In addition to the ability to sense, to develop, and to express a mood only one other ability, in any creative art, is absolutely essential. That is the ability to compose. Composition is the keeping of all parts in proportion and in position to achieve the desired whole — to make the parts unite, no single one left unneeded, all of them essential and contributing to an integral — often a centripetal — force. In reality, composing is an essential part of expressing a mood; yet it may be considered separately.

When so many people have learned to hear form in music; to know the difference between a mimic imitating sounds and a composer conceiving and delineating a symphony, it seems strange that so many people fail to see the difference between a commonplace illustrator drawing objects and an artist presenting a spiritual whole of which each form, each direction and movement is a balanced part, in proportion to the entire expression, growing out of a given emotional impetus.

Especially is it strange that composition in drawings often goes unappreciated even by people who can see the difference between the effect of furniture scattered aimlessly about a room and the same furniture arranged for a cohesive visual balance, for heights, weights, color intensities, and textures which give the eye a movement that returns upon itself to create repose, or unity and completeness, in a plan having centers of interest, opposing forces, and axes — the same framework features which in a drawing make a whole out of all the parts.

Without intelligent, sensitive organization — in addition to mood presence — no expression is art. In other words, composition is so important that no talent whatever can give an expressionist in any creative field the right to the name of artist without the ability to compose. This is one of the abilities which Roger Duvoisin has to a high degree.

The brush drawing of Marta, opposite page 184 in *Tales of the Pampas,* is one exceptionally beautiful composition in which I believe no one could fail to sense the cohesion, the interplay of all movements to one nucleus of effect and attention, the oneness and the completeness of the whole; and also the use of form solely to create a mood.

The trees are shown only as they add feeling to the drama. The observers, the grasses, the leaves, are indicated with complete adequacy for the purpose which brought them to the composition — but not presented as individually considered, separate units employed heterogeneously to fill up space, without regard to whether the composition demands sharp attention-calling detail in one position, or soft, retiring suggestiveness in another.

In the drawing of Marta the parts all compose in one satisfying unit. And the mood is overwhelmingly the major statement. Not the individuals. Not the trees and the log. Not the leaves and the branches. Not the gloom, even, beneath the trees in the woods. The reason for the drawing's being and its means of existence is the expression of a moment's compelling force between the universe and a heart. Oppressive tragedy is the mood; and every feature in the composition combines to express it.

The pen drawing on page 239 of the new World edition of *Robinson Crusoe* is again an obvious — though again a sensitive and intricate — composition. In this illustration the attention is sent back and forth and back and forth between two focal points of attraction, and is never tempted to wander aimlessly away to trivialities and hence out of the picture. There are no unrelated parts. The lines of the guns, the lines of the branches, the intricate movement of the disturbing, excited little figures in the middle distance, the strong horizontal lines of the far shore and the horizontal weight of the bluff keep a very active composition within its area — within its area of paper, and within its emotional area of excitement, battle, contest between the solid quiet power of adequate minority and a primitive distracted multitude.

Another Duvoisin illustration in which both composition and mood are plain is the drawing of hunter, dog and gun at the bottom of page 14 in *Moustachio*. In composition the movement grows from the lower left in strong divergent lines upward to the right. Their strength is made powerful by the simplicity of the shapes; by the sharp contrast between darks and lights; by the definiteness of every form in this central active featured part of the composition. The movement of the attention is stopped, turned back, and held within the picture by two vertical tree trunks at the ends of the drawing. These have stationary power by means of their vertical stability and their bulk; and yet they are so softly presented, and so netted about by a loose lacework of merely suggested foliage, that they do not vie for attention with the main statement.

How effectively the shape and position of belt and powder horn give the upward-and-to-the-right turn to the hunter's figure. The upward-and-to-the-right movements of the drawing's stressed forms are like those in the growth of a plant — reminiscent of the way long blades of grass, starting from one root, reach, curve, and separate as they grow away from their common nucleus.

The mood of the drawing is one of humor, with a slightly quaint and fantastic tinge. It is not a forced, exaggerated, or superficial humor. It is gained by the merest touches: the delineation of the dog's eye; of the eye and eyebrow of the man, the tilt of his hat, the cut of his beard, and his positive melodramatic stance.

Humor is one of the emotions Roger Duvoisin has expressed successfully in many varying shades. Humor in dogs, cows, and other animals has really grown into a new area through his work, from *Donkey-Donkey* down through the famous Lord and Taylor perfume advertisement which caricatured the names of famous scents and drew more fan mail to the store's advertising office than any other advertisement they have ever printed.

There is humor, when it is appropriate, in Duvoisin's people as well as in his animals: in his Old King Cole and his Little Bo-Peep of *Mother Goose;* in the maid and milkman of *At Our House;* in the organ-grinder in *A Child's Garden of Verses.*

It is not the affected humor of the superimposed wart, the root-shaped hand, the noticeable clothes, the cuteness of trite paraphernalia; the humor is in the way the person in the drawing feels, the way he lives, and the way these conditions of life translate themselves into form, through the tilt of a head, the widening of an eye, the drop of a jaw or perhaps by means of a gesture or a posture which through the delicate throw of a muscle gives a figure violence, confidence, hesitancy, or languid grace.

If we speak of color, there again Duvoisin has an ability which is exceptional. Perhaps his years of designing fine silks are partly responsible for the rich breadth and the maturity of his color sense; though, on the other hand, it is improbable, of course, that the finest silk firm of two continents would have brought him here from Paris at the age of twenty-three had he not had outstanding talent along that line from the start. The books of Duvoisin's which have had appropriate manufacture show his color work with a beauty not often seen between book covers.

The lush tropical color in *Riema* and the other Elliott books, the clear brilliance of the illustrations in *And There Was America,* the double-page paintings in *They Put Out to Sea,* the dramatic use of color on the *Tales of the Pampas* jacket, the fine breadth and depth in the simple two-color treatment of the illustrations for *Bhimsa, the Dancing Bear* are worth studying.

The abilities we have referred to so far are those of the artist as artist, or of the illustrator as illustrator. There are a number of specific applications of art to illustration for children, which work within limitations, or in accordance with releases, peculiarly their own.

Duvoisin says there are two ways of understanding and appreciating the child's viewpoint. One is through memory, the other through observation. If you can put yourself back into your childhood moods, or if you can watch children and tell them stories or read to them, you have a basis for selecting what will appeal to a child. He himself uses both of these methods.

As a boy in Switzerland, Duvoisin did a great deal of reading — as many imaginative children do. It was one of his parents' worries. Of course he would stop and draw — and his father, who was an architect, appreciated that; but, nevertheless, his parents thought he should get outdoors more than he did, on his bicycle, with his brother and sister, in the brilliant Swiss landscape.

His reading was in French, naturally. He knew no English except a little school English until after he came to this country. When those American days arrived, he used to return home at evening from Maillinson's design studios to a Brooklyn apartment, to read *Call of the Wild* as hard as he could in English, for the sake of the language training; but he was so excited over the story all the time that he could hardly wait to look up the unknown words in the English-French dictionary, as he felt he should.

The books he read in French during his childhood included Jules Verne, Kipling, Cooper, Mark Twain, Stevenson, *Mother Goose, Peter Rabbit, Uncle Tom's Cabin, Alice in Wonderland, Thousand and One Nights, Moby Dick, Little Women;* and many more English and American classics; as well as La Fontaine, Grimms' and Andersen's fairy tales, and all the other European masterpieces. He also read all the lurid current trash which he could obtain for small coins. He enjoyed this with the same extravagant appreciation he gave to the other books. He believes in letting a child read anything; in choosing books as in choosing friends the taste, he says, will develop, until in the end the matured judgment comes to distinguish between qualities which will wear and those which will not.

As a boy, Duvoisin saturated himself in tales of the jungles of India and in tales of the American plains with equal excitement. Each was introduction to a strange and wonderful land where bigness was immeasurably big, brightness limitlessly bright, and excitement without bounds. Cooper's Indians and Kipling's India, the doings of Buffalo Bill and those of some fabulous nabob, were played out on the same lofty planes of unreality.

When Duvoisin thinks now of those books he read as a child, he recalls the vastness, the wonder, the richness, and color which his child mind created; and in illustrating those or other stories he tries once again to live in the large lush land of imagination's childhood.

In watching children react to stories told or read aloud an author or an artist increases his sense of what feelings a child responds to most strongly and most quickly, Duvoisin says, telling of his own experiences with his children and their cousins. Things sad, happy, or funny, appeal to children most, he believes. The younger a child is the more he loves exaggeration and brash departures from fact. The older he grows, especially if he lives his hours among routine-ruled humdrum schools, the more he expects and even wants realism.

The vividness of Duvoisin's childhood memories are, without question, one of the greatest, if not the greatest, factor in making him a highly successful children's illustrator. His humor, his warmth, his imagination, his intellectual depth, and scholarly poise fit him for both this and his other lines of expression: his successes in adult illustrating — for the Heritage Club, for the first illustrated edition of W. H. Hudson, for *Fortune* and other magazines, for the *New Yorker* covers; for advertising for high-class magazines, for designing pottery and silks. But the ability to enter again into childhood's spiritual expanse is above anything else the thing which makes him peerless as an illustrator for children.

With a character who is as humanly pleasant as Roger Duvoisin, there is a temptation to speak at greater length about him personally; but the impulse is stayed by the fact that so many people in the world of children's books grow sentimental over picturesque or romantic details, real or fictitious, native or adopted, in artists' lives; neglecting study or appreciation of their work to drool over stories about their irrelevant personal traits, their homes, their families, their pets, or some trivial statement about the way they work; and they grow to think that when they have accumulated a few facts of this kind, they know an artist and have learned something of art. It is this tendency which leads to so much adulation in the children's book field for incompetent work and to such limited intelligent appreciation and attention for the work of artists of the caliber of Naomi Averill, Mary Dana, Joseph Low, Françoise, Artzybasheff, Bobri, Karasz, Weisgard, William Pène du Bois, Charlot, and many more of integrity and stature.

A factual outline of Roger Duvoisin's career may be found in *Who's Who in America. Illustrators of Children's Books,* published by The Horn Book, gives other data. To this might be added the statement that Miss Elizabeth Devoy of Scribner's was the first to bring Duvoisin's work into the book field, and that he has always done at least one piece of work for her every year since, if only a book jacket, in token of the first happy collaboration, when she accepted his *A Little Boy Was Drawing.* Samuel Lowe, then manager of Whitman's, likewise gave Duvoisin encouragement and helped to lure him into the book field. Many editors have since made fortunate opportunities for Duvoisin and themselves by bringing his versatile strong abilities to pages where children and adults alike may enjoy them, and where they can be preserved in all their competent variety between the covers of those precious, easily-stored, easily-handled packages called books — the most feasible units for art collecting or art enjoyment for most people of the present age.

THE CALDECOTT AWARD 1949

The Big Snow

illustrated by BERTA AND ELMER HADER

written by THE ILLUSTRATORS

published by MACMILLAN 1948

FORMAT

SIZE: 8½" x 10", 48 pp. (unfolioed)

ARTISTS' MEDIUM: Watercolor

PRINTING PROCESS: Offset lithography

ILLUSTRATIONS: Front matter, full pages and doublespreads in four colors and in black and white, partial-page drawings and decorations

TYPE: 16 pt. Lino Baskerville

BOOK NOTE

THE different animals of the woods prepare for winter when they see the wild geese flying south. Here are the cottontails, the chipmunks, bluejays, cardinals, robins and pheasants all making ready to stay with the mice and the deer. Then comes a heavy snowfall and unexpected need, but the wild creatures are cared for by two kindly folk in the country.

ACCEPTANCE PAPER

by *Berta* and *Elmer Hader*

New Approaches to Writing and Illustrating Children's Books

MOST of the problems confronting writers and illustrators of children's books have been well covered by previous speakers whom you have honored as winners of the Newbery and the Caldecott Medals. Most of you gathered here, as well as the librarians who are keeping the home fires burning, know much more about books for children than we do. You read and pass judgment on hundreds of books each year, whereas our chief concern is with one book, our own. Therefore, anything of interest that we might contribute on this occasion would be a few remarks on Hader books — how we got into the pleasant world of juvenile books and how we work together.

To begin at the beginning we shall have to go back many years. In our student days before the First World War, we lived in a world of paint and canvas. The road to fame and fortune was wide open before us and the world we knew was a beautiful place to live in. The First World War changed that picture. In the reconstruction period following the war, the path to success in the fine arts, never an easy one, became increasingly difficult. A problem which we shared with millions of others was to pick up where we left off when the war interrupted our lives. *We* chose that moment to join forces and prove that two could live as cheaply as one. Just how that miracle was to be accomplished had to be answered, and we put our heads together to think it out. That was the beginning of working together. In our search for a way to solve our problem, we noticed that the women's magazines of that period had a section devoted to the younger generation. We decided to try out a few ideas in that field. Fortunately for us, an editor of one of these magazines was a friend of ours and receptive to an idea for a special children's page. This launched us into the juvenile world, and we designed feature pages for children in several of the leading magazines. Starting from scratch, it was only natural that we learned to work together. During this period we made a series of drawings illustrating rhymes from Mother Goose for the children's page in the *Christian Science Monitor*. Little did we dream that these drawings, with a series of color pages we later made for *Good Housekeeping Magazine*, would be gathered together for our Mother Goose book published years later. Our stay in the magazine field was brought to a sudden end when, because of new postal regulations, children's feature pages were abandoned. We had just begun to build our house and our plans were upset by this unexpected turn of events. We had to make a new start.

About this time a few young women of ability and imagination entered the world of children's books. Louise Seaman, May Massee, Bertha Gunterman, Helen Dean Fish and Virginia Kirkus started the ball rolling and Doris Patee, Margaret Lesser, Eunice Blake, Rose Dobbs and a host of other editors have kept it rolling to build up the juvenile book departments to their present important place in book publishing. We are not unmindful of the big part librarians have played in developing children's rooms in libraries all over the country. And all of us in the book world know how stimulating the wise counsel and helpful suggestions of Frederic Melcher have been.

It was in these first formative years of children's book departments that we were asked by Louise Seaman to submit ideas for a series of small books for the very young. Neither of us had ever illustrated a book and we knew nothing of the do's or don't's of bookmaking. We had much to learn. Miss Seaman and the printer gave us helpful advice and guidance. We made dummies showing the placement of text and pictures. These we presented to Miss Seaman and hoped for the best. We had the good fortune to be asked to illustrate four of the titles. These were among the Happy Hour books and launched us into a new world, one that has been most pleasant to work in.

Experience has taught us that there is more than one way to approach the making of a book for a child. Some writers select the subject and the scene for the story. Then they visit the library and read everything that has been written on the subject. Librarians are most helpful to writers and artists at this stage of the work. This is the intelligent approach and one's knowledge of a great variety of subjects will be enriched by this method. But for those writers who like to feel that they are creating an original and unique book, it is apt to be a discouraging approach. Just glance at a list of juvenile authors today and note the imposing array of names of men and women who have distinguished themselves in many fields, and who have found time to write books for children. You will soon discover that children's books have been written on every subject under the sun and more than likely on the very subject you have chosen as your own original project.

Another approach is to arm yourself with a few salient facts from reliable sources and sit down and write. This method will not make you an authority on any subject, but it will leave you with that wonderful feeling of having created something original. This is our approach. We always start a new book in the happy state of mind that we are writing and picturing something quite unique in children's literature. This pleasant dream is apt to be shattered when the finished story is presented to a charming and intelligent editor. I quote what may be termed the usual remark.

" Oh dear! Why didn't you tell me what you were working on? Every publisher in the world is bringing out a book on snow," or cowponies or whatever the subject may be that you have selected. " But your story does have a little different angle and the makeup is interesting. Maybe some people will like it. . . . But I do wish you would talk over your plans with me before you get too far along."

This brings up another of our idiosyncrasies in bookmaking. We rarely discuss the subject we are working on with anyone until we have had our say. We know now that many writers observe this rule, but with us it was a carry-over from the days when we worked in that branch of the fine arts devoted to portraits and landscapes. Visitors to the studio would study the canvas of the moment on the easel. In its unfinished state the picture usually suggested something different to every observer, and most of them felt free to offer advice on how to finish the painting. These friendly criticisms and suggestions have a tendency to throw a switch in the artist's mind. The confusion led to many detours but we always found ourselves returning to the original creative impulse. We concluded that we would save time if we kept the unfinished work out of sight until we had developed our idea to the best of our ability. After that the canvas was fair game for any critic, and we would accept or reject the proffered advice.

We carried this working habit into the writing and illustrating of children's books. There was a difference, however. The making of a picture book was a new venture for both of us in the twenties. It was then that we learned to work together on the same project. The way in which two people work together on a book has always provoked a certain interest. Some of you may remember a little book called *Working Together* that The Macmillan Company gave away during the library convention held in 1937. In those few pages we explained in simple words and pictures our method of making a book. First, we discuss the subject for the book and outline in a general way the build-up of the story. We decide whether it is to be for the very young, the picture-book age, or for the not-so-very-young, those who are just beginning to read and to whom the story is as important as the pictures. This determines the probable length and the format of the book. Then we write and picture the story. What the psychological impact will be on the minds of possible young readers, we leave to the experts. Complete ignorance of this profound subject leaves us free to write and draw to please ourselves.

We have heard that many writers try out their ideas and stories on groups of children and profit much from their young listeners' comments and criticism. We have avoided that method, for we learned that comments and criticism from the younger generation can be very disconcerting if not altogether discouraging. Children's answers to questions are generally forthright and to the point. This was brought home to us very forcibly at a children's party held in Town Hall, New York. We had been invited to make a few water-color posters and explain to the children how easy it was to make a picture book. We finished our part of the entertainment, and as well as we could judge the children seemed to have understood the simple talk and quickly drawn pictures. They applauded or laughed as the spirit moved them. Then came the moment that greatly influenced our attitude toward young critics.

Mr. George V. Denny, Jr., who has since attained international fame as the founder and moderator of the Town Meeting of the Air, was the Master of Ceremonies for the party. He had been an interested spectator. In his enthusiasm, he turned to the children and said, " Wasn't that splendid? I am sure you all enjoyed Mr. and Mrs. Hader's talk." The children applauded. We were content, but not Mr. Denny. He tried for a bull's eye.

" Is there any child here who hasn't had a good time? " His question stilled the buzz and clamor of conversation. Much to Mr. Denny's surprise, and we must confess, to our own, a little girl in the front row held up her hand. Mr. Denny, feeling that she must have misunderstood, repeated the question. Again the little girl in the front row held up her hand. This really pleased the children and they laughed merrily.

Sharing the program with us was a young musical genius who was guest conductor of the Philharmonic Orchestra at the time. He was due to take over the program, but just as we bowed out, Mr. Denny was handed a note containing a telephone message from the young guest conductor who was at that moment standing on the sidewalk just east of Fifth Avenue and 43rd Street. The St. Patrick's Day parade was in full swing and no one could cross the street. Mr. Denny turned to us and explained the situation. He asked us if we could paint some more pictures to amuse the audience until he found some way of getting the young conductor across the street. Fortunately, we had plenty of paper and, of course, we were happy to help out. Also it gave us another opportunity to try to give the young lady in the front row a good time.

Since it was the Easter season we hastily decided that an Easter bunny would be a good subject. When we had finished the picture we turned to the sea of upturned faces, and here is where our inexperience showed itself. "What is it?" we asked, pointing to the little bunny which we had drawn much larger than life size, so that it could be seen by those farthest away from the platform. The answer deflated our egos completely. "It's a *dog*," the children shouted. Some barked, some whistled and we took that drawing off the easel in a hurry. Experience teaches, however, and we immediately decided to give the name of the animal we intended to draw. "We will now draw a cat," we announced loudly, before putting a line to paper. This drawing was recognized and we were pleased to see the young lady in the front row smiling. We have made it a practice ever since to rely on the helpful suggestions of editors and librarians and teachers who have close contact with children and know their needs.

Any writer who jots down an idea fresh from Parnassus or any artist who makes an inspired sketch knows how difficult it is to elaborate the thought or make a finished drawing and preserve the life and spontaneity of the original. Our approach to our works is emotional, but we strive to combine emotional content with good craftsmanship.

Perhaps a few remarks on the book you have chosen to honor with the Caldecott Medal will not be out of order. We try to have a book well in hand the year before it is to be published, but due to a series of unexpected interruptions, our plans went awry and the winter of 1947 found us still undecided as to the subject for our next book. The Christmas holiday passed merrily by and still no decision had been made. And then the snow came. That famous storm is history now, but we believe it will live long in the memory of all those who make their homes in the area of our country covered by that astonishing snowfall.

Ever since we started to build our home on the hill slope overlooking the Hudson, a few miles north of New York City, we have entertained ourselves by putting out food for the birds, squirrels, chipmunks and occasional wild creatures that stray from the parklands on the crest of the hill. As you know, these wild visitors often count on friendly handouts to help them through the winter months, and we try not to fail them. That the heavy snow would make the food problem a serious one was quite evident when the snow finally stopped falling. The feeding stations on the ground were buried too deep to be reached by the most energetic scratching and those hanging in the trees were heavily blanketed with snow that was turning to ice. It looked like a tough winter for the birds, and for all those who had to keep roads open to get in supplies. However, there is usually a bright side to every picture, so we put on our rose-colored spectacles and forgot all about blistered hands and aching backs, in the beauty of the winter landscape. Our feathered and furry friends found their way to the uncovered feeding stations and we all began to look on the Big Snow as an interesting experience. The food problem and the beauty of the snow-covered hillside struck us both as a good subject for a picture book. The models and the background for the pictures were right outside our windows. With the subject agreed on, the story seemed to write itself. Everyone spoke of the storm as the Big Snow, so this seemed an appropriate title for the book. Miss Patee liked the story and in due time *The Big Snow* came off the press.

Some of you have read our books when you were children. Some of you may have children of your own to whom you read Hader books. That we have been busy in this pleasant world of children's books for some time was made amply clear to us by an incident in a bookstore not long ago. A young woman customer picked up a copy of *The Big Snow* from a table. She glanced at the title and the authors' names on the jacket. She turned to the clerk in some astonishment. "I used to read Hader books when I was a little girl!" she said. "Are they still alive?"

This happy occasion answers that young woman's question very satisfactorily for us. Thank you all.

BIOGRAPHICAL PAPER

by *Rose Dobbs*

Personality into Books: Berta and Elmer Hader

THE first books for children illustrated by Berta and Elmer Hader appeared in 1927. They were *The Ugly Duckling, Chicken Little, Hansel and Gretel* and *Wee Willie Winkie*, four little volumes, published by Macmillan in their Happy Hour series. The publisher ran a competition for the first edition of the series. "It was the dummy for 'The Ugly Duckling,' done by the Haders, that stood out above all the rest of the artists' samples. It was so simple, so childish, so funny; the colors were so clear and bright; the ducks were well drawn; the layout was artistic without being arty."*

Almost twenty-five years and a long impressive list of Hader books later, these words take on special meaning. It is as if from the very beginning, the Haders knew exactly what would be *their* formula for a child's book: simplicity; a childlike approach; humor; clear, well-drawn, uncluttered pictures; and a presentation that was, as Louise Seaman so happily phrases it, artistic without being arty.

And yet, was not the formula inevitable? For, did it not spring from personalities that were in themselves simple, full of fun, possessed of the child's sense of wonder, and artistic without being arty? To spend time with the Hader books, from the little Happy Hour volumes to the lovely *Big Snow*, is a revealing experience. Seldom is personality translated so joyously into books for chil-

---

* Louise Seaman: "Berta and Elmer" and Their Picture Books. *The Horn Book*, August, 1928.

dren. An unusual sympathy for animals produced *Spunky, Midget and Bridget, Cock-A-Doodle-Doo* and the Caldecott Medal winner. A deep understanding of the universal world of childhood makes Jamaica Johnny and Pancho and Chuck-a-Luck as familiar as the children next door. Respect for tradition handles a beloved old favorite in a manner that is " freshly imaginative but entirely in the spirit of that strange merry world of Mother Goose."* A lively interest in people, places, things, gave children *The Picture Book of Travel, Green and Gold* and the phenomenal *Picture Book of the States.* A love of America crops up again and again in delightful pictures and stories about farmers in the dell, big cities and little towns, and picturesque individual regions of the land like Tommy Thatcher's Welcome Cove on Casco Bay in Maine and Billy Butter's Telegraph Hill in San Francisco, California.

Ordinary biographical facts about the Haders are to be found in several reference volumes, but the essential qualities of heart and mind that make up the Hader personality are to be found in their books. The reference volumes tell where the Haders were born, where they studied, how they met, married and came East to live and work. But they give no idea, for instance, of the Hader genius for making friends. The books do that. Practically every book was made with a particular person or happy occasion in mind. Perhaps that is why the books have such an air of warmth and friendliness. *Spunky* is " a pony for Louise "; *Midget and Bridget,* " two little burros for Lydia's children, Susie, Angie, Joe and François." *Billy Butter,* " an enchantingly pictured story," [*The Horn Book,* November, 1936] is dedicated " to Florence Babcock and the Lockhart School where Billy Butter received his education." *The Little Stone House* is " a surprise for Leota. " *Green and Gold,* the story of the banana, was made for " the banana planter's bride." *Tommy Thatcher Goes to Sea* is " affectionately dedicated to Betty and Bill, in memory of happy days on Goose Cove," and *The Skyrocket* is for " our little friend, George Russell Varian, who was born into a flying world."

*From a review of *A Picture Book of Mother Goose,* Mahony and Whitney: *Five Years of Children's Books.*

No less revealing than the dedications are the hilarious self-portraits which, for sheer fun because it amuses their freinds, the Haders place on dedication and copyright pages. Viewed in chronological order these present a rare, tongue-in-cheek thumbnail autobiography. Always in keeping with the book in hand, they show the Haders at home, farming, building, cosily sitting by the fire or digging themselves out of the snow; and abroad as travelers, sailors, tourists, vacationists.

Although the Happy Hour volumes were the Haders' first venture into books, by 1927 they were not unknown as illustrators and sympathetic interpreters of childhood. Since their marriage in 1919, they had been living and working first in New York City and then in the stone house they built in Nyack. Their children's feature pages and other illustrative work appeared in *Good Housekeeping, Pictorial Review, McCall's, The Christian Science Monitor, Everyland: A Magazine of World Friendship for Girls and Boys, Asia* and *The Century.* Imaginative and versatile (sometimes individually, sometimes together), they turned their hand with equal skill and humor from a featured cut-out series of paper dolls representing children in foreign lands to portraits for "A Gallery of American Myths," — some of the myths being Uncle Sam, Colonel Carter of Cartersville, and Paul Bunyan.

And all the time they were full of ideas of their own, clamoring for expression. Not all of the ideas were for books. One of them was for a shoe-box peep show in color. Complete with detailed and carefully worked out instructions for assembling, lighting, and performing, it was designed for and enthusiastically accepted by a national magazine. But, alas, unforeseen postal regulations interfered and the peep show appeared in only six issues. Nor did their busy schedule permit the Haders to do anything further with it. It is a pity, for few toys can claim such charming entertainment features. Some astute manufacturer of toys and games might do well to investigate the idea. Properly produced and marketed, The Berta and Elmer Shoe-Box Peep Show presents unlimited interesting possibilities.

It was not long before so fresh a talent began to attract the attention of book publishers. The four Happy Hour books were followed by three more the very next year. That year, too, saw the publication of *The Picture Book of Travel*, the first book "written and illustrated by Berta and Elmer Hader." They were now on their way, their popularity increasing with each book. A glance at their bibliography gives some idea of their schedule. In 1929, they did two books of their own and illustrated five others; in 1930, they did three of their own and illustrated six others; in 1931, they did three of their own and illustrated three others. And so on until they reached a point where they could afford to check this hectic pace.

In the early years of their career as artists-authors, the Haders' activities were not confined to writing and illustrating, building the stone house, seeing these United States and neighboring countries, and entertaining their friends. On occasion Berta and Elmer became part manufacturers of their books, spending long hours supervising the making of color separations and plates, hand-lettering picture-book texts when no appropriate type could be found, and checking the run. On other occasions, they became temporary booksellers. Their appearances in stores and libraries are still remembered as inspiring (and profitable!) events. In between, there was always a voluminous correspondence to answer and requests for autographed copies to take care of. To Berta and Elmer such a request was seldom a matter of a mere signature. More often than not, the signature was accompanied by a gay original sketch, making something personal and memorable out of something routine.

How do you work together? This question, often asked the Haders, was answered in 1937 in an amusing way. With The Macmillan Company, who publish most of their books, they produced a unique piece of advertising — a colorful booklet entitled *Working Together: The Inside Story of the Hader Books*. It was distributed free by Macmillan and is now something of a collector's item. In it the Haders tell about themselves and Willow Hill, their stone house on the Hudson. They answer such questions as, Who does the writing? Who draws the pictures? Where do you get your ideas? In it, too, they convey an astonishing amount of information about what goes on behind the scenes in an artist's studio and a publisher's office. Naturally they take advantage of this golden opportunity to poke fun, in their good-natured way, at certain editorial practices.

Emotion, Elmer believes, is perhaps the most important thing to consider when doing a child's book. If an artist must choose between emotion and technique, he would do well to choose the former. Here he is sure to be in entire control himself, whereas technique must always depend upon many outside factors. Bad engraving, poor paper and printing can make a shambles of the best art work. But nothing can destroy the intrinsic value of a book that is emotionally sound. Therefore the Haders always try to make their stories ring true, whether they are realistic or imaginative. Their humor is never sophisticated and their illustrations are always scaled to the child's level of understanding. The emotion thus called forth, whether admiration, joy, loyalty, gratitude or sheer pleasure, is always a true one, adding immeasurably to the child's enjoyment and knowledge.

For a factual book, their research is painstakingly thorough. There is an amusing story in this connection. When *Under the Pig-Nut Tree: Spring* appeared, one customer wrote the publishers saying he was surprised to find a serious error in a Hader book. Grasshoppers, he pointed out severely, did not come so early in the year as the book said they did. The letter, without comment, went to the Haders. Berta and Elmer were writing about Willow Hill grasshoppers, no others. They went out to their meadow, which was fairly jumping with grasshoppers, caught one cheerful plump fellow, put him into a box carefully lined with grass, leaves and cotton pads, and sent him, without comment, to their publishers. They, after recovering from the shock of the box's contents, repacked the grasshopper and sent him to their critical customer. In due course came a reply: " All right. I agree the Haders proved their point, but that grasshopper was pretty puny." Elmer tells the story with a twinkle in his eye. " He was anything but puny when we caught him," he says, " but I daresay he didn't exactly flourish during a long, confining journey. However, the customer is always right! "

Stories by other writers which the Haders illustrate are treated with the same scrupulous care which they give their own manuscripts. Some of their most interesting work, in black and white, is to be found in these books. Of their work in Louise Seaman's *Mr. Peck's Pets*, Anne Carroll Moore said: " Berta and Elmer Hader have outdone themselves in the pictures they have made for this book. They are full of character and fine understanding." [*The Horn Book*, September, 1947] The original drawings in soft pencil are beautifully reproduced. Few pictures anywhere can match the wistful charm and appeal of the two satiny dachshunds on page 16.

How Dear to My Heart by Mary Margaret McBride and *Down Ryton Water* by E. R. Gaggin, two " period " books, are illustrated by Elmer with sensitive pen-and-ink drawings which capture the elusive nostalgic quality of each volume. *The Wonderful Locomotive* by Cornelia Meigs, one of the first books Berta and Elmer illustrated, is loved by children almost as much for its authentic, expressive drawings in pen and ink as it is for the fine story itself.

But to speak of a Hader book is to speak of color — the clear, bright Hader color full of sunlight and blue of sky and sea. The Haders use color not only for its own sake but to establish background, evoke mood and atmosphere, and point up scene and action. The brilliant color in *Pancho* takes anyone who has ever been there back to the sun-drenched streets of Mexico. The hushed, muted loveliness of the snow-covered hills, meadows and valleys in *The Big Snow* is the very spirit of winter — peace and quiet and sleepy, patient waiting. *The Farmer in the Dell* makes effective use of color to highlight the climax in each section of the book, which is divided into four parts, one for each season of the year. The gay action, imaginative scenes and fascinating detail of *A Picture Book of Mother Goose* owe much to the beautiful rich color throughout the book.

One of Berta and Elmer's regrets is that they have more ideas for books than time to execute them. Some ideas are more persistent than others and sometimes one which has lain dormant for years will begin to beg for attention, giving them no peace until they turn to their drawing boards. *Little Appaloosa* is the result of a cherished memory. When Elmer Hader was a small boy, he and his brother used to spend their summers on a ranch in Monterey. Both boys loved all animals, but horses had first place in their hearts, especially in Elmer's. One wonderful summer a new arrival came to the ranch — a curious little polka-dotted colt. From the moment he saw him, and although he knew he could never own him, Elmer yearned for that horse. All through the years he never forgot him and never again did he see one like him. Recently, his brother, who now has a ranch of his own, wrote Elmer to say he had acquired an appaloosa, a polka-dotted Indian pony, for his young son. He couldn't begin to describe the boy's excitement and happiness. In picturing his nephew's delight, Elmer went back in memory to the time when he himself first saw an appaloosa, and memory, once stirred, refused to lie quiescent. No matter where he went or what he did, the polka-dotted colt danced before his eyes. An idea began to take shape, Berta and Elmer turned to old records and histories of the appaloosa, and gradually story and pictures emerged. The book is here now because once upon a time a boy loved an appaloosa but was not lucky enough to own one, and today there is another boy lucky enough to own a polka-dotted Indian pony whom he calls Pal.

It is very pleasant, on a lazy summer's day, to visit and reminisce with the Haders. Elmer smokes his pipe and talks about the good old days. Berta serves a delicious lunch topped by heavenly pumpkin pie and discusses their plans for the fall and winter, mutual friends, and Squirrely and Phoebe, Willow Hill's ex-star boarders. The squirrel, no bigger than a minute, was found by Berta in their own roadway. More dead than alive, he gradually revived under expert care, and grew up to be a mischievious little rascal. When he became too curious and restless, the Haders presented him to the Trailside Museum in Bear Mountain Park. After a while, the Museum authorities turned him loose in the thick woods and he scampered off, Berta hopes, to a full and happy squirrel life.

Phoebe, the bird, was found at the foot of a big tree. Like Squirrely, she was almost beyond help, but under the Haders' solicitous care gained strength daily. Soon she was flying happily all over the house and at first made no attempt to go out. In fact, her favorite perch was Elmer's finger, especially when he played the piano! As warm and sunny weather came, Phoebe began to venture outside. Each day she took a flight, increasing the distance every time, and one fine sunny day she flew off never to be seen again.

One comes last of all, because it is best of all, to the Haders' friendship with children. Berta and Elmer are great favorites with their small neighbors who love to visit them, making a party out of each visit. One Christmas a group of children, looking like holiday elves in their peaked winter hats, came to Willow Hill to show the Hader Christmas tree to their dog. Berta put on a peaked hat, too, and this so delighted the children they begged to have their picture taken " to keep for always." So, while the dog laughed to see the sport, the picture was taken.

Children who cannot visit the Haders write them constantly, individually and in groups.

As this summer drew to a close, literary and artistic activities quieted down at Willow Hill. Berta and Elmer turned their attention to pressing household matters such as the studio roof upon which carpenter ants were feasting. When last heard from, the Haders were " still on the trail of the carpenter ants. The pool has been repaired and we are about to put down the new flooring in the sun room. Otherwise all is peaceful on the hill." (From a letter dated August 26, 1949.)

THE CALDECOTT AWARD 1950

Song of the Swallows

illustrated by LEO POLITI

written by THE ILLUSTRATOR

published by SCRIBNER'S 1949

FORMAT

SIZE: 8″ x 9⅞″, 32 pp. (unfolioed)

ARTIST'S MEDIUM: Tempera

PRINTING PROCESS: Offset lithography

ILLUSTRATIONS: Front matter, full pages and doublespreads in four colors, and partial-page illustrations in two colors

TYPE: Memphis Medium

BOOK NOTE

PICTURES and text tell of the friendship of the boy Juan and Julian, the old bell-ringer and gardener of the Mission San Juan Capistrano, California. Julian tells the boy of the coming of the swallows on St. Joseph's Day in the spring and their departure in late summer. During the winter Juan makes a small garden in front of his house for the swallows, and the children celebrate their coming with games, singing, dancing and little plays, while Julian rings the Mission bell. Two songs of the swallows which Juan learns in school are given with the music.

ACCEPTANCE PAPER

by *Leo Politi*

Miracles in Olvera Street

It is a great pleasure and privilege to work with the American Library Association, that grand organization of the book world which is doing so much to bring happiness to our children and to build for them a better and securer way of life. I don't know how to express my gratitude to you for the honor given to my work.

This honor, awarded to me for my *Song of the Swallows*, I should like to share with my editor, Miss Alice Dalgliesh. Without her encouragement and help, I doubt whether the other books I have written and illustrated for her — *Pedro, the Angel of Olvera Street* and *Juanita*, as well as the *Song of the Swallows* — would ever have come into being.

In these books and in a new one coming out this fall — *A Boat for Peppé* — I have tried to bring out interesting customs and some of the traditions of California life; customs and traditions which I believe give color and charm to the past and are a part of the life of the state today.

Though these books are regional, I have tried to give them a quality of universality in the hope that children in other parts of the country might also enjoy them. The scene of the first two books is Olvera Street. I wish you might all see this quaint little street in Los Angeles, particularly during the Christmas and Easter festivals.

On the street I drew pictures and sold them and passed many happy years. I knew and loved the children of the street, and they and their elders took part in my books. When Pedro was not singing with his Grandfather, I remember the many times he came to watch me draw, and when I gave him some paper and pencil stubs he was so pleased because he liked to draw too. In the book, *Pedro, the Angel of Olvera Street,* because of his angelic voice, I had Pedro lead "Las Posadas." The impact and beauty of this Christmas festival can better be felt if one can hear the music and lovely hymns sung at this time.

Then I remember the happy young couple with the little daughter they kept so neat and clean. They were the inspiration for the Gonzales family in *Juanita,* the book with the blessing of the animals at Easter time. This beautiful ceremony as well as the Christmas one are suggestive and could be imitated in some way by children in other parts of the country.

In *Song of the Swallows,* I have embodied the charming and poetic happening of the swallows that leave the Mission of San Juan Capistrano for a period of the year and fly thousands of miles away to return punctually every spring to the same lovely mission. This is in fact one of the little miracles with which life is filled.

I should like to tell how I compose a book. I compose a book very much as if I were making a piece of sculpture. First I put down the bulk. When I feel the bulk has body and the right proportions, I begin to work on the detail. I work with the pictures and the text at the same time and make one supplement the other.

A quality I like is rhythm. The rhythm one can feel as he looks at the soft hills after sundown. There are peace and serenity and a rhythmical undulating movement in the lines of the hills. With the flow of pictures and words from page to page throughout the book, I try to convey this same rhythmical movement. I should like to tell of some other things I try to bring out in these books.

My love for people, animals, birds and flowers. My love for the simple, warm and earthy things, from the humblest house to a little tree to the tiniest seashell; for the things made by hands, the sewing of a dress, the painting of a picture; and for the singing of songs and the movements of the body in dancing — all those arts which are instinctive forms of expression. We take pride in these natural forms and they give us æsthetic and spiritual pleasure.

Today, unfortunately, this folk art is somehow lost and confused in a complex age of overabundance of material things and doubtful values. In schools everywhere I see teachers and librarians trying to keep these folk arts and the finer and sounder things alive, but they are faced with great odds from the outside world by the maddening output of tempting things for the children to see, hear, read; things which confuse and paralyze to a great extent their natural and creative growth. Some day, somehow, I believe that the work of these unknown but great teachers will emerge to shape and temper this modern age to values more æsthetic and spiritual.

Writers, artists and publishers will help, I believe, by thinking less of making books outwardly so attractive that they will sell millions of copies, and thinking more of making books which children will enjoy and which will at the same time be sound and constructive to their growth.

To the best of my knowledge this is the only type of book I care to write and illustrate.

BIOGRAPHICAL PAPER

by *Rosemary Livsey*

Leo Politi, Friend of All

ALTHOUGH I have known Leo Politi only over a period of a few years when his interest in books and children has brought him into our children's library, I count him my friend even as the children do. When he comes, after whatever length of days, conversation flows as though yesterday were his last visit. He bends his height to mine, leaning, elbow on lifted knee, one foot firmly planted in the seat of a sturdy low chair while he talks, listens, or watches the children busy around us finding their books. They, too, find it easy to stop to look at the books we are enjoying, to add their word to the conversation, feeling the friendly inclusion of his smile and his broad hand on their heads. These children, not unlike those he knew as a child, are the ones among whom he lives now on the great hill in the midst of Los Angeles. Mexican, Italian and Oriental — they are the children of whom he thinks and whom he sees when he makes his books for all children.

"From a playground we watch the children play," he writes. "Some are light, others dark . . . but they are all beautiful, all of them have a live force animating their little bodies. All of them run, play, laugh and cry, and yet if outwardly they look different, they have within the same emotions of life. Each enjoys living; all will later be in the arms of the mothers who love them, live for them, and raise them to be good and kind. If we can only understand this force that makes them live . . . the same love between mother and child, the same desire that you and I have to live; the love . . . aspirations . . . dreams like your mother with you, my mother with me, . . . then no dogmas, no prejudices, no fears can stand barriers between man and man."

Leo Politi was born in California in the sun-warmed valley of Fresno. His mother and father had come to this country from Italy. His father is very gay; he likes to laugh and sing; he is so friendly that he speaks to everyone and in no time at all is conversing with strangers as if they were friends of long standing. His mother is more reserved, but she, too, loves people and is always ready and eager to help anyone who is in trouble. Mr. Politi cannot recall ever having heard her speak of wanting money or material things; she is interested in all the fine arts and likes to write poetry. In Fresno they lived in a ranch house and his father bought and sold horses. Leo and his sister were most interested in the Shetland ponies; rode them all day long and then were heartbroken when the ponies had to be sold, sometimes after only a day or two on the ranch.

When Leo was seven, the family returned to his mother's childhood home, the little town of Broni, in the province of Pavia near Milan, in northern Italy. He remembers the excitement of the journey, — the train, the big cities, the long days on the ocean and the drive from Milan to his grandparents' home in an open wagon through white and glistening snow.

Clearest of all is his memory of the Indian chief costume, complete to the feathers, which his mother bought for him. It made an impression on the children he met in New York City. When they learned that he had just come from the West they wanted to know if California was filled with cowboys, Indians and bandits such as they had seen in the movies. Little Leo did not want to disillusion them, so he obligingly said California was just like that. He even made up exciting stories of his own in which he and his father were the heroes!

The Indian costume made an even greater impression on the children in the Italian village when Leo appeared for his first day at school. They could not conceal their wonder and admiration for *il piccolo americano* and followed him everywhere. He became the center of so much attraction that the teacher had to ask his mother not to let him wear the Indian suit to school.

He spent happy days playing, studying, and drawing everything that he saw, on scraps of paper, in his books, wherever he could find space. " I remember my favorite Italian book," he says; " it was *Pinocchio* with many illustrations by Attilio Mussino. It was the favorite book of all Italian children."

During those first years in Italy, Mrs. Politi was ill for a time and Leo was placed in a boarding house where an elderly woman and her daughter took care of him. They had a very large nanny goat which Leo had to take out to graze each night after school. Nanny was so eager to get to the greenest pasture at the top of the hill that the small boy had all he could do to cling to the rope. On the last stretch she went so fast that he could not keep up with her and, as he would not let go, he was invariably dragged up the hill.

To Leo each year of his childhood was much like the one before it. Even the year the family spent in London was not so very different, seen through the eyes of the little boy, for he lived among Italian children and went to a parish school. Some London incidents, however, stand out in his mind.

The school to which he went was a large one, but the playground was small; so each Monday the children were taken out into the country, to play soccer, cricket, and other games. It was the long streetcar ride to their destination that made Leo realize how large London was. He recalls also an old and very big theater where poor children with a few pennies could go. They took their lunch baskets because the show lasted almost all day. He remembers that during intermissions the children sang, all together. Charlie Chaplin's comedies were their favorites. They loved Charlie Chaplin; they sang a song dedicated to him; they imitated him and drew pictures of him on paper and on the sidewalks.

Sometimes the boys marched along the streets singing (we can imagine with what a jaunty air):

> We are some of the London boys,
> We are some of the boys,
> We never min'a
> We spend a tenna,

We are respected wherever we go.
We march along the old London road
With every window open wide.
This is the way we bang our feet,
Banga, banga, bang our feet,
We are the London boys.

Leo went often to St. Martin's Lane to watch the artists draw on the sidewalks. He was fascinated by "the deftness of their lines and the speed with which the colored chalk pictures appeared on the pavements."

It was not long before the family returned to Italy.

At the age of fourteen, encouraged by his mother's enthusiastic belief in his ability to draw, Leo entered a competition for a scholarship to the National Art Institute at Monza near Milan. Among the students who competed from all over the country, he was the one chosen from northern Italy. For six years he lived and studied at the Art Institute which was housed in the Royal Palace, formerly the residence of King Umberto the First — a beautiful old building set in a great park with gardens, trees and even a zoo. Much of the students' time was spent out of doors sketching animals, flowers and the countryside. Here, too, Leo studied sculpture, architecture and design, which have played such an important part in the composition of his later work. At twenty-one he was graduated with credits that allowed him to teach art in Italy but he did not attempt to think of teaching, for he was eager to create for himself.

With a school friend he worked at textile and tapestry designing and did his first book illustrations. He is amused when he thinks of these now. "It was not my job," he says, "but my friend was too busy, so, instead of him, I did the pictures for a textbook to be used in schools for deaf and dumb children. It was a government book. It did not bear my name, nor did I ever see it in print."

After fourteen years Leo returned to the United States, sailing through the Panama Canal on his way to California. He was enchanted with the Central American countries and with Mexico which he visited later. The gentleness and beauty of the Latin Americans filled him with a desire to learn more of these people for whom he felt great admiration and kinship.

It was natural, therefore, that when we and Helen Fontes were married, they should make their first home in that colorful section of Los Angeles, Olvera Street. There the Mexican craftsmen's little shops still continue near the Plaza and the Mission Church in the midst of the great city. There the religious festivals of the people still take place. Leo Politi knows all of the families who have shops in Olvera Street, he has watched their children of yesterday grow up and knows their children today.

Life was not easy for the young artist and his wife who lived simply and worked endlessly. "What were you doing then?" we asked him; he spread his arms in a broad expansiveness. "Everything." That "everything" included painting murals for the green room of the State College theater in Fresno; night sketching of the sightseers as they wandered up and down Olvera Street; carving beautiful wooden figures, primitive and simple in feeling; and working at his drawing board night after night to earn a living.

His real entrance into the field of book illustration came as a result of work for Rob Wagner's *Script*, a magazine that is part of the Los Angeles tradition. Pancho, the little Mexican boy, was familiar to us long before he became a part of the book, *Little Pancho*, for we had watched for him and for the other Mexican children appearing under the signature *Leo* as spots and covers in *Script*.

"That Pancho, he was very bad," says Leo. "I had always drawn him for fun, and one night I started to draw him running and he ran all over the page and right into his own story. In one night I had completed the idea. It was not good drawing — too heavy — but Pancho made my first book and brought me to my first publisher, the Viking Press, and to Miss Massee, who was very kind to me."

Leo Politi enters with naive sympathy into the mood of the books he illustrates. The childlike quality of wonder and reverence which he gives to the humble, industrious family in Ruth

Sawyer's *The Least One* and the mocking pomp of military splendor in the background of Helen Garrett's *Angelo the Naughty One* give distinction and personality to each of these books. Always his strong sense of composition and design give rhythmic beauty both to his panoramas and his simplest drawings. However, it is to the books which he has both written and illustrated himself that one turns to find Leo Politi's full strength.

It was Alice Dalgliesh, juvenile editor for Charles Scribner's Sons, who gave him the incentive to do *Pedro, the Angel of Olvera Street*. To her, as to other of his chosen friends, he had sent as a holiday greeting a drawing of one of the Mexican children with angel's wings for Christmas. Why not do an entire Christmas book, with angels, Mexican children and Olvera Street? The idea did not come to fulfillment immediately, but once started it was inevitable, for " the best time of all the year for Olvera Street is Christmas time. Then the Street looks so gay, all decorated for the Christmas procession called La Posada. . . . The Posada is a procession which, like a Christmas play, tells the story of the journey of the Holy Mother Mary and Joseph to Bethlehem. It tells how they sought shelter (posada) from the dark night and at last found refuge in the humble stable where the Christ Child was born." The story of Pedro who sang like an angel and walked at the head of the procession is dedicated to the children of Olvera Street.

Two years later, in 1948, Leo Politi repeated his success with an even more childlike and appealing story of the children of Olvera Street celebrating the blessing of the animals on the day before Easter. *Juanita*, with its fresh springlike quality, is the endearing story of the little daughter of Antonio and Maria Gonzales whose "*puesto* was more than a booth where they made and sold wares. To them it was also a little home filled with dear and pleasant memories, for in here they had watched Juanita grow up to this day." When Juanita was four years old, she took her birthday dove and walked with all the people and their animals through the Street to the patio of the old church where the kindly Padre blessed each pet saying, " Bless, O Lord, these animals so all will be well with them." Never do church bells ring out their songs more gladly than in a Politi church tower. Never are children in or out of a book happier.

To the children, living near Olvera Street and knowing the Easter blessing of the animals, this book was of themselves. To our great delight a group of small children drew their own pictures for the story of Juanita, leaving out no pet of their own, remembering the high city buildings and the pushing traffic bordering Olvera Street and the little church across the Plaza.

These pictures were especially appealing to Leo Politi, who feels strongly that children should be encouraged to draw, unhampered by outside influence or adult interference. Because children are direct and sincere with the object or impression they want to convey, he feels their drawings are filled with fresh imagination and delight. Instinctively they are well composed in color and design. He tells with amused pride of his little son, Paul, now in kindergarten, who loves to draw and paint with his father. " Nani, as we call him at home, draws both sides of his little boys," says Leo, " the back on one side of the paper and the front on the other." Suzanne, the baby, is too young to paint. Both children, though perhaps unconsciously on the part of their father, appear in many of his drawings.

Myron Nutting, art editor of *Script*, writes of Leo Politi: " The most striking quality of his work is a gentleness that comes only to those who have known and seen the bitterness of life and can still accept it. Like the youngsters who said that ' a friend is one who knows all about you but still likes you,' Politi knows about life but still loves it. He meets it with a sort of Franciscan faith and good cheer. It does not occur to him to propagandize or try to reform. A spirit of kindness pervades his work, and God knows this would be a different world if that spirit were more pervasive. His little world is full of it, and makes any arguments as to its limitations futile. . . . He is eager, he is searching, in an unforced and unpretentious way."*

* *Script*, October 26, 1946, p. 12.

In *Song of the Swallows,* his new book of this spring, Leo Politi has moved a few miles south of Los Angeles to the Mission of San Juan Capistrano. There against the scene of the old Mission and its gardens, through the friendship of the boy Juan and the old caretaker Julian, he has told of the arrival of the swallows on March 19 — St. Joseph's Day — and their departure on October 23.

Along with the simplicity and goodness inherent in all of Leo Politi's work, there is a conviction and a vigor. It can best be expressed in words he himself used while turning the pages of one of his books: " I am proud of this page. It tells what I feel of a family counting its happiness in little things. I would like my children and all children to seek security less in material things, and more in the spiritual and the æsthetic; to know what it means to enjoy working with their hands; to be reasonable in what they want, and generous in what they have to give."

It is for this simple sincerity that he is to each of us " my friend, Leo."

The Egg Tree

illustrated by KATHERINE MILHOUS

written by THE ILLUSTRATOR

published by SCRIBNER'S 1950

FORMAT

SIZE: 7¾" x 9¾", 32 pp. (unfolioed)
ARTIST'S MEDIUM: Tempera
PRINTING PROCESS: Offset lithography
ILLUSTRATIONS: Full pages, partial pages and doublespreads in four colors and in two colors, decorative borders in one color with black text
TYPE: Caledonia Bold

BOOK NOTE

A picture story for Easter, growing out of a Pennsylvania Dutch custom. The story tells about the time when Katy and her brother hunted for colored eggs, hidden by the Rabbit, and their grandmother showed them how to make a tree on which to hang the eggs, as well as how to decorate them.

ACCEPTANCE PAPER

by *Katherine Milhous*

The Egg Tree
and How It Grew

THE last time I spoke before a large audience was upon graduating from high school. My mother had to administer a large dose of aromatic spirits of ammonia to get me up on the platform.

Tonight I am going to try to speak without benefit of aromatics, for I know well that I am among friends, and no friend of mine ever expected me to be an orator. In awarding me the Caldecott, I like to think that you have also honored my state, Pennsylvania, and my native city, Philadelphia. Just before coming here I walked from my studio down to Independence Hall. The old Georgian building glistened with fresh white paint in honor of the 175th anniversary of the signing of the Declaration and its brick base was brilliantly punctuated by flags borne by the color guards of the thirteen original colonies.

Then followed a ceremony of superb symbolism. To the beat of drums the color guards, wearing traditional uniforms, marched to the speakers' stand, each bearing an urn containing the earth of his native state. This earth was then mixed with soil from Independence Square, and the mingled earth is even now on its way to be distributed among the capitals of all your states.

Something of this kind of co-mingling — a pooling and redistributing of ideas — is taking place here in Chicago as the A. L. A. celebrates its 75th anniversay. I am so *pleased* that my book rides on the wave of such an important occasion. AND I am *delighted* with the way you have helped my little egg tree to blossom from coast to coast. Thank you very much.

As far as I know, I am the only born Philadelphian to have been awarded the Caldecott Medal, so perhaps you would like to know how your artist works in that not too Quakerish city.

When I first heard the glad news that I had won the Caldecott Medal for *The Egg Tree,* I was speechless! An artist always is on such occasions. I wish I could say thank you with brush and paints and lots of color splashed all over the place. I wish I could take you into my studio to watch the picture grow. But you would have to take a lot of sound effects with it, for I do not work in an Ivory Tower.

My studio is in the heart of Philadelphia on a narrow traffic-jammed street. Behind it, across the alley, are rows of music studios. Beethoven, Brahms and be-bop bend the air waves. Into this cacophony I, myself, introduced an old clock which ticks like a metronome heard through a loud speaker.

But dominating all these sounds and blending all together as a leitmotiv is the sound of the printing press in the adjoining room. All day long — and into the night — I hear the thump, thump, thump of the press. I like to hear it. The sound of a press was my first lullaby, for my father was an old-time label printer. The family lived above the shop — an old Philadelphia custom. It is a sound that has followed me all my life or else I have followed it. Even during the war years, when I was designing books for Scribner's, my work took me down in the city to stand beside the great offset presses for the proving and printing of the books. I love the sound. But when I am at work in the studio, I love less the screaming of the printer above the press as he tells his helper how he could run the government, or explains to a constant stream of clients that their jobs will be finished tomorrow — tomorrow — and tomorrow.

All in all, the atmosphere of my studio may be summed up by the words of Hyman Kaplan, the night school student, in his misquotation of Shakespeare, " The world is full of funny sounds and phooey."

Just before writing this paper, I had acknowleged a great sheaf of letters sent me because of *The Egg Tree.* It had been a pleasure. Also I had finished belatedly a picture book for which I had drawn a good section of our Mummers' parade and, it seemed to me, half the populace of Philadelphia. I was quite spent and felt the need of some oasis, some hiatus, before giving my Calde-cott Acceptance speech. But there was not time to get away. I looked wildly about the studio. Help! Help!

And then I saw my rows of books marching in peaceful pageantry around the room. Books! "Books Are Bridges." Wasn't that the slogan of one of the Book Week posters? I would find a book to take me away from the studio, without my even having to leave it, and another book to bring me back. The journey led me far afield, and what I discovered along the road meant so much to me that I want to tell you about it.

But first I will tell you about my book, *The Egg Tree*, and something of how it came into being. It came after a long quest which, like any real quest, was exciting. It began ten years ago, after I had finished my first picture book, *Lovina*. I wanted badly to do another Pennsylvania Dutch picture book, making use of their traditional ornament as I had done earlier in my series of Pennsylvania Dutch posters. These were the posters which Alice Dalgliesh saw on exhibit during a library meeting in Philadelphia in 1938. She wrote me at once, asking whether I would do a book for Scribner's. This was fortunate for me, because if Alice had stayed in her New York office at the time of that library meeting there would have been no book called *The Egg Tree*.

After finishing *Lovina*, I read everything I could lay my hands on about the Pennsylvania Dutch. One day in a scholarly vol-ume I came upon a picture showing an egg tree. It was a lovely thing, its white branches hung with many colored eggs. Greedily I read the text, hoping to find an account of a charming Pennsyl-vania Dutch custom. My enthusiasm was quickly deflated. The egg tree, the author pointed out, was a subject to be shunned. When pressed, old-timers admitted having seen such trees, hung always with undyed eggs, in the yards of isolated farmhouses. In every case the woman of the house was childless. The egg tree is a symbol of fertility. You don't have to delve into Frazer's *Golden Bough* to draw your own conclusions. I drew mine — no story for children here. Into the basket went my hopes for a book about an egg tree — forever, I thought. I concluded that the tree in the photograph represented an isolated case and I had wanted a traditional tree.

I went on to other things. There followed some delightful years spent in illustrating Alice Dalgliesh's books. But all this time, and even during the years when I was writing my own books, the urge to do another Pennsylvania Dutch book kept nagging at me. If not a book about an egg tree, why not a book about eggs — those decorated eggs with the traditional Pennsylvania Dutch designs? I began to collect egg lore.

Helen Papashvily "put her trusty operatives into the field" with the result that I went to Quakertown and sketched the eggs later shown in *The Egg Tree*. I worked on a dummy, showing on each right-hand page a large-scale drawing of a decorated egg, with the text opposite. It would make a very nice Easter book, I thought, until I saw in a bookstore window the Easter book for which Leonard Weisgard painted those huge, handsome, decorative eggs. So into the wastebasket went *my* egg book.

Then, several summers ago, Frances Lichten and I were invited to autograph books at the Reading Bicentennial. The temperature was 108° and people stayed away in droves. This left plenty of time for talk, and, remembering the egg tree I had seen in the book so long ago, I asked our hostesses if it was not in Reading that there used to be such a tree. "Why, yes," they said, "and people come from everywhere to see it. We will let you know next spring when it is to be on exhibition in the Historical Society."

At Easter time they not only sent me word, they also sent a newspaper clipping showing a photograph of the egg tree. One look at the picture and I dashed for a train to Reading. The tree itself was a fabulous, fairy-tale thing, towering high above one's head and blossoming with eggs of every color of the rainbow. What if the making of the egg tree isn't a folk custom, I thought, I will make a book anyway about an egg tree and how it grew. I talked it over with the woman who had trimmed the tree for over twenty years — Carrie May Umberger Palsgrove. Being a person of lively imagination and generous sympathies, she gave me her blessing and said, "Happiness to others is my goal, as I love people and their doings."

Scarcely was the book published when a tempest in an egg cup arose. Was the making of the Easter egg tree a traditional Pennsylvania Dutch custom or was it not? Readers and book reviewers, with a few outstanding exceptions, jumped to the conclusion that it was a custom, perhaps because of the traditional designs in my book. But it was in the Pennsylvania Dutch country itself that the tempest raged most furiously. Learned professors delved for hours into old German manuscripts and emerged to write articles denying that the egg tree was traditionally Pennsylvania Dutch. To be sure, they admitted, there is still celebrated in Germany, as of old, the Spring Festival on Laetare Sunday, shortly before Easter. Youths and maidens wind in procession around the town *platz*, carrying staves trimmed with evergreens, all entwined with parti-colored ribbons and hung with apples, pretzels and blown and colored eggs. But still no written record of an Easter egg tree has been found anywhere in the old sources.

Something had to be done about all this. When I wrote *The Egg Tree*, I told a simple little story of a grandmother who made an egg tree for the children. I made no claim that it was a Pennsylvania Dutch custom. Yet, here I was, put on the spot because I couldn't prove that it went back to the days of Freya and Wotan. All this time I did believe in my heart that the making of the Easter egg tree was a custom — an expiring one, certainly, and perhaps never a general custom, but still a tradition which dated far back in time.

Intuition, it is said, is only a quick, unconscious reasoning. Now I began to reason consciously. Of all peoples on earth, I believe the Germans are the most holiday-loving and certainly the most tenacious in holding to their traditions. In the Pennsylvania Dutch country no old-world symbolism ever quite dies out; the scholar keeps it alive by conscious devotion to cultural heritage, the farmer, unconsciously, through his very isolation.

I see in my mind's eye a farmer's wife of the old days. In the fatherland, where she was born, the life of her people, poverty-ridden and persecuted as it was, was nevertheless rich in the pageantry and the still-flourishing symbolism of the early Christian era. Now she lives in a strange country — not a neighbor in sight, not a church within miles. Comes spring with memories of the gay festivals of her girlhood. *Her* children will never march in procession, carrying the little egg-trimmed evergreens. Here there is no Spring Festival; there is only Easter Day. What goes for the children's Easter? An egg hunt, maybe, but what else? "Vell, now," she says to herself, "there makes here no grand Cathedral square for the kinder to walk around mit the *Sommertagsstecken,* and for me it makes no never mind that in the old country the Spring Festival comes sooner. Here we do all on one day — Easter." So she makes do with what she has — eggs from her own henhouse, dyed with onion skins and beet juice, hung on her own little tree. "Nice, ain't? "

I can't prove, of course, that this was the way it happened. But lack of proof is not proof either, though this is often a pit into which the professors fall. Those of you who have read *Kon-Tiki* will understand what I mean. I continued my quest for egg trees hung with colored eggs. Autographing trips gave me a good opportunity to talk to native-born Pennsylvanians. "Have you ever seen an Easter egg tree? " I kept asking. "No," said a lady in a Victorian mansion, "but when I was a little girl, my grandmother said she would make one for me if I would visit her on her farm at Easter time."

"Have you ever seen an Easter egg tree? " "Why, yes," said a librarian who sat next to me in a cafeteria. "Where? " I asked, and nearly burst with excitement when she mentioned a charming tiny crossroads outside Lancaster, for I remembered having visited the place the previous summer. The artist who later drove me there told me he knows of certain sections around York where egg trees are displayed both indoors and on porches. Another friend wrote me of a traveling man who last year had come upon the old lady proprietor of an inn in the very act of making an egg tree from a thorn bush.

A clipping from a Pottstown newspaper showed an egg tree,

hung with six hundred and fifty eggs, made by an elderly couple living near Pittsburgh. They have made an egg tree on their lawn for nearly fifty years. Colonel Henry W. Shoemaker, State Archivist of Pennsylvania, remembers, as a boy, seeing an egg tree in the kitchen of the tenant farmers of his old homestead. He asserts that in some localities the Easter egg tree is even more cherished than the Christmas tree. "People who deny that there are egg trees make me sick," he says belligerently. "Just refer them to me."

From an outstanding collector of Pennsylvania Dutch antiques came a most welcome letter. When he was a boy some fifty years ago, his mother told him about the Easter egg trees she had had as a child and those which her mother and grandmother always had at Easter time in York County. The family came to Pennsylvania from the Palatinate in 1730. This record takes the egg tree back well over a century. Whether the tree was of Germanic or other ethnic origin, I can now say with authority that egg trees have blossomed in many counties of Pennsylvania from the eastern to the western even as far as Mercer County near the Ohio border.

I know from firsthand experience what it means to make an egg tree. I ought to know, for I made fifteen of them when my book came out and sent them to my good friends in libraries and bookshops in adjoining states. With the help of Frances Lichten, I blew out, dyed and decorated about six hundred eggs for these trees. We each decorated the eggs with designs from our own Pennsylvania Dutch books. It was lots of fun. It is even more fun to know that others have carried on where I left off. Judging from the photographs of egg trees that have reached me from all parts of the country, there are some beauties. One such tree brought a hundred new subscribers to the library which exhibited it. So, long live the egg tree!

And now, for the journey I took without leaving my studio, across the bridge of books. It was a very real experience which left me with certain convictions.

First, I want to make a plea that all kinds of children's books, barring trash, of course, should be available to all kinds of children. The book I loved most in my childhood, and for which I forsook all others, was *Bimbi* by Ouida. In its pages I found all the things I lacked and many others I had not known I lacked. I owe it much. Today it is not to be found anywhere in my own city except on the shelves of certain research libraries. Although it is subtitled "Stories for Children," I doubt if modern children would read it. Perhaps I would not have read it myself if I had had a well-adjusted childhood. Today I am thankful that I had not, for artist children have a way of thriving on rocky soil. They need few roots and draw their sustenance from other sources. To a child who grew up in a country town, without a library, without music, painting or sculpture — a child who, nevertheless, wanted passionately to become an artist — *Bimbi* was full of sustenance.

The other day I re-read *Bimbi*. It is a book of preposterous plots, of child geniuses, child saints, child devils, of children who risk their health, their lives even, for a cause, for a friend, for an animal, for a porcelain stove. As the word "vocabularize" was unknown in 1882 when *Bimbi* was published, the book is full of extravagant verbiage, of adult phraseology, of Italian, French and German phrases, of technical terms having to do with painting, ceramics, architecture.

But in spite of — or perhaps because of — all this, there are passages of great descriptive beauty. One is aware of the author's devotion to all things beautiful and to their makers; and over and over is the message repeated: "It is good to be loyal and to endure to the end." And so I am loyal to this book which gave me courage to become an artist and which first made me thrill to the fascination of foreign places and peoples.

The other author I want to mention is Willa Cather — and a greater contrast to Ouida would be hard to find. Miss Cather's books are quiet and go deep, and one can't define why they are so beautiful any more than one can put into words the reason that a shadow on a rock, a pioneer at the plow or the last days of an archbishop are beautiful things. Willa Cather was not speaking of herself when she said, " Whatever is felt upon the page without being specifically named there — that, one might say, is created." But this is true of her own work — utterly true.

Impossible as it sounds, this is true even of pictures. Otherwise we should have nothing but calendar art. There everything *is* on the page — moonlight, firelight, lamplight, grandma, the dog, the baby on the rug. Nothing is left to the imagination. Good art has always had an intangible, indefinable force, something felt rather than seen. This applies equally to a cave drawing, an icon, a madonna in mosaics, a landscape, a bit of ornament — and to a picture book.

There are artists who are by nature Whirling Dervishes and there are those who are St. Simeon Stylites. Good books have been written by Quakers in prisons and by poets in taverns. The main thing is that you hew to your line. If you are a Whirling Dervish, then, for Heaven's sake, whirl! If you are a St. Simeon, sit tight on that pole! But whatever your subject — sports, science fiction, modern family life, historical novels, folklore — " you can't " and here I am quoting my editor, " ' just toss off another little book for the kiddies.' " If you do, they will toss your little book out of the window and you with it!

Real writers know this instinctively. James Boswell, writing in his Journal of the children's stories he hoped some day to write, (but unfortunately never did) says — " It will not be a very easy task for me; it will require much nature and simplicity and a great acquaintance with the humors and traditions of the common people. *I shall be happy to succeed, for he who pleases children will be remembered with pleasure by men.*"

BIOGRAPHICAL PAPER

by *Frances Lichten**

Katherine Milhous

In my copy of *Lovina*, Katherine Milhous's first book, she wrote,
" To my severest friend and best critic — and vice versa." This
inscription delights me, for it succinctly outlines a relationship
that has survived three decades of working together in the same
studio. Besides being a testimony to a long friendship, the inscription conveys Katherine's wit and happy satiric touch.

Katherine Milhous could have been a caricaturist. She catches
the salient features of persons and things, and at one time in her
life drew caricatures speedily and deftly. But that ability quickly
slips away unless the acrid art is followed steadily. Years of
serious work in mural designing, in sculpture and in the world
of children's books left little time and less inclination for the
more frivolous approach. The caricaturist's peculiar viewpoint,
however, cannot be shed easily; today it bursts out, not in sketches,
but in her precise, close-fitting word pictures. " Mrs. Dream-
feathers," for instance, calls to mind all those lady watercolorists
we used to meet in Europe — those indomitable females in broad-
brimmed hats and trailing veils who floated about vaguely, searching for subjects fit for their peculiar delicate brushwork. " Aunt
Clara Closet-Banger " is myself — a name given in recognition of
my domestic proclivities, but even more so in protest against my
banging ones, which disturbed our author or artist (whichever
she was at the moment) at her work.

* FRANCES LICHTEN calls herself a " dyed-in-the-wool Pennsylvanian," and
says that ever since the days of her first painting lessons she has been much
interested in the folk art of her native state. From 1936 to 1941 she was State
Supervisor of one of the outstanding Federal Art Projects, the Index of
American Design, now permanently housed in the National Gallery of Art
in Washington. She is the author of the distinguished *Folk Art of Rural
Pennsylvania* and *Decorative Art of Victoria's Era*.

Like many humorists, Katherine has a sober, almost impassive face. It is constructed of smoothly modeled planes, and her profile could be laid over that of a Piero della Francesca Florentine lady with scarcely a deviation from the standard of fifteenth-century beauty. There is even the high forehead, then so fashionable that, if lacking, it was achieved by shaving back the natural hair line. But as the twentieth-century taste in coiffures has changed, Katherine conceals her Tuscan brow under dark bangs — a hairdo which brings out her striking resemblance to another author (also a " K. M."), Katherine Mansfield.

Unlike her pale, serious prototypes, the ladies in Florentine painting and sculpture, Katherine smiles. Only rarely, however, does she laugh aloud. When she does, one doesn't forget the occasion. I remember clearly a day in London when we were sitting in Hyde Park, soaking in the sunshine. She suddenly caught sight of a pop-eyed, bearded apparition on a leash — a cross between an insect and a scrawny canine. The creature stopped, shook its beard and glared at her. Katherine, faced by this cartoonist's dream come alive, went into shriek after shriek of laughter, for she was convulsed by her first glimpse of that most bizarre of canines, the Belgian griffon.

Katherine was born in Philadelphia. It is natural that her books deal with Pennsylvania, for her roots are here. Though one side of her family were shipbuilders in New Jersey, the others were among the early Quaker settlers of Chester County, Pennsylvania. In an out-of-the-way spot in this most beautiful of Pennsylvania counties, settled so long ago that the countryside with its solid stone houses has a patina similar to that of the English landscape, there is a small rose-colored brick edifice known as New Garden Meeting. A placid, willow-dotted graveyard surrounds this meetinghouse, and snuggled up close to it are the tiny headstones on the graves of the first Milhouses — Quakers from Ireland who settled in this region in 1729. From these Quaker ancestors Katherine has as heritage an awareness of the eternal values in life. Indeed, if she found herself sharing the hard life of that Colonial couple, Thomas and Sarah Milhous, she would not be too uncomfortable. Many of her habits and working methods smack of pioneering days, for she runs her life — by choice — with the simplest of equipment. She walks rather than rides, and is never beguiled by the idea of modernity *per se*. She lights her cigarettes with matches, uses a broom instead of a vacuum cleaner, and grinds her coffee in an antique coffee mill held between her knees, exactly as did her great-great-grandmothers. And were she confronted with the large fireplace of her ancestors, and the housekeeping problems pertaining to it, she could face the situation with composure — even pleasure — for she takes great pride in building and maintaining a fire. Jeered at affectionately as " Old Handmade Herself," she nevertheless adheres to the pioneering simplicity of her ways.

Sturdily built, she has a liking for physical work such as gardening and carpentering. This taste she undoubtedly inherits from her forebears. " K. M." (as she is often called) frequently says she likes furniture that she can take a saw to. From time to time she does just this, altering the studio pieces to fit her changing needs. And they do change somewhat, for in the thirty years we have shared a studio, it hasn't always been the same one. First it was a tiny cell. Then we graduated to a large, impressive affair, skylighted and glass-ended. Its pleasantest feature was the high sloping ceiling always associated with attic studios in literature. Today we occupy a third, practically the twin of the second. Because they are always filled with plants, the great glass windows are a landmark on a mid-city street. The walls are a warm yellowish-gray, a good background for watercolors. At present, the protean furniture is painted in various shades of pinkish tan.

Katherine has acquired a separate studio on the floor below. This became necessary when we both, after being artists, began to write. Immediately we found that writing was a more jealous mistress than drawing.

Call it stability or Philadelphia slowness, as you will, but unquestionably we can lay claim to the longest tenancy in the neighborhood. To have shared a studio for such a length of time indicates that the occupants' methods of working are in harmony.

Katherine is orderly, systematic, thorough. None of her possessions, her papers, ever gets mislaid; she keeps them under exquisite control. There is file after file filled with material which furnishes her with the background she needs before she begins a book. Perhaps no trace of it is evident in the finished book but its contribution, nevertheless, is there. As several of her books lie in the field of Pennsylvania folklore and folk art, an area in which the learned professors range, she is occasionally challenged. Having thoroughly grounded herself in whatever she attempts, she can always meet these challenges.

A student by temperament (she was probably known as a "greasy grind" in her high school days), she went beyond the studies required. Most students consider one foreign language a trial, but Katherine worked not only at the prescribed German, but taught herself French and even attempted Greek. Astronomy, too, was on her extra-curricular list. A map of the stars clipped from the *Philadelphia Evening Bulletin* and a bicycle lamp to see it by were her equipment; her observatory, a chilly stance behind a chicken-coop in a flat, snowy New Jersey field. For two years in preparation for a trip abroad she studied Italian under the tutelage of an Italian clergyman. And very useful it was, for during a six months' stay in Italy, Katherine's Italian extricated us from many of those predicaments in which the unconducted tourist finds herself. From that year's trip abroad, taken between the two World Wars, we returned with portfolios bulging with drawings and paintings of old-world towns.

Her urge for self-improvement is a verdant one. After much work in black and white, she felt the need for further study. During the depression, she concentrated on sculpture at the Pennsylvania Academy of the Fine Arts. Sculpture poses infinitely more problems than do the graphic arts; nevertheless " K. M." mastered them so well that she won a Cresson Traveling Scholarship in 1934. All that summer she traveled alone in Italy and France, studying the world's sculptural masterpieces. As her approach to transportation is as simple as her approach to living, her friends were concerned whether she would ever return from her faraway destinations. But she set out dauntlessly with their blessing:

> " Last seen
>   Wandering vaguely:
>   Quite of her own accord,
> She tried to get down to the end
>   Of the town — Forty Shillings Reward! "*

However, she came back, and with the look of added experience seen on the face of the cat who " walked alone, waving its wild tail."

Whether she always reached the precise destination she set out for has never been disclosed, but her books tell us that what she saw and felt was added to her rich store of impressions. *Lovina* was woven from materials observed in her own state, yet a casual glance gives one the impression that it is based on a European folk culture, so keenly has she been aware of the cultural heritage of the Pennsylvania Dutch farmer.

Though born and now living in Philadelphia, Katherine spent her school years in Pitman Grove, New Jersey, a small town located in a flat, fertile terrain. This region, though known as the " Truck Patch of the East," furnished but meager soil for an imaginative child's intellect. The core of Pitman Grove was an old Methodist camp-meeting ground, the hub of which was The Auditorium. From this center, the streets bordered with tiny frame cottages radiated as the spokes of a wagon wheel. When Katherine lived there, there was no library, no evidence of any interest in cultural subjects; Pitman Grove nourished itself on religious faith. To a child, the camp-meeting grove itself was an exciting place in summer but in winter a lonely one, for then very few of the tiny cottages were occupied. At night the light from their kerosene lamps made cheerful golden spots on the snow in this grove of towering chestnuts and oaks. Sometimes Katherine lived with her grandmother within this wheel of devotion; sometimes with her parents in another part of the town.

* Copyright, 1942, by E. P. Dutton & Co., Inc., from *When We Were Very Young* by A. A. Milne.

There was very little money in either household. But there were books – mostly English classics and fairy tales. How she looked forward to Friday nights (when there was no home work), to the fascinating world that reading revealed to her! Books furnished her with ideas which she translated into actions. Once in her reading she came across the pretty custom of making May baskets. As a result, several old couples, opening their doors on May Day, were mystified to find a tiny basket filled with wild flowers suspended from the knob. The child, Katherine, knew no one else to give them to, since she was somewhat young to have a " true love." Besides, she loved old people and still does.

The child who takes pleasure in this type of imaginative playfulness is often a solitary one. I, myself, was such a child. " K. M." and I became friends during art school days. There we found that, in spite of our disparate backgrounds, we could do a good job of teamwork in carrying out the ideas we had loved in books. The most venturesome was one implanted by much reading of English novels – a caravan trip. We brought this to pass, not in England but in Pennsylvania – a caravan trip with horse, wagon, camping and all its concomitants. It was the most delightful of vacation trips, taken at the time when the model T's were kings of the rural roads. Long afterward I drew on this excursion into genuine farm life for background to my *Folk Art of Rural Pennsylvania*. Katherine made entrancing use of the caravan trip in *Herodia*. Much of her experience was woven into this story about a traveling puppet show; and in it, too, there is much evidence of that sense of childish wonder which she still possesses. The Pennsylvania mountains through which her puppet caravan travels are terrifyingly dark, the waterfalls tumble from great heights, the distances seem to a child endless, endless. The gypsy camp is transmuted from the hobo camps she stumbled into during many early wanderings in woods and fields. *Herodia* is a book that would have delighted Katherine, the child. In truth, it is written for every little girl who ever loved to read, or rather, *lived* for reading.

Katherine loves the country, the ever-changing aspects of nature. These she studies even in the city, though they be no more than a brash ailanthus tree trying to survive on a cinder roof outside the studio window or as much as she can glimpse of the shifting panorama of clouds in the little patch of sky between ever-encroaching skyscrapers.

Above all an artist, Katherine lets no element of beauty escape her. She will describe with admiration the effects of light on New York's great verticals, for she loves the modern; or speak with equal affection of the softened lines of Philadelphia's Colonial brick. She used to paint excellent watercolors for exhibition purposes; now, busy with the writing, designing and illustrating of books, she files the pictures away in her mind. Although no antiquarian, she loves to wander in the streets and alleys of Philadelphia neighborhoods established in pre-Revolutionary days — some of them sections no visitor ever sees. Viewed as slums by the social worker, to such an artist-writer as Katherine these humble backwaters are the actual soil of America's history, a lively picture gallery and a seedbed of future inspiration.

Finders Keepers

illustrated by NICOLAS [MORDVINOFF]

written by WILL [LIPKIND]

published by HARCOURT 1951

FORMAT

SIZE: 8¼″ x 10⅞″, 32 pp. (unfolioed)

ARTIST'S MEDIUM: Acetate color separations for line reproduction

PRINTING PROCESS: Offset lithography

ILLUSTRATIONS: Front matter, full pages, doublespreads and partial illustrations in three colors and in two colors.

TYPE: Century Schoolbook

BOOK NOTE

THE story, told in the manner of a lively folk-tale, concerns two dogs, Nap and Winkle, who seek help from other animals in trying to decide which of them found a fine bone first and so should have it. It was a Big Dog who threatened to take it away from them who made them see the wisdom of sharing it between them without more ado.

ACCEPTANCE PAPER

by *Nicolas Mordvinoff*

The Best and Not the Sweetest

I REMEMBER some time in February when I had spent the better part of the night working. By early morning I was asleep and having a dream. I was mounting up into a boxing ring. In the opposite corner was a huge, fierce-looking prizefighter with cauliflower ears and no nose to speak of. The bell rang. I jumped. But it was my doorbell. The mailman was bringing a special delivery letter at seven o'clock in the morning! Being but half awake, I tossed the letter onto my desk and went right back to bed. Then it occurred to me that I might relapse into the same dream. And the last thing I wanted was to see myself confronted again with that ferocious pugilist. "Might as well take a look at my mail," 1 said to myself.

And there it was, the announcement of the Caldecott Award! You can guess that this woke me up. It was still very early in the morning. But the first thing I did was to call and wake up Margaret McElderry. All I said was " *Viva Zapata!* " And she knew right away what had happened.

It seems to me that in human nature, fulfillment of a lasting desire very often comes too late or brings some sort of disillusionment. Once, I remember, for a long time I had wanted to own a horse. And at one time, circumstances being favorable, I realized my desire. But who likes to ride alone? I had to have a second horse. Now, when you have two horses, there is always one of the two that has something wrong, a sore of some kind, a lost shoe, a split hoof. I felt obliged to get a third horse. And to take care of three horses and as many saddles, various bridles and harnesses means a full-time job. Therefore, I could not paint or draw any more. It was a great relief when I succeeded in getting rid of them all.

I had also wanted to have a car. As a result, I spent one entire summer vacation sitting in a smoky garage while mechanics kept on discovering new things to repair. It was the most expensive vacation I ever had!

Shall I admit now that I hoped some day to win the Caldecott Medal? I did. And I am very happy about it. This time there will be no disillusionment, I am sure. I shall not have to groom the Medal like a horse, and there is no leather harness or bridle attached to it. Neither are there any mechanical parts that will have to be repaired. Instead, it will be a source of pride and continuing pleasure and a constant stimulus to strive for finer picture books.

A picture book must have complete unity in text and pictures. And I cannot well imagine working in any other way than Will Lipkind and I do. We work in such a close relationship that when a book is finished, it is sometimes hard for us to remember who was responsible for what idea. Story, pictures, design, type and even color are conceived as one whole. It is fascinating to see the book grow from the first miniature dummy, through many phases, to its last run through the printing press, to its binding, and sometimes, as today, to the Caldecott Medal. At no time is it a quick or easy process and the work is never in any proportion to the material reward. It is a work of love.

No matter how long the creative process may take, to be convincing the final result should retain its spontaneity and freshness. A portrait painter who had just spent a long time finishing a picture said of me one day, " No wonder Nicolas likes to do picture books. He does one in one evening after dinner." I wish it were true. As it is, I am glad if it appears that way.

By definition no creative work can escape criticism and dissension. Divided opinion is better than none. Only mediocre creations can rally a majority through indifference. But some criticism can be entirely beside the point. I know I am often amused at some of the remarks about my paintings or books.

I remember once in Tahiti during the last war I had all my etchings seized by the police and almost went to jail myself for reproducing in one of my etchings a backyard wall on which was the inscription, "*Vive de Gaulle.*" Such things generally happen in critical periods. At that time, France was tragically split into two factions: for Maréchal Petain or for General de Gaulle. The Gaullists were very strong in Tahiti. I was as ardently for de Gaulle as any of them. But because the local politicians had no particularly glorious deeds or events to fill up their time, they turned their attention toward my etchings, seeing a lack of respect for the General where I saw only a picture, and if anything else, a tribute to his popularity.

All art forms are subjected to what could be called a *confusion of values.* Book illustrations are no exception. Thus, among some people, there is a tendency to believe that anything destined for children should be sweet and not too unconventionally imaginative or not realistic in the true sense of the word. For example, in illustrations grown-up people should not be shown smoking or mistreating an animal, and they must be more than decently dressed. Why? Just think of the pictures children see in magazines, newspapers, and on the screen today. Of course, there is a great difference between encouraging bad instincts and simply mentioning casual facts of everyday life. Many people smoke, most change their clothes at least once a day. Some occasionally kick a dog. I have seen it done. And most children have — or will, anyway! It is surprising that we have not yet seen candy-covered picture books. But children, like grownups, cannot thrive on candy alone.

Do not misunderstand me. I am not saying that illustration cannot be at the same time sweet and good, as it can be rough and good. Unfortunately, often it turns out to be sweet and bad or at times rough and bad, as, for instance, in the comic books. Never enough sincere effort is made in between these extremes. Often timid attempts to free or "modernize" a style result in illustrations with static, lifeless figurines. No wonder they can't smoke.

Maybe I should give a clearer definition of what I would call sweet and not so good. To be described as *sweet* is, I think, a left-handed compliment. The word is hardly sufficient to qualify a well-balanced individual. We are saturated with saccharine sweetness around us. Sweet is the smile of the pin-up girls, but not the one of the Gioconda. Sweet the calendar scene with a willow, but not the poplar trees in Van Gogh's painting; the apron-clad kittens on the greeting card, but not the cats of Goya; the pink babies on advertising posters, but not the children of Velasquez; the framed lithograph in grandmother's room, Easter bonnets for little dogs, most popular love songs and magazine romances, baby talk, half-baked baritones, toothpaste and soft-drink posters, and chewing gum sentimentality. Such sweetness is a substitute for feeling and intelligence. As a matter of fact, good things of this sort are quite rare.

Misconceptions or confusions of values of that order are mostly due to insufficient ethical and æsthetic training. Producers and sponsors of the kind of art I have described often lack judgment themselves and speculate on the so-called popular taste for commercial purposes.

In contrast, how marvelous, sweet and imaginative are the story of *The Little Prince* by Antoine de Saint Exupéry, *The Pirate Twins* by William Nicholson, Leo Politi's bambinos, Roger Duvoisin's foxes — to mention but a few.

And marvelous and sweet are just about all God-created young animals — puppies, kittens, colts and lambs, birds, rabbits, mice and butterflies, the tiniest creatures endowed with real life.

To please on the surface is no more than to attract attention by a bright display in the window of an empty store. It is a form of treachery. Any form of art to survive has to be lively, sincere, honest and truthful. Art is life and life is no candy.

If a distinction is to be made, one can imagine the field of book illustration as standing in a place by itself somewhat between the so-called pure art and commercial art. Although in its essence it is attached to the former, the production end of it relates it to the latter. It is not unimaginable that it can touch both sides at once. It has been done before, as, for instance, with the old illuminated manuscripts and more recently in the case of the French art dealer, Ambroise Vollard, who turned publisher just to see beautiful books illustrated by the greatest artists of his time – Picasso, Derain, Chagall and others. It is told that one day an American art lover insisted on buying a small painting by Cézanne from Mr. Vollard. "*Un petit Cézanne.*" But the dealer was reluctant to part with it and asked an excessive price. The customer inquired how much he would reduce the price if he took two paintings instead of one. "Oh, in this case," replied Vollard, "each painting will cost twice as much, because, you see, I love them."

All through the history of art, great artists have contributed to the world of book illustration and have often made the book immortal. It occasionally happens in our time. But usually when money is considered as the ultimate goal, art bows and deserts the field, and artists go away from it. I think it is a mistake to consider book illustration as a métier in itself. It is of course a medium in the sense that it requires a great deal of technical knowledge, an understanding of printing techniques, a feeling for types and an interest in general bookmaking.

The best art teacher can only give his knowledge, not his heart or his talent. I like the advertisements that guarantee a successful art career after a six-week course. "Earn while you learn." I have seen people taking such courses just to find out if they had any gifts. Well, I have been at this for more than twenty years and still don't know what it is all about. Perhaps talent (although I do not like this word) can be called a gift, a gift in the manner that dark or blond hair is a gift.

Talent, if we have to call it that, is a state of mind, sometimes a form of chronic anxiety and, in the plastic arts, an almost painful hypersensitivity of visual organs. I think that art can be considered as a relaxation only by Sunday painters, doctors and statesmen with tidy paint boxes and folding easels.

An illustrator is primarily an artist. An artist is a man whose urge for expression makes him unable to find any other purpose in life. You have certainly noticed that the greatest or most important artists in art history are less remembered for their skill or technical virtuosity than for a new, unprecedented approach in the way of seeing life itself.

A problem in book illustration is created as soon as mass production is involved. Bookmaking in general, and illustrated books for children in particular, is a difficult task. The increasingly high cost of printing and production cripples the initiative of many an editor. I must say I admire everyone connected with children's book publishing, from the editing to the production and sales departments, but I imagine that some publishers are not entirely free of a tinge of jealousy when they look at the soap and cereal manufacturers.

True, there is nothing to say against book mass production per se. The danger is of depriving the book of its most inherent quality: dignity. But mass production and quality *can* go together, an enviable goal to reach. There are some inexpensive books that are thoughtfully and excellently produced. The fact remains that more often such books are published with the primary idea of reaching a mass public. A vast public is neither selective nor discerning. The choice, therefore, lies with the producer. What a unique and wonderful opportunity for the publisher with large means of distribution to guide and clarify common misconceptions, to give to children the best and not the sweetest!

It would open new horizons, new possibilities. It would free writers and illustrators from many latent inhibitions. It would attract new recruits from other fields of art expression. Numbers of the best contemporary painters would welcome an opportunity to try their brushes at children's book illustration. It would be ideal if fine artistic achievement could find its place in the domain of mass production.

Yet someone has to ring the bell. A train would never start if it had to count on just one more eventual passenger appearing at the gate.

And so Art could die. But this will not happen. Never in our field have there been wider perspectives. A new enthusiasm seems to be spreading. More and more editors and librarians, writers and artists, seem to be attracted by these new horizons and possibilities. Likewise more parents and more children appear to respond. Undoubtedly awards like the Newbery and the Caldecott have done much for the cause. But it takes courage, perseverance, understanding and true love of books; and it takes the fine qualities and unselfishness of a man like Mr. Melcher.

Two years ago I went abroad. And nowhere in Europe, with a few exceptions, did I find as many or as good children's books. We have the greatest means and the largest audience. We have the best children's books in the world. The future is bright.

BIOGRAPHICAL PAPER

by *Henry C. Pitz*

Nicolas Mordvinoff

Nowhere does the American melting pot steam more busily than in the field of book illustration. One cannot begin calling the roll of first-rate illustrative talents without being struck by the large proportion of foreign names; and even the list of native-born artists suggests most of the races of mankind. As might have been expected, something rich, varied and vital has sprung from this complex amalgam. And particularly in the field of children's books, this pool of multi-racial talent and skill has given America's children a pictorial pageant that is unrivaled for color, invention and diversification.

Nicolas Mordvinoff, the 1952 winner of the Caldecott Award, is one of our foreign-born artists who has made an individual contribution to American illustration. He has been working quietly but ably for a number of years; the Award has focused the spotlight on him and given us an opportunity to review his work. Many of us knew him through two of his early books, *Pepe Was the Saddest Bird* (Knopf, 1944) and *The Ship of Flame* (Knopf, 1945). They had no unusual sales record, but they went quietly into the collections of those who look for the fine and unusual in illustration.

Here was obviously a talent that was different. It was not only confident and competent; it was strangely flavored, full of provocative overtones and unusual insights. We discovered that the artist was a Russian living in Tahiti, and when he arrived in New York about a year later, he was disclosed as a man of polish, culture and charm. He was more than a little bewildered by the sudden transition from the slow day-by-day existence of the South Seas to the push and impatience of America. The adjustment to the new land was not made overnight; there is a tightly packed history of change and development, of trial and error, between *Pepe Was the Saddest Bird* and *Finders Keepers,* the Caldecott prize book.

Nicolas Mordvinoff's art is now the story of a racial urge modified and quickened by a dozen other pressures and influences. He was born in Leningrad (then Petrograd) September 27, 1911. His grandfather was Admiral Alexander Mordvinoff and his earliest years were the indulgent and luxurious ones of an upper-class Russian family. But with the revolution came hardships and danger — days which he still remembers. When scarcely seven he fled with his parents to Finland and then to Paris.

He grew to manhood in Paris, studying at the Lycée Jeanson de Sailly and the École des Roches, and drawing, always drawing. His first love was for horses and he watched them pulling the heavy carts and trotting with elegant carriages, and then rushed home to draw them. Unconsciously he was training one of the illustrator's most precious assets, his visual memory.

He was given a continental, classical education, receiving his degree in Latin, Philosophy and Languages from the University of Paris. All through his school years he continued to draw, and his desire to be a painter continued to grow. While studying at the University he began to contribute cartoons and illustrations to some of the French newspapers and magazines. After the University he began to paint intensively under Fernand Leger and Amédée Ozenfant.

He was caught up in the swirl of fads, fashions and cultural currents of the Paris of the early 30's and he felt the need of distance and leisure to resolve his doubts and work out his own stylistic language. In 1934 he left for the South Pacific where he was to live for the next thirteen years. He moved about, from island to island, painting and thinking, grateful for the slow pace of the native life.

It was while living in Tahiti that he struck up a friendship with William Stone, the writer. Stone was finishing a book manuscript for an American publisher and he persuaded Mordvinoff to make pictures for it. When the drawings were sent with the manuscript to the American editor, Lillian Bragdon, she recognized the stamp of a new illustrative personality.

That first book, *Thunder Island* (Knopf, 1942), introduced Mordvinoff to the American public. There were some complimentary things said about the pictures, although they excited no overwhelming interest. But the small public that keeps alert for the new and the superior had found a new name.

This was followed by two more Stone books, *Pepe Was the Saddest Bird* and *The Ship of Flame*. They proved that here was no flash in the pan but an arrived talent.

The two books are quite different in mood and technique, although both are South Pacific tales. *Pepe* is an ingratiatingly humorous story for children. It is half text, half picture, with an illustration on every other page. These are in pen line, the work of a free but assured draughtsman. Each page is a beautiful design. There is an astonishing variety in them; some are dark, richly textured in native patterns, others are of great simplicity with a few significant forms around which white spaces circulate. Mordvinoff early discovered the eloquence of white paper.

The Ship of Flame, a beautifully told story, based upon a great Polynesian legend, is a large book. The original pictures are monotypes, which were reproduced in sheet-fed gravure. The monotype is a very rare medium in illustration, but here it proved to be an ideal vehicle for the dark enchantment of the story. The pictures are painted in monochrome on metal plates and transferred to paper under pressure. It is a difficult and chancy method, for the impression is in reverse and there is always an element of gamble in the transfer.

These Mordvinoff monotypes received excellent reproduction and they revealed for the third time his rich sense of compositional invention and his power to cast a pictorial spell.

The success of these books induced Mordvinoff to come to America in 1946. He brought his paintings with him and had his first one-man show in a 57th Street gallery in New York.

Meanwhile began the task of getting adjusted to American life. He tried two extremes of living. One year was spent on a small island off the Massachusetts coast with scarcely anything but sheep for company. A longer stay was in an old, roomy apartment looking out on bustling St. Mark's Place in New York City.

Here came about the collaboration that has resulted in his two latest books. A friend and writer, Will Lipkind, was invited to stay with the Mordvinoffs while his own apartment was being painted. As often happens when artist and writer get together, they talked of collaborating on a book. This dream got beyond the talking stage, however. Outside their windows was the rich life of St. Mark's Place and this gave them their theme. There would be a red-haired boy and a red cat against a setting of St. Mark's Place backyards. Lipkind's story grew and Mordvinoff's dummy developed into finished pictures and finally *The Two Reds* (Harcourt, Brace, 1950) appeared, to become a runner-up for the 1950 Caldecott Award.

The second book is always a test, with great danger of a letdown, but *Finders Keepers*, of course, not only won the Caldecott Award but has become one of the most important children's books of the year.

A glimpse into Mordvinoff's integrity and struggle for perfection is given by his editor, Margaret McElderry. She tells of his bringing to her the finished art work for *Finders Keepers* — months of work — in the spring of 1950. She was excited about the pictures and began work on the book while Mordvinoff sailed for Europe. When he returned, he took one look at the proofs of his work and announced that he would redraw the entire set. Some more months of effort produced an entirely new book.

The illustrations for *The Two Reds* and *Finders Keepers* seem, at first glance, radically different from the pictures for the early books. They are big, bold statements, utilizing strong, flat-color masses with the skill of a poster designer. The all-over feeling of delicacy has been replaced by a more instantaneous pictorial impact. But the line is still there, less haunting, but with more body and more directly expressed. Under the more aggressive technique is the same winning creation of character and mood and there is still the same flair for composing a page. Mordvinoff has learned to work within the limitations of flat-color line reproduction and can now indulge himself in the freedom born of mastery of the method. Obviously this freedom is not an instantaneous thing; it comes of hard ground work and considerable trial and error.

Looking back through the nine or ten books that Nicolas Mordvinoff has illustrated, including the fine recent *Cezar and the Music Maker* (Knopf, 1951), one is immediately conscious of variety. Here is an artist who seems concerned with approaching each problem freshly and without prejudice. Bound up with that desire for a continuing new vision is undoubtedly a search for himself. He has experimented and discarded more than he has retained. Through all the changes, however, certain strong characteristics persist — an instinctive sense of design that orders the elements of each picture into a pleasing and personal relationship, accomplished draughtsmanship that is supple and obedient to mood, and finally the intangible qualities of charm and character.

Almost certainly the ten picture books already planned for the future will reveal further search and change. The third of the Will and Nicolas books, *Even Steven,* will appear in the fall. Here Mordvinoff goes back to his early childhood love, the drawing of horses. Pictures for a new type of book have also been completed. This is a science-fiction tale laid in the future after the near annihilation of mankind.

The Caldecott Award brought to everyone's attention that Nicolas Mordvinoff had outlived being cataloged as a South Sea Island artist alone, that he has assimilated the material of twentieth century America and that his future is bound up with that of his newly adopted country.

The Biggest Bear

illustrated by LYND WARD

written by THE ILLUSTRATOR

published by HOUGHTON MIFFLIN 1952

FORMAT

SIZE: 7¾″ x 10½″, 88 pp.
ARTIST'S MEDIUM: Opaque watercolor
PRINTING PROCESS: Offset lithography
ILLUSTRATIONS: Full pages in black and brown
TYPE: 16 pt. Futura Medium

BOOK NOTE

JOHNNY Orchard decided to shoot a bear so that his farm should not be the only one without a bearskin nailed to the barn. He found a little bear and took him home for a pet. When the bear became a big bear and began to pillage the neighborhood, Johnny tried in vain to return him to the woods, but the bear would not stay there. Finally Johnny sent him off to a Zoo and often went there to feed him maple sugar.

ACCEPTANCE PAPER

by *Lynd Ward*

The Turning of the Page

I AM grateful for this opportunity to say publicly to the librarians of America how much I appreciate this vote of confidence in my work. This does not, of course, begin to acknowledge all of the things for which I am in your debt, nor does it indicate the many friends and those who are more than friends whose share in my work has been so great. A moment like this is something for which an artist's day-to-day life ill prepares him. In spite of the embarrassment that results from being suddenly pushed into so bright a spotlight, there is this salutary result — you become very much aware of how little a person is by himself, and how much of what he is comes from others.

In my case this may be less than a startling revelation because more perhaps than that of almost any other artist working in this field my life has been, without punning, an open book. The things that I have believed, the things that I have learned, are all there on the pages of the books on which I have worked.

The association with the many writers with whom I have been privileged to work is something for which there can be no adequate acknowledgment. It is true that the worlds of the writer and the artist have their differences, but the extent of those differences has been too often exaggerated. I do not know what the artist can give the writer, but I am sure that any artist will be the richer for absorbing something of the writer's broad horizons, his insistence on dealing with what is intelligible and his basic premise that art is, first of all, communication between people. What I owe my editors is much more than the sum of their friendly encouragement of new projects, their willingness to consider different ways of doing things, their tolerance of the crises recurring in that never-ending battle between the picture that will not come out right and the calendar that will not wait.

All of these qualities which in publishers make possible the work we do were present in full measure and overflowing in Houghton Mifflin's relation to *The Biggest Bear*. There is, moreover, one point at which their understanding of their responsibility as publishers went far beyond the most exacting call of duty. I knew that Boston still abuts on the great primeval wilderness and that the people at 2 Park Street include among their number some who can do almost anything you can mention, but I was still unprepared for the arrival, just before Christmas, of a package which, when opened, contained a very special copy of *The Biggest Bear*, bound in bearskin! Mary Silva Cosgrave has not yet told me how it was accomplished, or who the mighty hunter was, but they have succeeded in creating an heirloom that will be an object of wonder among the Wards for as many generations as moth-proofing and summer fur storage will allow.

I must confess, however, to some misgivings and moments of doubt that have still to be resolved. You will understand what I mean when I mention that some years ago Mrs. Ward and I were staying for a few days at a little hotel on the Elbe River in Upper Saxony. We were almost the only guests and when the sun was warm enough our meals were served in a little courtyard overlooking the river. During the course of those several days we made particular friends with a little chicken who put in an appearance regularly to gather crumbs that fell from the table. We came to expect this friendly companionship, but on Sunday there was no feathered visitor. It is understandable that we had no appetite for the roast chicken that crowned that Sunday dinner. So far I have been unable to find out from Johnny Orchard whether his bear is still safe and sound, eating his maple sugar in the zoo.

I have said that an artist is ill prepared for this sort of thing, but in one way I stand before you with a special kind of embarrassment. A long time ago I published a book that was not quite so wordy as *The Biggest Bear*, and meant for a slightly older age group. If there are any among you who can remember so far back you will recall that *Gods' Man* was based essentially on the argument that creative talent is the result of a bargain in which the chance to create is exchanged for the blind promise of an early grave. This theory of course was the result of a youthful brooding over the lives of such diverse characters as Vincent Van Gogh, Toulouse-Lautrec, Keats, Shelley, and Aubrey Beardsley. But, having long since passed the age implicit in that theory of the quick ascent, the bright light, and the speedy fall, I naturally have some doubts as to whether I should be here at all. However, like the drowning man who reportedly sees his old life pass before his eyes in quick review, I can, at least, pass on to you some of the experience that goes into the making of a book.

It is one of the dogmas of our age that what we are as children, the pressures we are subject to, the frustrations we endure, the many little things recorded from day to day on the endless magnetic tape of the subconscious, combine to make us what we are when we are no longer children. Childhood thus is the first mile on the road that leads to violence, crime or the psychiatrist's couch.

In the case of a book artist, of course, it is no secret that the road usually leads to a book. But it requires a special combination of experiences to bring about this fate. We can sort out some of the factors that are in the combination. Whether they add up to a total picture will still be anybody's guess. First let me say that so far as I know I am not Johnny Orchard. It is true that at one period in my life I was an enthusiastic hunter, and, while squirrels, rabbits and partridges were about all that fell victim to my twenty-two, there was one evening when my twenty-two and I did meet a bear on the way home through the woods. However, that bear was much bigger than the one Johnny met, and I had reached, fortunately or unfortunately, what among hunters would be called the age of discretion.

It is not always the bear that you meet face to face that you see most clearly. I recall an afternoon much earlier, long before I was old enough to be in school, when our whole family went to pick raspberries across the lake through the woods to a clearing near an abandoned lumber camp. My excitement in this expedition was heightened by knowledge that, not long before, one of the

Watsons, farmer friends of ours, had here rounded a big pine stump and come smack up against what was, as he told it, the biggest bear ever seen in that part of Canada.

Raspberry picking for a family involves establishing a base of operations to which we all return when it is time for the picnic supper, and from which we all set out independently with pail yawningly empty to seek those elusive and as yet unknown spots where the berries grow thickest and largest. The hillside beyond the old lumber camp had been cut over and then burned over, and the stumps of the big pines were scattered over the hillside as far as a child's eye could see. With the peculiar logic of raspberries it was around these old stumps that the bushes grew thickest and the berries were largest.

An afternoon like that becomes inevitably one of the major times of one's life. The better spots are always a little farther on. You are soon absolutely alone and you move to each new stump with the full awareness that right on the other side of where you are picking is the biggest, blackest, fiercest bear that ever lived. It may be that the bear I didn't see that afternoon has ended in a book.

There are other experiences far less direct that also have a part in a thing of this kind. On the lake behind our place there was only one summer camp. This was the habitat of a sportswoman named Mrs. Bass whose only passion in life was fishing. All day long, every day, she was out on the lake in that search for the biggest trout, the search that never ends, and that only fishermen understand. Since this was long before the invention of the outboard motor, she hired one of the farm boys to do her rowing for her. Because she tipped the beam at about three hundred pounds, while the lad would scarcely scale seventy-five, this poor fellow was constantly rowing uphill. To see Mrs. Bass out fishing was, I suppose, one of those unforgettable things, and she would probably be quite horrified to know that she had contributed in any way to *The Biggest Bear*.

From all this you will realize that much of those early summers in the Canadian woods has been the raw material of experience that, however deeply submerged and sublimated, has been building up pressure under the crust. A major part of my feeling about the woods up there at Lonely Lake was the awareness that came when I was old enough to go to school, and gradually to pierce the mysteries of maps — that we were literally on the edge of the frontier, that due north from where we were the forest and lakes stretched on without break to the shores of Hudson's Bay.

I suppose there is always the question of the relation between experience and art, and, although there must be a beginning somewhere, the artist most likely to make a totem pole is the one who has seen totem poles in his village ever since he can remember. I can remember that on Sunday afternoons in the winter, because of the rules of conduct governing the children of a Methodist minister, we were not allowed to read funny papers as were less underprivileged groups. I am not sure that there is a moral in this for publishers, but I remember that it was to books that I turned in this extremity.

I recall with a clarity which must mean that the experience was important, those long Sunday afternoons lying flat on the floor on the living-room rug. There were two volumes that were my special favorites. One was a book in which there was a story told with a picture on each page, and about three twelve-line verses of rhyme to keep you abreast of the action. But the poetry was printed in such small type, probably about eight point, that I never bothered to decipher it. Turning the pages and seeing the story unfold in pictures was enough for me.

My other favorite was Doré's *Gallery of Bible Pictures*, in which again I rarely bothered to read the accompanying letterpress, but I can still remember the violence of my emotion as I turned the pages and moved through the book absorbing those images and living with them. I knew when I got to a certain point that the next picture was going to be that of Saul falling on his sword after his final defeat in battle. Each time I looked at that page my identification with what was happening in the book was complete and the sword that pierced the side of the human figure in that old wood engraving ran deep into me each time I turned that page. From those two books I suppose I was learning, without realizing it, what it is that makes the book a unique form of expression.

No other medium in which the artist can work has that particular element to offer, and it is that one thing that makes the book a form something different for the artist from what it is for the writer. It is true that the writer works with a succession of words, paragraphs and chapters that because of their sequence in time have a significance completely dependent upon that time sequence; but the turning of the page is not essential to that sequence, and, save at the end of the chapter, is more often than not likely to be an interruption that is tolerated rather than utilized for its own sake. For the artist, however, the turning of the page is the thing he has that no other worker in the visual arts has: the power to control a succession of images in time, so that the cumulative effect upon the viewer is the result of not only what images are thrown at him, but the order in which they come. Thus the significance of those coming late in the sequence is built up by what comes earlier.

This great potential of the book is not unique with our generation, but the last twenty-five years have seen a growing awareness of its importance as an art form capable of involving the best talents of which we are possessed. At a time when influences in most of the other plastic arts are emphasizing unintelligibility and the emotion of the decorative and nonobjective, the concern of the book artist is of necessity with making sense and communicating with his fellow men. This not only makes him a functioning part of the community but it also makes him feel that the things he is doing have value in the scheme of things. Thus it is possible for an artist to grow so that what he does today is better than what he did yesterday, and what he does tomorrow will, by the grace of God, be an advance over both.

I feel a great debt of gratitude for having had the chance, during these past years, to work, and, I hope, to grow. For that I give you all my thanks.

BIOGRAPHICAL PAPER

by *May McNeer*

Lynd Ward

WHEN *The Horn Book* asked me to write an article about my husband I thought — why, how can I? I know too much — and too little. Although I have lived in the scent of turpentine, ink, paint, and other noxious artist fumes all of my life, still, I know so little about art! I am not an art critic and the language of art washes wildly about me without leaving a mark. My mother, my husband, my older daughter and now my son-in-law — all artists! We have one other daughter, however, who finds it more fun to read than to write or draw and she can, and often does, give us valuable criticisms of our efforts.

Lynd appeared a bit dubious, too, when I timidly mentioned the fact that I had been asked to write about him. He gave me one of his sideways looks and said, "Do it at your own risk." I think he meant at his own risk. So here goes. After all, I have seen every one of Lynd's books in production, and so might be able to tell a little about some of them, and about him.

He was born in 1905 in Chicago, and lived in Oak Park and Evanston, Illinois, before moving to Newton Centre, Massachusetts, and then to Englewood, New Jersey. I have been told by the most reliable sources that he first thought of becoming an artist when, in the first grade, he made the astonishing discovery that the name Ward was really Draw turned backwards.

He has been known to admit, reluctantly, that commercialism cropped up in connection with his talent when he was nine years old. At that time he was given an order book from some store. On his way to school he used to pass a shop with a sign saying, "John Morris, Shoes Repaired While You Wait." So, one morning, Lynd wrote on the order book a sign which read, "Lynd Ward, Artist, Pictures Painted While You Wait," and set it up on his desk.

When he received no orders he went back to art for art's sake, and that, in his case, meant painting bandits. The next best thing to being a bandit was to paint bandits, and so his earliest efforts are mainly portraits of a red bandana below two eyes and a Stetson hat.

Lynd studied art at Teachers College, Columbia University, graduating there in 1926. He did many of the drawings for *Columbia Jester,* and was editor-in-chief during his senior year. We were married the week we received our diplomas and sailed immediately for Europe, where we spent a year. Lynd studied at the Leipzig Academy for Graphic Arts. He entered the Academy with plenty of courage and determination, and no knowledge of the German language. He knew no one there who could speak English, except one *werkmeister* whose knowledge was very slight. Every night Lynd studied German, and every day he made use of each word that he learned, much to the amusement of his fellow students. He spent most of his time in the etching classes, but did some work also with wood engraving.

When we returned to the United States and Lynd began to make the rounds of publishers, he had a portfolio of book illustration samples made in Leipzig and a strong desire to do a novel in woodcut, without words. That was later published as *Gods' Man.* The first books that he illustrated were *The Ballad of Reading Gaol,* for George Macy, then of Macy-Masius, and *The Begging Deer,* a book of Japanese stories for children, for Louise Seaman of Macmillan.

I think that it was Louise Seaman's enthusiasm and encouragement that first gave Lynd his intense interest in children's book illustration — an interest that has not only lasted but has grown with the years. Our first collaboration book was *Prince Bantam,* also for Macmillan.

Since that time Lynd has worked continually on books, with so much pleasure in it that his work is really a part of living for him, as natural as breathing, although not so easy. Every day he comes up with one to six new ideas for books. They seem to generate in his head during the night, for he brings them forth at the breakfast table. He has illustrated well over a hundred books, both in the adult and children's field, and this list includes six stories in woodcut. He also makes prints in wood engraving and lithography. He is an Associate of the National Academy of Design and a member of the Society of Illustrators and the Society of American Graphic Artists.

One of the strongest influences in Lynd's life has been the Canadian woods. This dates from early childhood and has given him a love for outdoor work; he likes everything about it from chopping wood to building a complete house with an enormous stone fireplace. In fact, one of his hobbies, in which he seldom has time to indulge now, is stone work and he is blissfully happy with his feet in wet cement and his hands hoisting granite boulders. If the mixed cement is not used up by dark he rigs up a light out of doors, forgets his dinner and sets stones until midnight.

Another hobby is the accordion. He bought his first one, just a little fellow, in Paris when we spent a winter there in 1930. Now he has a larger one that goes with us in the car or in the rowboat, by land and by sea. Lynd's playing is mainly by ear, and his repertoire is made up, largely, of folksongs and selections from the 1890's.

Lynd works in an old barn at the back of our lot, where he has converted the carriage room into a studio. The remainder of the barn, the loft and stalls, is filled to the roof with community property, such as costumes for the Leonia Players Guild, flats for the Woman's Club yearly art show, a marionette theater for the Girl Scouts, and other things. He spends most of his waking life in the studio, in a faintly lingering scent of old leather and horses, mixed with the sweet smell of casein paint and the acrid odor of turpentine. His working hours are, nearly always, from nine in the morning until midnight, seven days a week. When he is not composing drawings he enjoys company, and so friends come to sit and talk and the Players Guild often rehearses plays in the studio, as Lynd quietly works in a corner. The only unfortunate result of the latter is the fact that Lynd absorbs all the lines of the play and quotes them to us for weeks afterwards.

People ask about likes and dislikes, so I will mention that Lynd likes travel, both in America and abroad, children, animals, puns, loud socks and enormous salads. He dislikes hats, neckties, hominy grits and argumentative people. Artists are supposed to be temperamental, but not so Lynd. He is even-tempered and cheerful and can come into the house, after working all night to meet a deadline, with one of his jokes and the solemn look that goes with it.

Lynd has sincerity, honesty and thoughtfulness, and these are a part of his work as well as his character. He is painstaking and energetic, and he sets a standard that he will not lower. If a drawing does not seem worthwhile to him it goes into the wastebasket, even if it delays completion of his work. It is useless to argue with him about it, in spite of the fact that it causes his family to tremble and his editor to totter on the verge of insanity. Once he threw away a whole set of drawings for a book, the work of three months. When he was doing *The Biggest Bear* he discarded the first ten finished drawings and did them over. One drawing he did over six times.

Another characteristic quality in Lynd's approach to his art work is thoroughness. Whenever he has used a new type of technique; or a new method of reproduction, he has set about learning it in every detail. He is never satisfied to learn just enough to get by, but must know exactly how everything is done, and why, and what the results will be. He never approaches a job with an estimate of the time it will take, but only with a desire to do it well, and to learn as much as possible.

For all his exactitude in preparation and in execution, Lynd is an imaginative artist. Even when he does an engraving from a sketch that he has made of a landscape, the final print is not the same as the sketch. He has never drawn from models, and is able to remember details of places, of people's appearance, and of factual photographs with surprising ease. If he has any doubt about accuracy, however, he will spend any amount of time searching and checking on the point.

Working with Lynd on a book is to me a privilege as well as a pleasure, for from it I never fail to learn, each time that I do it, a little more of the meaning of a high standard in quality and self-discipline. I feel that his work has always had sensitivity and great strength. He feels he must make the next book better than the last one — for the last one was not good enough.

THE CALDECOTT AWARD 1954

Madeline's Rescue

illustrated by LUDWIG BEMELMANS

written by THE ILLUSTRATOR

published by VIKING 1953

FORMAT

SIZE: 8¾" x 12", 56 pp.
ARTIST'S MEDIUM: Brush, pen and watercolors
PRINTING PROCESS: Offset lithography
ILLUSTRATIONS: Front matter, pages in full color, and in two-color line
TYPE: Bodoni

BOOK NOTE

A second book about Madeline at school in Paris with Miss Clavel in charge. The rescue is accomplished by Genevieve, a dog, who is immediately adopted as a " pupil " of the school and remains until the awful day when the Trustees decide that Genevieve must go because of the children's constant quarreling over her ownership. The overwhelming sadness of the little girls changes to joy when " suddenly there is enough hound to go all around." The full color pictures are of Paris in scene and atmosphere.

ACCEPTANCE PAPER

by *Ludwig Bemelmans*

And So Madeline Was Born

My deep gratitude to the members of the American Library Association for the Caldecott Medal.

Now we shall talk about art.

There is one life that is more difficult than that of the policeman's and that is the life of the artist.

I have repeatedly said two things that no one takes seriously, and they are that first of all I am not a writer but a painter, and secondly that I have no imagination. It is very curious that, with my lack of these important essentials, the character of Madeline came to be. It accounts perhaps for her strength; she insisted on being born. Before she came into the world, I painted. That is, I placed canvas or paper on an easel before me and made pictures. I found in this complete happiness and satisfaction.

The unfortunate thing about painting is that the artist must exhibit, and at exhibitions, along with his work, exhibit himself; that he has to see his work, which is as his children, sold; see it wrapped up and taken away. I felt sorry for many of my pictures and those of other painters. I wish that there were a way of acquiring dogs or paintings other than by walking into a store and paying for them. The art market, then, the faces of the people who come and look at pictures, the methods of arriving at success, which entail self-advertisement and the kissing of hands, were not my dish.

I looked for another way of painting, for privacy; for a fresh audience, vast and critical and remote, to whom I could address myself with complete freedom. I wanted to do what seemed self-evident — to avoid sweet pictures, the eternal still lifes, the pretty portraits that sell well, arty abstractions, pastoral fireplace pictures, calendar art, and surrealist nightmares.

I wanted to paint purely that which gave me pleasure, scenes that interested me; and one day I found that the audience for that kind of painting was a vast reservoir of impressionists who did very good work themselves, who were very clear-eyed and capable of enthusiasm. I addressed myself to children.

You will notice in *Madeline* that there is very little text and there is a lot of picture. The text allows me the most varied type of illustration: there is the use of flowers, of the night, of all of Paris, and such varied detail as the cemetery of *Père la Chaise* and the Restaurant of the *Deux Magots*. All this was there waiting to be used, but as yet Madeline herself hovered about as an unborn spirit.

Her beginnings can be traced to stories my mother told me of her life as a little girl in the convent of Altoetting in Bavaria. I visited this convent with her and saw the little beds in straight rows, and the long table with the washbasins at which the girls had brushed their teeth. I myself, as a small boy, had been sent to a boarding school in Rothenburg. We walked through that ancient town in two straight lines. I was the smallest one, but our arrangement was reversed. I walked ahead in the first row, not on the hand of Mademoiselle Clavel at the end of the column.

All this, as I said, for many years hung in the air and was at the back of my mind. Madeline finally began to take shape in France, where I had gone to paint. My daughter Barbara was about Madeline's age when we went to the Isle d'Yeu for a summer vacation. This was then an island without any pretensions, and has since become famous as the place of detainment of Marshal Pétain. There was the usual *Hôtel des Voyageurs* and the *Café de la Marine*. The house we rented was twenty-five dollars for the season. It had its own private beach and the beds were always full of sand. A few miles away lived a man who owned a few lobsterpots and a fishing boat, and I bicycled there regularly to buy the makings of a *bouillabaisse* or a fish stew.

One day, pedaling along the road home with the sack of seafood over my shoulder, both hands in my pockets, and tracing fancy curves in the roadbed, I came to a bend which was hidden by some pine trees. Around this turn, coming the other way, raced the island's only automobile — a four horsepower Super Rosengart belonging to the baker of Saint Sauveur, the capital village on the island. This car was a fragrant, flour-covered bread-basket on wheels. I collided with it, and it threw me in a wide curve off the bicycle into a bramble bush. I had taken the car's doorhandle off with my arm and I was bleeding. I asked the baker to take me to the hospital in Saint Sauveur, but he said that according to French law, a car that has been involved in an accident has to remain exactly where it was when the crash occurred so that the gendarmes can make their proper deductions and see who was on the wrong side of the road. I tried to change his mind, but he said: "Permit me *alors, Monsieur;* if you use language like that it is no use at all to go on with this conversation."

Having spoken, he went to pick up his *pain de ménage* and some *croissants* that were scattered on the road, and then he spread the branches of the thicket to look for the handle of his Super Rosengart. I took my lobsters and went to the hospital on foot.

After I had waited for a time, an old doctor came, with a cigarette stub sticking to his lower lip. He examined my wound, cleaned it, and then with a blunt needle he wobbled into my arm. "*Excusez moi,*" he said, "but your skin is very, very tough." I was put into a small, white, carbolicky bed, and it took a while for my arm to heal. Here were the stout sister that you see bringing the tray to Madeline, and the crank on the bed. In the room across the hall was a little girl who had had an appendix operation, and, standing up in bed, with great pride she showed her scar to me. Over my bed was the crack in the ceiling "That had the habit, of sometimes looking like a rabbit." It all began to arrange itself. And after I got back to Paris I started to paint the scenery for the book. I looked up telephone numbers to rhyme with appendix. One day I had a meeting with Léon Blum, and if you take a look at the book, you will see that the doctor who runs to Madeline's bed is the great patriot and humanitarian Léon Blum.

And so Madeline was born, or rather appeared by her own decision.

Now we come to the sequel, which is the bearer of this Medal and the reason why I am here tonight. . . .

In this story Madeline shares the pages with a dog. This dog came about in a strange way. My wife's parents live in Larchmont, and in a house next door to them is a family of outwardly respectable folk — that is, no one in that solid community would suspect that this quiet and respectable surburban house was occupied by a poet. Her name is Phyllis McGinley and she writes for *The New Yorker*.

She has two little girls, and they said, "Why don't you write another *Madeline?*" So I offered them fifty cents apiece if they would give me an Idea, for I was paralyzed with lack of imagination. The children did not even go out of the room. They came with hands held out, and after I paid them they stated the plot:

"There's a dog, see — Madeline has a dog. And then the dog is taken away but it comes back again, maybe with puppies so all the girls can have dogs."

That was tight and clever dramatic construction, and now there remained the dog to find. I said, "What kind of a dog? "

" Oh, any kind of a dog."

I went back to Paris and started to look for any kind of a dog. And of that breed Genevieve is a member.

I had a studio at the time in a house on the Seine at number one *Git de Coeur*, and I walked down to the quay and promenaded along there. Under one of the bridges there lived an old man with his dog. He loved it very much and he combed its fur with the same comb he did his own hair, and they sat together watching the fishermen and the passing boats. I started to draw that dog, and observed it. It loved to swim.

I now had the dog and I sat along the Seine, and thought about the new book. But as yet there wasn't a plot I could use, and the little girls who might have done it for me were in America.

Then one day something happened. An object was floating down the Seine, and little boys ran along the quay, and as the object came near it turned out to be an artificial leg. One of the little boys pointed at it and said, " *Ah, la jambe de mon Grand-père!* "

At that same moment a long line of little girls passed over the bridge *des Arts,* followed by their teacher. They stopped and looked, holding onto the iron rails with their white-gloved hands. The leg was now very close, and the dog jumped into the Seine and retrieved it, struggling ashore and pulling it from the water by backing up the stones.

There suddenly was a great vision before me. The plot was perfect.

There are many problems ahead. Who are Madeline's parents? Who are the other girls, what are their names, what new disaster shall Mademoiselle Clavel rush to? The next *Madeline* on which I have been working for two years concerns a boy called Pepito, the son of the Spanish Ambassador who lives next door to the little girls and is a very bad hat.

I'm looking for him now. That is, I've been to Spain three times and searched for him and for his house. As yet, nothing has come up, but with patience it always does, for somewhere he is, lives and breathes. The portrait of life is the most important work of the artist and it is good only when you've seen it, when you've touched it, when you know it. Then you can breathe life onto canvas and paper.

BIOGRAPHICAL PAPER

by *May Massee*

Ludwig Bemelmans

EVERY writer leaves bits and pieces of his own story in his books whether he knows it or not, so I thought I'd look through some of Ludwig Bemelmans' books to see what he says about himself here and there. The trouble is, I find a paragraph that shows what a good story teller he is and half an hour later I realize that I've just gone on reading and haven't written a word about Ludwig.

I'll begin again, with *My War with the United States*, the first book he published for adults, after he had written *Hansi* and *The Golden Basket* for children. Those books showed that he could tell a simple story with clarity and sparkie which with his pictures made the whole book sing.

The chapters of *My War with the United States* (Viking) were translated from the pages of the German diary he kept during his service in the United States Army. He must have been about eighteen and he had been in this country only two years. Here are unforgettable characterizations and descriptions that show an eager young mind learning to understand the American character, so different from the German, and recording pictures of everything he saw.

"The Field Hospital, Unit N, to which I belong, was recruited in New York. The men are mostly college students or graduates, not ordinary privates. Some of them are older, and professional men; for example, the one who has his bed next to mine in the barracks is a Professor of French at one of the large universities. . . . I am very glad of his friendship; he seems to take the whole business we are engaged in as if it did not concern him, as a vacation, never has a serious thought. . . . But he is happy, and most so when we push a wagon with bread from the bakery back to the barracks every evening; then he sings and says that this is the best time he has ever had, that he is completely happy. Perhaps he has been in some terrible life and now feels happy because he is away from that. He tells me that Schopenhauer states with authority that Happiness is the absence of Unhappiness, which is so obvious and foolish that a backward child could make this observation, but he says I must think about it. I looked this up and it is right; only Schopenhauer says the absence of '*Schmerz,*' which is pain, and in German the word pain covers more than just pain — it means sorrow, trouble, unhappiness. And so Professor Beardsley is perhaps right. . . .

" In our free time we go to motion pictures and entertainments for the soldiers. One is as dull as the other. On Sundays we go to churches, and afterwards people ask us to their houses for dinner. In all these houses is a soft warm feeling, a desire to be good to us, and the food is simple, good, and plentiful. We also take walks together, and Beardsley has pointed out a piece of scenery which he named 'Beautiful Dreck.' It was a bitter landscape composed of railroad tracks, signal masts, coal sheds, a factory building and some freight cars, a gas tank, and in the background some manufacturing plant, black with soot. Some of the windows of this building were lit by a vivid gray-blue light and yellow flames shot out of several chimneys. 'That is,' he said, 'beautiful Dreck, and we have lots of it in America.'

"*Dreck* is a German word for filth and dirt but it also means manure, mud, dirty fingers. It is a large, able word, *patois*, almost bad; it covers all that was before us, and thereby it can be seen that Professor Beardsley knows much. He told me St. Louis had a particularly good portion of 'Beautiful Dreck,' but that the best he knew could be seen in the Jersey Meadows, where it covers almost a whole countryside."

I wish we had space to quote the story of the time one of the prisoners he was guarding took Ludwig's gun to pieces to show him how it worked and Ludwig couldn't put it together again.

It's all very unorthodox and very soberly told as true comedy should be. And there is deep tragedy here too as must be in an army hospital for the insane. The young man observed and studied about it all and his judgments were wise and kind. There is a beautiful chapter "Tirol in Buffalo," full of almost unbearable homesickness, that gives the Austrian background the boy loved.

In short, if you would know the young Ludwig you could not ask for a better script than *My War with the United States*. The diary must have been written in 1917-18. The book was published in 1937. The twenty years between had been crammed with living and working — the banquet manager, storing up more tall tales of hotel life, the artist perfecting his own style of drawing, the traveler shuttling from New York to the West Coast or from New York to Europe and back again. His restless energy can never let him alone — he has so many skills that he is driven from one to another and in between he writes a play or opens a restaurant or takes a Mediterranean cruise — it's all the same to Ludwig.

Hansi (1934) and *The Golden Basket* (1936) and *My War with the United States* (1937) established Ludwig as an important writer-artist or artist-writer with a cosmopolitan genius all his own. He has written many brilliant, witty, amusing books from then to now. But *Father, Dear Father* (Viking, 1953) is my favorite and to me is the best portrait of Ludwig today — probably because it is largely the story of a trip to Europe with his small daughter, Barbara, and a remarkable miniature poodle, Little Bit. Barbara asks searching questions and her father's answers give background, philosophy and hopes. Here is a sample:

" 'Some of the people you write about are awful — most are.'

" 'Yes, some are awful, and I have portrayed them as best I can. I have written some very bitter social satire.'

" 'Well, I'm sorry, Poppy, but I never got that. You make them all charming and too, too utterly divine.'

" 'I'm not a prosecutor. I don't condemn. I put the form, the shape, the being, on canvas and on paper, and I let the reader decide for himself.'

" 'Well, maybe you start out that way, and then, no matter how awful, you fall in love with your characters, and they all turn mushy and nobody is really bad — they're just odd. In fact, sometimes the bad are much more lovable than the good. And now that I come to think of it, almost always. Anyway, it's not social satire.'

" ' Well, maybe it's not social satire but comedy of manners — and in a world in which there are less and less manners, especially among the young, it's a very hard thing to write. As for hating people, I'm sorry, but I find it hard to hate anybody, and impossible to hate anybody for long.' "

Another day they had been talking about Ludwig's Austrian accent which he has never lost, and Barbara asked:

" ' Do you think in German? '

" ' That's another thing that puzzles me — no, I don't.'

" ' In English? '

" ' No, I don't think in either. I think in pictures, because I see everything in pictures, and then translate them into English. I tried to write in German; I can't. I made an attempt to translate one of my books, and it was very difficult and sounded awful. Then the Swiss publishers Scherz engaged an old lady, the widow of a German general, to translate the book, and when I read it I said to myself, " How odd! It's another book." I liked it, but I never could have done it myself.'

" ' What do you mean by pictures? '

" ' Well, when I write, " A man comes to the door," I see it as a movie — I see the door, precisely a certain kind of door, and I see the man.'

" ' In color? Do you dream in color? '

" ' That depends on the subject. Happy dreams are usually in color, especially flying dreams.' . . .

" ' You love painting more than writing? '

" ' Yes, I would rather paint than write, for writing is labor.'

" ' Do you think you could be a great painter? '

" ' Yes, the very best.'

" ' But why aren't you? '

" 'Because I love living too much. If I were unhappy as Toulouse-Lautrec was, or otherwise burdened, so that I would turn completely inward, then I would be a good painter. As is, I'm not sufficiently devoted.'

" 'Is it the same with writing? '

" 'Well, yes. My greatest inspiration is a low bank balance. I can perform then.'

" 'To make money? '

" 'Yes, to make money.'

" 'But that's awful! '

" 'Well, it has motivated better people than I.'

" 'For example, whom? '

" 'For example, Shakespeare.'

" 'And if you had all the money in the world would you just be a café society playboy and waste it? '

" At such turns in the conversation I impose silence.

" 'Poppy — '

" 'Yes, what now? '

" 'About the people you write about.'

" 'We've had that argument before, and I'll run through my little piece again for you. I was born in a hotel and brought up in three countries — when I was six years old I couldn't speak a word of German, because it was fashionable in Europe to bring up children who spoke nothing but French. And then I lived in other hotels, which was a very lonesome life for a child, and the only people you met were old ones, below stairs and upstairs. In my youth the upstairs was a collection of Russian grand dukes and French countesses, English lords and American millionaires. Backstairs there were French cooks, Roumanian hairdressers, Chinese manicurists, Italian bootblacks, Swiss managers, English valets. All those people I got to know very well. When I was sent to America to learn the hotel business here, I ran into the same kind of people, and these I know very well and I can write about them, and one ought to write about what one knows. I can write about you, or Mimi, or a few other people, but I can't write about what you call " ordinary people " because I don't know them well enough. Besides, there are so many people who do, and who write about them well.'

" ' Could you write about German ordinary people? '

" ' I can write about Tyroleans, and Bavarians, whom I have known in my youth, woodchoppers, teamsters, boatmen, peasants, and the children of all these people.'

" ' But how did you find out about them, and understand them, when you didn't speak their language? '

" ' Oh, I understood them, as a foreigner does.'

" ' When you were older? '

" ' Oh no, in my childhood; or better, when I started living and occasionally ran away from the hotel.'

" ' And did you like that more than the hotel? '

" ' Of course. The hotel was like an all-day theater performance and one played along, but the other was real and important and something you never forget. I ran away often and played with other children, but I was always brought back.'

" ' Do you speak German with an accent too? '

" ' Yes, of course.'

" ' Do you speak any language correctly? '

" ' Well, I have the least accent in French, or else the French are very polite, for they always say how very well I speak it for a foreigner.'

" ' That's all rather sad, Poppy.'

" ' Well, it has its advantages. It's like being a gypsy, belonging everywhere and nowhere. When you are in Paris you want to be in New York and vice versa.' "

Right now he is in this country to accept the Caldecott Medal but tomorrow he flies back to Paris.

THE CALDECOTT AWARD 1955

Cinderella,
or The Little Glass Slipper

illustrated by MARCIA BROWN

published by SCRIBNER'S 1954

FORMAT

SIZE: 8″ x 10″, 32 pp. (unfolioed)

ARTIST'S MEDIUM: Watercolor and crayon

PRINTING PROCESS: Offset lithography

ILLUSTRATIONS: Front matter, full-page and partial-page illustrations in four colors

TYPE: Bembo

BOOK NOTE

PICTURES delicate in color accompany this re-telling of the well-known tale, freely translated from the French of Charles Perrault.

ACCEPTANCE PAPER

by *Marcia Brown*

Integrity and Intuition

AN artist cannot help feeling deeply honored to receive an award bearing the name of Randolph Caldecott, one of the happiest spirits in children's books. Prizes and awards seem to be gifts from the gods, unless they are given for measurable performances, such as jumping. Perhaps this one has been given for sheer persistence in running up. The book so honored is neither better nor worse than it was before, but the illustrator has grown in that you have added to her your confidence in her and her work.

It is also a great pleasure to receive an award given by librarians. Public libraries have been a part of my life, as long as I can remember. When our family moved to a new town, my sisters and I made a trip to the library to make friends with the librarian and get our library cards before our parents had a chance to unpack the china. One of the first books that came home from the library in Cooperstown was *Clean Peter and the Children of Grubbylea*, suggested purposely, I am afraid, by an older sister. We were near enough of an age to share a pleasure in the same books. One night when I was five and she and I were alone, to amuse me she read aloud Andersen's fairy tales. Three of us sat in our old, black leather Morris chair — she on one side, our good-sized airedale on the other, and I in the middle, feeling the warmth of each as an antidote to the sadness of the Little Match Girl.

I shall never forget our excitement when later on we discovered *Otto of the Silver Hand*. A child brought up on Howard Pyle and the Lang fairy books can hardly help acquiring some feeling for the Middle Ages. Reading books and listening to music were as normal parts of my childhood as eating and playing. I can never look on those Carnegie buildings in small towns — the red brick, the golden oak, the cool, dim corners behind potted palms, the smell of the stamping pads, the peculiar, cozy smell of worn buckram and pages that felt as soft as old flannel — without thinking of what that place is meaning to some child who thinks of it as a second home, a kind of last stand of privacy.

On the top floor of that library in Cooperstown was a small museum, containing, among others, two wonderful things — one, an exact model of James Fenimore Cooper's house. "Through the little windows you could look right into the rooms." The whole thing seemed a glorified doll house to my sisters and me, who spent a good deal of time leaning on the table, looking in those windows and imagining a life inside. I always had a passion, like Tag-a-long Too-Loo's, for little things, chiefly boxes and dolls. The other wonderful object in that museum was a primitive little doll carved by an Eskimo from walrus ivory. She was only about two and a half inches high and had almost no face. I wondered if she was aware of my devotion, or of the many trips I made to the library just to go upstairs alone to look at her. Like most children, I never told my love.

No one can know the influence on a child of those first books and their pictures, good and bad. Reproductions were then all I saw of the great paintings of the world. Most of these were on slides borrowed from the State Library by a wise and enterprising seventh-grade teacher who, when we were restless, would often suddenly say, " I think we need some slides." Down would come the dark curtains of the schoolroom windows, and off that seventh grade went, transported and refreshed by " The Wedding of Aurora " or Botticelli's " Primavera."

From the time when I first wanted to illustrate books, and that was quite early in my life (it all seemed more possible somehow when we moved to the parsonage where Maud Petersham had lived as a girl), I was interested in books for younger rather than older children. The greater attractiveness of those I saw in the former group and the often disappointing dullness of those

I saw in the latter made me feel that way. I remember a keen resentment that a book was illustrated at all when the pictures were inadequate compared to those pictures that formed in the mind.

A young child shares with the primitive an extraordinary power to identify himself with the people, animals and things of this world, and this power makes him extremely accessible to the magic power of symbol. This same power carried into adult life enables the artist to enter the feelings of his subjects and draw and paint them in such a way that not only do they look as if they felt a certain way, but they also make the spectator feel that same way. Young children have a profound sense of the mysterious, but if the mood of our work is to speak to them, it must relate to other realities they know. The child cannot gape forever at the juggler or shiver endlessly with the tightrope walker. After the circus is over the arc of his own ball in the air will be more beautiful, the sureness of his own foot as he walks the curb will give him pride. He contains his experience.

A picture book really exists only when a child and a book come together, when the stream that formed in the artist's mind and heart flows through the book and into the mind and heart of the child. Before starting to make the book, an artist must be sure the story is worth the time, his time and love spent in illustrating it, and the child's time to be spent in looking at it.

Once the story is chosen, what is its texture? What are the large patterns of action? These might be the very meaning of the story itself.

A picture book is somewhat related in its effect to that of a painting. The whole is greater than any of its parts, but all the parts must relate directly to each other in harmony. The young child might be more receptive to the intuition of the artist than the educated adult, who might be an ignoramus in art, for all his conscious knowledge. But the pictures must be blessed with real intuitive quality for them to speak to him.

The clearest exposition of the creative process I have yet found is Jacques Maritain's *Creative Intuition in Art and Poetry*, in which he tells of inspiration (and those who scoff at its necessity to a work perhaps have never felt it) springing from the dark night of the soul in vibrations that he calls "pulsations," "wordless songs," then assuming form as one begins to think of the work in question, and finally being subjected to conscious reason. As an artist develops he gradually becomes aware of the presence of this night, and to trust in it; for it is there, not at the surface of his mind, which deals with the problems of existence, but deep in those waters that contain the resources of his spirit and intellect, that his intuition has its birth. That is why, I think, when only vague feelings are beginning to form, an artist should be left alone to let them gradually rise to the surface and take form as visual idea. And that is also why the feeling of others can hardly be incorporated or even listened to at this point if the finished work is to have the integrity which means that it sprang from an artist's own sensibility. His sensibility, of course, has been enriched by his thinking, his seeing, his feeling, his living — all his life up to now, and that is what is drawn on, not the impulses of last week. That might be another reason why the time spent on creating a book in its first form, that is, making the dummy if there is to be a visual plan, can be very short or very long. I have never been impressed by tales of the extraordinary length of time that it took to produce books or paintings. An art student's laborious drawing of a month will not compare with a one-minute impression of a Picasso. All one's life has been spent in preparation for the work at hand. When the greatest amount of inspiration is brought to bear, the least amount of work will bring the idea to realization. Inspiration — no minute in making a work should escape it.

In our modern world beauty is often dismissed in favor of hard labor. People will respect the hours consumed in a project without ever questioning the use of the time spent in the first place.

The artist is overcharged, and works to find a relief, ease for his burden, so that he can take up another as soon as he is able. At his most relaxed he is often most unhappy; at his most tense, difficult as he might be to live with, he is often experiencing one of his deepest joys, for he is finding his way back into himself. This region is so subjective that he is often hardly aware it existed, but he knows, if he has listened to music, that it exists in others. Rhythms he feels there are old as time and tide, but they are part of the bloodstream of all the morning subway riders. Colors take their meaning from first awareness of light, blue vastness of sea and sky, hot warmth of fire, the sun and his own blood. Sounds, movements, all these rise to the surface to be called into use to speak to the same feelings in another human being. These feelings or this intuition, if it is strong enough in a person, demands to be expressed in work, even if that work is never understood by others. Its strength is such that it will drive an artist to live the life of greatest hardship in order to nourish it, and allow it to have its way with him.

The question of integrity has a direct bearing on one's choice of subject matter for a book. Who knows when an idea can light a match? A sight of children playing in a city street; meeting a stalwart Cape-Codder of three who that day had fallen off a dock when the tide was in and had walked in to shore, as his brother told us, " by hisself "; hearing an old rhyme read or a sly old folk tale; or having one's editor suggest illustrating a tale, the feeling of which, if not the exact images, had persisted in the mind since early childhood; any reason can exist, it seems, for making a picture book. But, and this I believe most strongly, the reasons have to be a part of the person and his feeling before he attempts the book. Contrivance and fad-following impress only those who are unaware of their superficiality.

A good editor knows the stage at which authors and artists must be left alone if their work is to be their own best expression. I have been most fortunate in my editor, Alice Dalgliesh. As an outstanding writer for children, and a very kind friend, she has given me more than usual understanding and consideration during times of stress.

The whole process of actually getting a picture book ready for the printer usually takes me about five months. It is sometimes difficult to maintain the same high pitch of excitement that was there when the work started, but it must be done. The original idea must always be the aim. In almost all cases, it is the one with vitality and truest feeling toward the text.

Why is it that the paintings of children often have qualities of intensity of expression, beauty of color, and depth of feeling that make us feel that they are works of art? By his desire to say something, to force the meager means, the meager knowledge at his disposal, the child is able to draw what he has to say so vividly that his drawing speaks to us. All during the work on a book, all during his working life the artist will be forcing *his* means to say what he has to say. The means will always be determined by the subject at hand, and that is why I feel that each book should look different from the others, whether or not the medium used is the same.

The simplicity of a very young child's pleasure in a little street carousel, a tale of a roguish cat that is colored by the sophistication of the Sun King's Court, the longing and immolation of a little tin soldier, the freshness of a lovely young girl's dream as opposed to her stepsisters' delusions of grandeur, and they more waspish than wicked — how could one feel the same about such different books? A technique learned as a formula to apply willy-nilly to any subject often knocks the life out of the subject. The vitality, the quality peculiar to the subject should dictate the method to follow. Is the subject to yield to the manner, or the manner to the subject?

Whatever the means, the only pictures that will arouse interest and love in a child are those created in the same interest and love. Each word, each gesture counts toward giving the fullest value of the feeling. White space, in which the mind rests or fills in its own images, can be as telling as drawing, and will certainly be more effective than empty decoration. Research is done simply to aid in picturing the idea, bringing it into objective being, never for its own sake. Incompletely absorbed research results in costume plates or journalism, not creation. How do the colors speak in this telling, not how many colors are there. One accent rightly placed, whether color, shape or line, can be worth a hundred small forms. One small area can suggest the design of a whole curtain. The mind continues where the pictures end.

A horse is not drawn in a stroke or two because the artist wanted to show his skill. But, feeling strongly, he got the horse down fast, and there it was — in two or three lines. Why add more and get the horse ready for the taxidermist?

We often hear it said of an artist that he or she has developed no personal style yet. One of the most unfortunate pressures put on young artists in this country that sets such a premium on novelty, often while the artist is still in art school, is to develop a distinguishing style to apply to his work.

To me style is the way you walk and talk, what you are as a person. The discerning eye will notice certain traits of personality, certain ways of feeling that will show up in the work. These help to make a person's style, not a technique that is put on like a garment. *Style,* in the larger sense, is something quite different. We live in a world eager for recipe or formula, which, not finding it, hands over its birthright of independent thinking to the self-styled expert who imagines he has it. Any effort to coddle originality is to end by stifling it in self-consciousness. An artist's primary preoccupation is his own *development,* the perfection of himself as an instrument — whether he be singer, dancer, or painter — the better to sing his song. He is faced with all of life, but the mirror he holds up to it can be no bigger than his own mind and heart.

I have never felt that children needed any particular kind of drawing any more than they needed any particular kind of writing. The clarity, vitality of the message, the genuineness of the feeling — that is what is important.

After a book is done, it passes from the artist and has a completely separate and, we hope, strenuously active life of its own in the hands of children. But now it is something apart. Only by putting the feelings that were specifically tied up with it completely out of mind will the artist be free to be ready for something else, to grow by feeling all over again, by trying to look at the new book as if he had never done another. To forget the old solutions, to refuse to copy not only what he has seen, but also his own work, is one of the greatest problems of an artist, but only by meeting its challenge can he avoid his own clichés.

I have always felt that good drawing is more important than color in a young child's book. Yet color and its symbolism speak very directly to children. Color is often most rich when it means something perhaps too subjective to be put into words, when it is the expression of some life value. Only a hypothetical child brought up in a hypothetical vacuum without the sense of sight, even without that marvelous sight behind the eyelids that little children know in their daydreams, could be impervious to the meanings of color. These meanings are old as life itself. The passion of little children for red has an earthy origin not to be denied. Blue sky, blue sea, green and brown earth, red fire — their world radiates from very simple color relationships. By color they can be led into a greater sensual enjoyment of the visible world, as well as that between the covers of their books.

The choice of a color combination for a picture book will often have been associated with the book from its first imaginings.

Gold of the summer fields, gold of a small boy's thatch of hair, gold of his dream of London, the sunrise when he heard his destiny ring out in Bow Bells, gold of his treasure and of the chain of his office of Lord Mayor, — gold was the color for Dick Whittington.

When I was in the Virgin Islands, the unbelievable turquoise water of the Caribbean, the mahogany-skinned people, brilliant white sand, coral-colored houses and bougainvillea, deep green of welcome shadow, chartreuse of leaves filtering sunlight — the colors for *Henry-Fisherman* chose themselves.

The colors for *The Steadfast Tin Soldier* I felt could speak to children on several levels. "Red and blue was their beautiful uniform." "... a bright spangle as big as the whole of her face." Red, blue and gold, and black for type became a blue violet that could tell of steadfastness, infinite longing; the red became rose for passion and sacrifice; the gold a minute glitter on the surface; black became charcoal for the somber note of the Troll's warning and the ash in which was found the little tin heart and the burnt black spangle.

But how to get all one's colors to speak? In the past few years we have seen more and more books using a crayon and line technique, with the drawings reproduced directly from the artist's own color separations by means of a contact method with no camera work. Any process which throws the illustrator back on his own resources is good for him, because if he is not to do the same book over and over, regardless of the subject, he must push what he knows farther and farther in order to encompass the feeling of the new work at hand. By making their own plates, by exploring the variety of effects possible with hand-graphic techniques, illustrators can develop the freedom of fine artists in their print-making. Color separations are a step, a crucial one, in a long creative process that begins with feeling and should end with feeling. Illustrators are engaged in making books that are usually collections of offset lithographs, not originals that a printer must print exactly. In America we have just begun to tap the vast resources of the medium. The highly imaginative approach of artists like Roger Duvoisin, Nicolas, and Hans Fischer is an inspiration to the rest of us. In his color separations the artist has a chance to correct, to simplify, always with the aim to get back and clarify his first dreams, never to "finish." When a work is completely finished it is dead. What can the child or anyone else bring to it that will complete the feeling and give it second life? By work the artist effaces traces of work. It is not pleasant for us to agonize with him. We care nothing for the hours he took. Why does he bother us with them? Let's hear his story now, listen to his song.

My editor, Alice Dalgliesh, and the distinguished art director at Scribner's, Margaret Evans, have been as anxious as I to make picture books as beautiful as ingenuity and budget will allow. A beautiful type page, quality of binding cloth, color harmonizing with, playing against, or repeating a color in the book, a cover stamp that conveys some of the spirit of the book, end papers, if used, that both summarize and introduce the mood of the story or in design and color set a period — all these details help to make a book what it is. In spite of ever-increasing bindery and production costs, artist, editor and designer look on their work as a challenge. The end in view is always to make the book a unified and beautiful object, each part expressive of the spirit of the whole, each part complementing the other toward this end.

The book as a beautiful object will pass from our scene unless children and adults are taught to love and appreciate it. Today, institutions and products that were brought into being because of some individuals' intense personal interest, are being leveled out to meet the demands of a hypothetical universal public taste, under the mistaken notion that you can please all the people all of the time. It is very discouraging to an artist to hear that schools and libraries often buy unbound sheets, have them " pre-bound " in covers of color and texture not only out of harmony with the feeling of the book, but often downright ugly. How can a child sense the loving care that went into the creation of this book? The argument given for such a practice is that the book will last longer. But figures tell us that thus bound it costs almost twice as much. Why not give the child the book as it was originally planned and when it wears out give him another fresh copy?

When I was a child, thinking that I would like one day to illustrate books for children, I always thought of the fairy tales that I loved. It was some years before I felt ready or capable of attempting illustrations for Andersen or Perrault. When an illustrator attempts the interpretation of a folk or fairy tale that already stands as an entity, the problem of adding a new dimension and bringing the whole into harmonious unity is great. Illustration becomes a kind of visual storytelling in the deepest sense of the word. As a storyteller ideally submerges himself in the story until he loses his own identity and becomes a medium for the revelation of the story, the illustrator must likewise submerge himself in the feeling, so that what comes through is an interpretation and intensification of meanings. The big meanings, the big masses, big movements and rhythms must hold the same relationships as in oral telling. Rhythm of speech is echoed in rhythm of line and color. Never must there be a mere recounting of the event. None of these things may be consciously aimed at; yet I feel they are part of the illustrator's feeling as he attempts to make a picture storybook of a fairy tale. The pictures can convey the wonder, terror, peace, mystery, beauty, — all he is able to feel or might convey if he were telling the story in words.

The popularity of certain types of subject matter rises and falls, but children remain basically the same, with the same gaiety, eagerness to feel, the same clear-eyed wisdom and wonder in facing the world. Educators and experts on child study, who sometimes seem to have been as supple as straws in the wind, quick to bend to this or that breeze or fad, for a time decided that children no longer needed fairy tales. Not for a moment did the children who came of their own accord to public libraries and were free to choose their own books, desert their heroes, the personification of their dreams. The calls still came for Cinderella, for stories about giants and princesses, for simple people raised to high station because of their own gifts. Some of these stories appeared horrifying to adults, who seemed to lack the balance of the children in these matters. The children looked beyond the horror to the battle between moral forces. The heritage of childhood is the sense of life bequeathed to it by the folk wisdom of the ages. To tell in pictures, to tell in words, to tell in dance — however we may choose — it is a privilege to pass these truths on to children who have a right to the fullest expression we can give them. Neither so self-conscious as a parable nor so contrived as an allegory, fairy tales are revelations of sober everyday fact. They are the abiding dreams and realities of the human soul.

This very day some rogue has by his quick wit opened a new world to his master and helped him win the princess of his heart, to whom he was entitled by sensibilities if not by birth.

Today a staunch soldier, through circumstances not of his own making, goes through terrible trials, but remains steadfast in his devotion to his ideal.

Tonight somewhere Cinderella, through the magic of kindness, has been enchanted into greatest beauty; tonight Cinderella goes to her ball to meet her prince.

BIOGRAPHICAL PAPER

by *Alice Dalgliesh*

Marcia Brown and Her Books

THE three little Brown girls, Helen, Janet and Marcia, lived for several years in a parsonage in Cooperstown, New York. It was a delightful place to spend one's childhood, for there was Otsego Lake with woodland paths to be explored and, best of all, Natty Bumppo's cave. The girls had a good deal of freedom and *could* explore — Marcia remembers that they liked to play in the Episcopal Cemetery; it seemed a tranquil place, and they would go to see James Fenimore Cooper's grave.

All three girls liked to draw, and there was a Christmas when they had been given crayons, and bent earnestly over sheets of paper trying to draw angels flying over a red barn. They liked to make things, too. Janet made wonderful paper dolls. Marcia would go down to her father's workshop in the basement and try to make elaborately jointed puppets — puppets being an interest that would go over into her adult life.

In school Marcia drew whenever she had the chance. She even drew in the margins of her books. Her seventh-grade teacher was particularly understanding and let her draw during class, provided she could keep her mind also on the school work in hand!

Of course there was the local library with books to be brought home. The librarian was a little surprised that twelve-year-old Marcia wanted to spend so much time with the picture books. She was beginning to want, even then, to illustrate books and to paint. Realizing that here was a child with a really passionate interest in illustrated books, the librarian allowed her to go into the closed stacks where the art books and illustrated books for adults were kept. There Marcia found the Doré, Dulac and Rackham illustrations and others. I am sure she was as absorbed and earnest about these first experiences as she is about her painting and her bookmaking today.

When she went to the State College in Albany, where she trained as a teacher, Marcia carried on her many interests, with art always in the foreground. Summers especially gave her the opportunity to develop various creative projects. In college she designed and painted stage sets, and one summer she was at the White Horse Beach Theater in Plymouth, Massachusetts. There most of her waking hours were spent in the scene shop.

By now she was fully determined to be an artist. She went to see Judson Smith, who gave her a scholarship. She studied under him for two summers at the Woodstock School of Painting and profited by his very individual method of teaching.

She drew and drew and drew — painted and painted. Meanwhile she was also teaching English and dramatics, but always her painting, her desire to illustrate books, was in her mind.

If she wanted to illustrate children's books, then New York was the place for her to go. She came down and was fortunate enough to find a part-time position in the New York Public Library. This gave her an opportunity to work with children and books, and many opportunities for storytelling in city playgrounds.

New York was exciting. She lived in an apartment on Sullivan Street. From her window she could see the busy life of that largely Italian section — the children playing in the street, on roofs and fire-escapes. Pictures and a story began to come into her mind. *The Little Carousel* began to take definite shape, its central theme the traveling carousel that was such a delight to the city children. It was just after the war, and when soldiers returned, green, red and black Italian streamers were everywhere in that district. *The Little Carousel*, you will notice, uses those Italian colors.

I don't know how much concentrated work went into the making of the dummy of that first book. Experience with Marcia's later work makes me know that many illustrations may have been drawn and discarded. But when it came to me, the dummy had all the freshness of the most spontaneous drawing. She reminds me that the day she brought it to us I was "too busy" (editors, beware!) to see her, and she withdrew with much sadness. She and the dummy climbed the stairs to another editor's office, as there was an elevator strike. It happened that the editor had *not* climbed the stairs that day, and so, fortunately, Marcia and the book found their way back to Scribner's. I accepted it — not without thinking it over for a short time, as one does before adding a new artist to the list. But I felt that here was an artist with great originality and many possibilities for future work. I liked the clever, simple use of flat color — so many young artists present their first work in too elaborate technique and color. Authors and artists worry about first books, but so do editors! An editor sending out a book by a new author or artist has all the feelings of a mother sending her child to school for the first time. Such a big group — will the child be noticed? Such a big country, so many books — will this one make its way? *The Little Carousel* made friends immediately.

At that time — still not too long after World War II — we were going a little cautiously with color, and I was pleased that Marcia's next book, *Stone Soup*, was in limited color. Limited color, but such humor and spirit and gaiety of feeling! An old folk tale retold, *Stone Soup* appealed to children everywhere. It was the first of Marcia's books to be a runner-up for the Caldecott Medal, as all her books were to be until *Cinderella* won the award.

By this time she had spent two summers on the island of St. Thomas, then *Henry-Fisherman* arrived in our office. We began to realize that here was an artist who brought something entirely different to each book. Here were the bright colors of the tropics, bold patterns in five flat colors. I look at the pictures now, and those perfectly beautiful end papers with their semi-abstract pattern of palm trees, the charming patterns made by sea and boats and fish throughout the book, and wonder why, why *Henry-Fisherman* did not have quite the general appeal of the other books. Children of the Virgin Islands in the West Indies and Negro children of this country love that appealing little brown boy who wanted so much to be a fisherman. They love him because Marcia really understands Henry and his family. I'd never noticed until this book came out how many reviewers lack words for color. *Henry's* colors were usually " pink and light blue, yellow and brown." We called them " coral and turquoise, gold and chartreuse and brown " — the commercial firms who make such products as textiles know the value of descriptive color words. And *Henry is* color!

I watched *Dick Whittington* grow, as I've watched a number of books grow, on the big working table in my barn studio in Connecticut, when Marcia was spending a summer there. *Dick Whittington* in its first appearance was in pen line with four colors. The story — first printed in an English chap book — called for a bolder treatment, however. Marcia had been working on wood blocks at The New School for Social Research under Louis Shanker, and linoleum blocks in two colors seemed to be the treatment for this particular story. Cutting a block for each color (and you can't cover up the mistakes of a cutting tool — you have to start all over again) was a long process, but resulted in one of the handsomest books we have published. It reflected Marcia's interest in the Middle Ages, which had begun long before with Howard Pyle's books, and had continued through college, where she studied medieval music and poetry.

The books went on, with *Skipper John's Cook,* made after many summers on Cape Cod, and *Puss in Boots,* who won much acclaim for his swashbuckling airs. *Puss* really began with a puppet that Marcia made, a very gay and gallant little cat with red leather boots and a plumed hat. *The Steadfast Tin Soldier* followed. It seems to me to be one of the best of her books, with its skillful suggestions of mood and feeling. She had always wanted to illustrate an Andersen story, but hesitated to attempt it until she felt ready for it. The translation to be used was given much thought, too. She selected the one by M. R. James because it is excellent, informal and suited to storytelling.

Then came *Cinderella* — with careful work on the translation and the research that went into the period setting. *Cinderella* has humor and gaiety and magic. It is the *Cinderella* I would, as a fairy-tale-loving little girl, have loved to own and read over and over.

It is an experience to see Marcia at work, to see her following her many art interests. She has never taken a complete commercial art course, but has selected many classes at The New School for Social Research, and this year a class at the Art Students' League. Her prints have been exhibited, and the Library of Congress has purchased one for its permanent collection. It is even more of an experience to see her with a group of children, drawing and telling stories, and to note her easy, friendly relationship with them. That is where her training as a teacher and her library work with children stand her in good stead — as they do also in planning her books.

With her background in dramatics it was natural that puppet shows should be an outstanding interest. She uses hand puppets, which are flexible and easier to handle than strung marionettes. Her stage sets are pages of her books come to life. If only she could take her charming shows all over the country! But she has also to have time to work on books, and picture books take time, especially if an artist makes color separations. Perhaps some of her puppet show experience in Jamaica, where she spent a summer teaching puppetry at the University College of the West Indies, will sometime come into a book to be shared with many children. She has told me much about taking her puppet show into small villages where the children had never seen one, but so far there is no plan for a book. Some of what she saw in Jamaica went into the line drawings she did for Philip Sherlock's *Anansi Stories* (Crowell), adding an authentic setting to the tales.

But what is Marcia Brown herself like, you may ask? Is she like Cinderella, always " good and sweet "? Haven't you written about her as if everything were perfect and went easily for her, as if there were no struggles, no " temperament "? There are struggles — dummies made over *(Dick Whittington* had three), times of discouragement, and no artist is placid as a millpond; at least I've never known a good one to be! But Marcia has a wonderful sense of humor that carries her through difficulties. While she has an absorbing interest in her work, she is not an "ivory tower" artist, but one who is almost as eager about many other things as she is about painting and illustrating. Music is one of her great interests: she loves concerts, the opera, ballet, and finds time to go to them. She plays the recorder and is learning to play the flute. It is all "refreshment," she says, and all helps with the making of better books.

THE CALDECOTT AWARD 1956

Frog Went A-Courtin'

illustrated by FEODOR ROJANKOVSKY

text retold by JOHN LANGSTAFF

published by HARCOURT 1955

FORMAT

SIZE: 8⅜″ x 10⅞″, 32 pp. (unfolioed)
ARTIST'S MEDIUM: Acetate color separations for line reproduction
PRINTING PROCESS: Offset lithography
ILLUSTRATIONS: Front matter, full pages in alternating four-color and
  two-color
TYPE: Bulmer

BOOK NOTE

A rendering from several sources of an old Scottish ballad telling
of the wedding festivities of Frog and Miss Mousie. The feast is
attended by many animals and insects, but unfortunately is broken
up by an uninvited guest.

ACCEPTANCE PAPER

by *Feodor Rojankovsky*

Mysteries of Art and Nature

I AM deeply touched by your generous reception and by the magnificent Award that has been bestowed upon me. I wish I were eloquent enough to express adequately all my feelings and all my gratitude, but I am afraid that my words will be only a pale semblance of my actual emotion. I am really handicapped as a speaker. In the first place, as you have probably noticed, my English pronunciation is not exactly that of a Sir Lawrence Olivier or even that of a New York radio announcer. And in the second place, I am a painter, not a writer nor a poet, and I am used to dealing with visual images and not with words. I am at home with lines, colors and shapes, and I am rather embarrassed when I have to make a speech. So please be indulgent to an artist who is compelled to play the part of an orator.

When I began to wonder what I was going to say tonight, I remembered all the letters I have received in this country and all the questions my readers — young and old — have asked me. Many of them wanted to know how and why I became an illustrator of children's books. Maybe you would ask me the same question. And tonight more than ever before I feel like telling you this story. I wish I could illustrate it but I am afraid I shall be able to give you only the text of the story — and no pictures.

I suppose that in my case, as in that of any artist, the roots of my vocation are to be traced back to my childhood and to my family. I must say that we were quite a family. When people ask me, "Where are you from?" I answer, " From Russia." Then I feel that I owe them an explanation. My father was a teacher and administrator of high schools and his changing jobs took him across

Imperial Russia. My sister was born in Kishinev, which meant that she became Rumanian when the city was taken by the Rumanians. One of my brothers was born in Odessa and therefore became a Ukrainian or a " Little Russian "; the other brother was born near Moscow and therefore he was a " Great Russian." My second sister was born in Esthonia, and I in Mitava, Latvia. So we had five nationalities in one family. When I tried to explain that to an officer of the Immigration and Naturalization Service, he held his head with both hands and then grabbed an aspirin. I told him the story of a Jew who tried to explain that he was not a Pole. " But weren't you born in Poland?" asked the officer. " Listen," answered the poor man, " if a sparrow is born in a stable, that does not mean he is a horse."

Despite the fact that we were Rumanian, Ukrainian, Esthonian and Latvian, we felt very much like Russians and there was a remarkable unity of atmosphere and spirit in our multi-national family. " I do not want you to become rich," my father used to say, " but I want you to be well educated." There was no danger of our becoming rich, with five children who were all to receive the best education on a teacher's salary which in those times was no higher than it is today. Yet we were all happy, and we were all extremely interested in the arts. Music, painting, literature were the family's daily and most beloved fare. My sister Alexandra went to St. Petersburg Conservatory. She had a lovely contralto voice. My brother Sergei studied law but he was a brilliant draughtsman and made excellent posters. The other brother, Pavel, an engineer, devoted his leisure to painting, and his water colors were so good that the Imperial Academy bought them. And my other sister Tatiana, who was a pupil in the aristocratic Catherine Institute for Noble Women, became a concert soloist and conducted church choirs.

My father did not want his children to become professional artists because at that time Russian gentlemen looked down their noses at artists, but he could not help dabbling himself in painting and drawing. I remember that he accompanied his translations of Greek and Latin poets by naive and sometimes funny illustrations or made jocular portraits of his sons — in one of his drawings he represented me as gobbling buckwheat porridge.

Two great events determined the course of my childhood. I was taken to the zoo and saw the most marvelous creatures on earth: bears, tigers, monkeys and reindeer, and, while my admiration was running high, I was given a set of color crayons. Naturally, I began immediately to depict the animals which captured my imagination. Also when my elder brothers, who were in schools in the capital, came home for vacation, I tried to copy their drawings and to imitate their paintings.

There was another source for my artistic inspiration. After the death of my father, when I was five, the family passed through hard times but we never parted from Father's valuable library. We kept it up and stuck to it in all our wanderings and misfortunes — and it took a revolution to destroy it. There were big books in this library and I sat for hours admiring them. I remember so vividly Milton's *Paradise Lost* and *Don Quixote* with the magnificent illustrations by the great French artist Gustave Doré. And, of course, there was the Bible with the impressive drawings by the same Frenchman. One does not need to study Freudian psychology to understand the impact of these early experiences on the formation of artistic imagination and sensitivity. The whole environment in which I was brought up pushed me toward artistic expression. I was eight or nine when I started, together with my sister, to draw illustrations for Defoe's *Robinson Crusoe*, one of my favorite books. I am sorry to say that this first great work of mine was lost during the turbulent years of war and revolution.

Later when I went to school in Reval Tallinn, an ancient town on the shores of the Baltic Sea, my love for art was enhanced and strengthened by a passion for nature. Tallinn was surrounded by forest. The sea presented wonderful opportunities for excursions and study of sea life. But there were also steamers, sailboats, flags, and all the excitement of a port. This was no less exciting than playing Red Indians or reading James Fenimore Cooper, the beloved author of all Russian children before, during, and after the Revolution.

What helped me enormously in my attachment to nature was an excellent teacher in the high school who initiated his students into the secrets of woods and fields and lakes, and developed in us the power of observation. While I was rather poor in classes of design because I did not relish copying clay models of a pseudo-classical kind, I put all my ardor into compositions we had to write for the class in natural history, and I accompanied my enthusiastic descriptions of plants and animals and insects with no less enthusiastic images of what I saw and loved. One such illustrated composition received the highest grade. This was my first award in art, and I was then thirteen — it has been a long way from that to the Caldecott Medal, but I was proud and happy that day, too.

I think that my training in observing nature — including such innocent things as collecting butterflies and minerals and plants and leaves, and fussing around with pet animals, and spending hours in observing wild life in forests or in Reval's 18th-century park — that all these early contacts with nature played a decisive role in my development as an artist. All my life I continued to be interested in those very things I became spellbound by as a child and as an adolescent. I believe that children who like my books feel instinctively that I see nature with the same wonder and thrill that they do.

Later other factors were added to my first initiation into the mysteries of art and nature. I worked hard to acquire skills and techniques, and this work filled me with joy. I always loved my profession and my work. I found that creativity, particularly artistic creation, is a real blessing, and nothing else gave me such pleasure and satisfaction in life, even though I like all the good things on this earth.

I was full of joy when, as a boy of 17, I was painting murals for a small theater in the Crimea, the Russian Florida, or doing some other half-professional jobs. By that time — on the eve of the First World War — everything became clear to me. I wanted to be a painter. An exhibition of paintings I saw in Moscow made me so happy and enthusiastic that I decided to present myself in the examination contest for the Moscow Fine Arts Academy. I won it, and I entered as a student in one of the best Russian institutions of higher artistic education. The course of my life was now defined. Since that time many things have happened to me: the First World War broke out, I became a combatant and an officer in the Imperial Army, I was wounded, I went through the fires of the Revolution, I lost people who were dear to me, but I continued to paint and draw. Wherever I was I felt that my duty to my vocation as an artist compelled me to remain faithful to my artistic goal. I became an illustrator of children's books. I did it because I was an artist and loved nature and loved children.

BIOGRAPHICAL PAPER

by *Esther Averill*

Unfinished Portrait of an Artist, Feodor Rojankovsky

THE FEBRUARY, 1932, issue of *The Horn Book Magazine* carried an article which introduced the work of a Russian illustrator whose first children's book in France had recently appeared. His name was Feodor Rojankovsky.

The August, 1956, issue of *The Horn Book* published the speech delivered by Mr. Rojankovsky when he received the Caldecott Medal for 1956. The award, won by his illustrations for *Frog Went A-Courtin'* by John Langstaff, places Rojankovsky in the ranks of other distinguished "Caldecotters" who, after coming to live in America, have brightened our children's books with talents stemming from cultures other than our own.

Rojankovsky, in his acceptance speech, tells us of his early happy life in Russia, his uprootings, and the forces that have shaped his art. I can merely add a few recollections and impressions.

My first glimpse of him was caught in Paris, long ago in 1929, when the modern movement in the graphic arts was in full swing. A catalogue illustrated by an unknown artist, whose signature was Rojan, had taken my eye. It was a de luxe catalogue done for the Grande Maison de Blanc, and even now I can recall its gay Russian colors, its smartness and highly decorative style. And since I worked at that time for Thérèse Bonney, the journalist-photographer whose office was a kind of clearinghouse of information on contemporary arts, we sent for Rojan, whose full name, we learned, was Rojankovsky.

The interview took place in the front office. I toiled in the wings. But presently our secretary came to me and said, " The man is nice. Oh, really nice. And you should go and see."

Instinct prompted me, and I walked softly through the rear of the front office. By doing so, I was rewarded with a view of Rojankovsky's back.

I met him face to face a few months later after I had left Miss Bonney and hung out a shingle of my own. My chief account was an American stationery manufacturer who wished to modernize his papers, boxes and Christmas cards. On this project I became associated with another American who lived in Paris, Lila Stanley. Rojankovsky was among the artists we called in to help us. He furnished us with drawings that enchanted us. They had color, gaiety and humor, and revealed how thoroughly he understood the graphic possibilities of the medium in which he worked. But his heart lay elsewhere. He wished to illustrate a children's book.

Unfortunately, French publishing for children was at a low ebb. France had had nothing to correspond with the great publishing movement begun in the field of American children's books as far back as the early 1920's. Job and André Hellé were still alive but they belonged really to a former period. It is true that lovely juveniles cropped up from time to time, but only when the spirit moved. Rojankovsky helped to change all that and tribute should be paid him for sticking to his vocation, even when the road was rough.

I know how rough it could be, for Miss Stanley and I were the publishers of his first children's book in France — his *Daniel Boone* which appeared under my imprint, Domino Press, in 1931.

This series of brilliant colored lithographs caused a stir in Europe. Its best support, however, came from the United States, where a sustained interest in children's books had been developing. Three Americans in particular helped wherever they could, and they will always be associated in my memory with *Daniel Boone*.

They are Anne Carroll Moore, who was then head of children's work in the New York Public Library, Bertha Mahony Miller, whose Bookshop for Boys and Girls in Boston gave *Daniel Boone* a home, and Frederic G. Melcher of *Publishers' Weekly* fame — he whose Caldecott Medal has gone this year to Rojankovsky because of *Frog Went A-Courtin'*.

Now, back to Paris.

In retrospect I see more clearly. In working on this paper I have searched for facts and dates to place Rojankovsky properly in his period in France — the period of pre-World War II.

I find that in 1929 appeared the remarkable *Regarde*, written by Colette, illustrated by the distinguished Méheut, and published by the youthful J.-G. Deschamps who was endeavoring to do something new and truly beautiful for the children of his country. But this book was issued in a limited, de luxe edition which only bibliophiles felt they could afford to buy.

In 1930 the Nouvelle Revue Francaise published André Beucler's *Mon Chat*, illustrated by Nathalie Parain, a Russian with extraordinary feeling for the dynamics of a picture book. *Mon Chat* cost fifty francs, if memory serves me. (At any rate, its price was higher than the average Frenchman wished to pay for a child's book.) Our *Daniel Boone* of 1931 cost even more.

Still, Rojankovsky in believing he could make a career out of illustrating books for children had not been wrong. He had caught something in the air, as artists often do.

Over at the great publishing house of Flammarion sat Père Castor, sizing up the situation. He solved the selling problem by devising a series of simple picture books for young children which could be printed in such quantities that the retail price would suit the French. Yet one never has a feeling that Père Castor was catering to an indiscriminating public. His books were edited with artistic taste, and they offered a fine medium for Rojankovsky's talent as it burst into flower.

Rojankovsky's first work for Père Castor appeared in 1932 and his last in 1942. During that period the artist created such little masterpieces as *Panache* (the Squirrel) and *Frou* (the Rabbit), along with other memorable beasts and birds. He was doing what he likes best to do — putting down upon paper his observations of the world of nature.

I have always had the impression that he lives in close communion with the creatures he brings into being. My impression is confirmed by Margaret McElderry, children's editor at Harcourt Brace, publisher of *Frog Went A-Courtin'*. In a paper published elsewhere she speaks of the many frogs that decorated Rojankovsky's letters to her and of the feeling he gave her that frogs filled his working hours and haunted his sleep.

He himself has been likened to a happy squirrel, because in his hours of social relaxation he seems to keep in constant motion, darting here and there as lightly as a ballet dancer. (Early in his life Rojankovsky was strongly tempted to become a dancer.) But this activity makes me think rather of a hummingbird or a bee, and the image of the bee recalls a verse which reminds me very much of Rojankovsky:

> Where the bee sucks, there suck I:
> In a cowslip's bell I lie;
> There I couch when owls do cry.
> On the bat's back I do fly
> After summer merrily.
> Merrily, merrily, shall I live now
> Under the blossom that hangs on the bough.*

Obviously Rojankovsky's habitat is not the city but the country. His present home is a white house in Bronxville, near New York. Here he lives with his Russian-born wife and their enchanting little daughter, Tania, whose drawings help decorate the rooms.

Outside on a slightly wooded incline stands Rojankovsky's studio, which is a joy for any visitor to enter. Low bookcases contain the books he constantly collects and studies. Here and there on the light spacious walls are specimens of art from various regions of the world.

* From Shakespeare's *The Tempest*.

Overhead there is a sloping roof in dome-shaped plastic, crystal clear, so that, when working at his drawing table, Rojankovsky may look up into the tree tops. Trees are dear to him. They remind him of the forests in his native Russia.

How did it happen that he came to live among us?

This illustrator of tremendous talent and productivity entered New York Harbor on the S. S. *Navemar* in 1941. Paris had fallen; populations once again were on the move. As I understand it, an American printing firm which eyed children's books in terms of mass production brought Rojankovsky here.

In any event, Rojankovsky for the next ten years worked exclusively for the Artists and Writers Guild whose editorial office is in New York City. They were the printers of his *Tall Book of Mother Goose* which appeared in 1942 under the Harper imprint. This book, which sold for one dollar, swept the country and brought joy to innumerable children who had never encountered such gaiety as it possessed.

However, *The Tall Book of Mother Goose* marked a change in Rojankovsky's style and touched off a controversy which has not ceased to rage around him in circles steeped in the fine book traditions of the past. The change in style was probably due to his wish to give his books appeal for the mass markets of this country. (These markets would seem to have a taste quite different from that for which he worked in France under Père Castor.) This matter of popular taste is extremely complicated, and I for one am not qualified to comment, though I realize its great importance in these times in which we live.

What concerns us here is the ultimate effect upon the artist himself. I find that in many Golden Books which the Artists and Writers Guild has produced for Simon and Schuster, Rojankovsky's work is of unequal value. This, of course, is to be expected of an illustrator whose output is so vast.

More serious, to my way of thinking, is the fact that Rojankovsky was typed, and let himself be typed, just as an actor in Hollywood often gets poured into a mold. And certainly this was at the expense of his great lyric qualities and his own brand of gentle humor which springs from nature rather than from the world of man.

Many of us felt happy when Rojankovsky finally obtained his freedom to work also for publishers who deal in smaller editions and represent a more traditional kind of bookmaking. This opportunity should permit him to develop further his unique talents. To date these publishers include Viking, Holiday House, Scribner, Harper, and Harcourt, Brace where Margaret McElderry with great acumen introduced him to the manuscript of John Langstaff's *Frog Went A-Courtin'*.

THE CALDECOTT AWARD 1957

A Tree Is Nice

illustrated by MARC SIMONT

written by JANICE MAY UDRY

published by HARPER 1956

FORMAT

SIZE: 6⅜″ x 11″, 32 pp. (unfolioed)

ARTIST'S MEDIUM: Watercolor

PRINTING PROCESS: Offset lithography

ILLUSTRATIONS: Front matter, doublespreads alternating in 4 colors and black and white

TYPE: Garamond and hand-lettering

BOOK NOTE

BRIEF text, one line up to four lines on alternate pages, and illustrations tell many ways in which trees are " nice."

ACCEPTANCE PAPER

by *Marc Simont*

An Illustrator's Art Is a Craft

WHEN I first received the news of the Award I was stunned. When I recovered from the shock, I did what I believe any other person would have done in my place – I celebrated. When all the legitimate reasons for celebration were exhausted, I thought up some less legitimate ones. Then, with the idea in mind that I'd have to write a speech, came the sobering up.

At first I thought of the many fine children's books that are done every year, how the choice must be nip and tuck as to which is the best and how lucky I was that mine happened to be chosen. When I began to prepare this speech, I was almost moved to tears at the sound of my own humble eloquence. Then it was as if someone tapped me on the shoulder and said, "Simont, you are a phony – you know jolly well that the reason you're feeling so good about this is because enough members of the Children's Library Association thought you'd done the best picture book of 1956 to merit the Caldecott Medal."

It seems appropriate to me that I should have received this medal for a Harper book because Harper's, and specifically Ursula Nordstrom, constitutes my longest and most consistent association in the field of children's books.

Of course, all I've been doing during the last few months hasn't been just celebrating. For one thing, I've had to answer so many requests for my life history that my biography is beginning to sound as if it were about somebody else. Then there are all the requests I've received for my views and theories on art and books. It seems you have to be up against a situation like this to become aware of your deficiencies. It isn't that I haven't had plenty of theories in the past, but I have very few of them going. Theories seem to supplant one another, and I can't remember what the others were. That lapse of memory, incidentally, has the advantage of cutting down this talk by at least two hours.

Although we are forever amazed at the beautiful pictures children can make, still, their intention is not to make a beautiful picture at all, but to tell a story. You've seen them, huddled over a piece of paper with crayon in hand, muttering fantastic doings to themselves — " and the lion comes running down the hill, and the cowboy is galloping on his horse, and he's shooting at the lion, and the Indians are hiding behind rocks, and . . ." All their intent is in realistic storytelling, but the end result is closer to the abstract.

Considering the astounding results they get, it would be taking coals to Newcastle to aim solely at making beautiful pictures. What one can do, however, is offer pictorial clarification of a story. This can be done because of two things: one, because art with the illustrator is a craft, and the other because, having lived longer, we have accumulated more information about things they want to know.

After children go through a picture book, the chances are they won't remember very many facts about it. But they will retain an impression, and if the book has been presented to them with clarity and taste, it's reasonable to assume that the impression will have been a good one. That, it seems to me, is as much as an artist can hope for.

The reason a person writes a story is that he is touched by something he has experienced, and consequently, if it's a good story, those who read it will be touched in the same way. Unless the artist feels this when he reads a manuscript he shouldn't undertake to illustrate it, because in this field there's no room for cynicism or tongue-in-cheek. If it turns out to be a good story with bad pictures, or a bad story with terrible pictures, in either case the result is a bad book.

For the artist, then, the most important factor is for him to be completely sympathetic with the basic idea behind a manuscript;

all the rest, by comparison, are details. Once the artist under-
takes to illustrate a story, psychologically it becomes *his* story
— this is a risk an author must take. When the artist makes the
story " his own," so to speak, he is free to invent without getting
out of character, and thus his pictures will complement — or establish harmony with — the text. Otherwise the pictures will merely
supplement, which is like saying the same thing twice.

In *A Tree Is Nice,* Janice Udry had given me everything an
artist could want in a picture-book manuscript. The idea of *A
Tree Is Nice* is so fundamental and uncluttered that when I first
read it, I said to myself, " Now, why didn't I think of that? "
Well, that's what they said about Columbus' voyage to America.
The trouble was it only occurred to them after he'd gotten back.
A Tree Is Nice had a solid basic idea presented with simplicity
and charm; all I had to do was keep pace with it.

Where technique is concerned, an illustrator's viewpoint is
always changing. The only time it must stand still is when he's
working on a specific job. But it is impossible to arrive at " the "
solution for all illustration situations. Every job he starts must
be approached as if it were his first.

I consider your awarding me the Caldecott Medal as your approval of this point of view and, with thanks to you and Mr.
Melcher, accept it as your vote of confidence for the work that
lies ahead of me.

BIOGRAPHICAL PAPER
by *Elisabeth Lansing*

Marc Simont

DURING the fall of 1940 my mother boarded her parrot with Mr. and Mrs. William Behn in Cornwall Bridge, Connecticut. Why the Behns consented to shelter this soulless bird is not now clear to me. Mr. Behn is a blacksmith, specializing in quadrupeds. Mrs. Behn is fond of animals, but even she could not love this morose misanthrope. The Behns were happier, I am sure, with a second boarder. He was Marc Simont.

I remember this in particular because the parrot escaped to a pine tree one day that fall and we went down to see whether he could be lured back to his cage. The parrot was in the pine tree all right and Marc was under the tree trying to whistle him down. He didn't succeed. That was my first introduction to Marc and the only time to my knowledge that he has failed to charm bird, beast or man. But then it must be acknowledged that this parrot was, and still is, quite without grace.

Marc had come to Cornwall to work with Francis Scott Bradford, a noted muralist, on a hurry-up commission. The work was meant to be temporary, but Cornwall is a haven for the literary and artistic and it is not strange that Marc found the atmosphere there congenial. In any case he has lived in Cornwall off and on ever since and there is no doubt at all that the inhabitants have found him a compatible spirit.

Cornwall, Connecticut, is a far reach from Paris, France, where Marc was born of Spanish parents in 1915. His father, José Simont, is a well-known illustrator who has been awarded the Spanish Golden Pencil and a French Legion of Honor for his work on the continent. In 1920 Mr. Simont came to America where he "earned lots of money" illustrating for the glossier magazines, a distribution of rewards that is highly satisfactory to him and reveals something of the differences between the European and American sense of what is due an artist. So it was by tradition as well as design that Marc became an artist.

Marc's early years were spent in Barcelona where he began what he claims to have been a "very spotty" education. "I was so bad in school," he says, "that I never thought of being anything but an artist. I was always more interested in what the teachers looked like than in what they said."

The fact that he attended six schools and crossed the Atlantic four times during his scholastic years may account for this sense of educational irregularity. In spite of this chronic state of inattention to the three Rs, Marc now speaks four languages fluently.

In 1926 the Simonts spent ten months in New Rochelle, New York, where Marc attended high school, drawing caricatures of his teachers and presumably still deaf to the flow of professorial wisdom. When he left high school he went to Paris to study at the Academie Julian, the Academie Ranson and the Lhote School, an artistic education that was far from "spotty" and where his academic vagaries found a more comfortable setting. By 1935 his formal schooling was over and Marc could settle down to being what he is — a natural-born artist.

His single-minded devotion to art was interrupted by a three-year tour of duty in the Army, but Marc was able to turn even this inartistic career to his advantage. It was during the war that he met and married Miss Sara Dalton of Reidsville, North Carolina.

"And she," says Mrs. Behn, who should know, "is just the right girl for Marc."

Thus even in the marital field Marc pursued his natural bent, for, as any man knows, finding a wife who is both pretty and intelligent is an art in itself. In 1951 they bought a house in Cornwall where Marc has a studio, carefully planned for the execution of the many illustrating commissions that come his way. The Simonts also have a nine-year-old son, Doc, whose career so far seems to involve the not-so-carefully planned exploits of a lively small boy.

In writing about Marc it is nearly impossible to separate the man from his art — they are so happy a complement to one another. If he were to be characterized by a single word, *empathy* would have to be that word. It is this quality that is strongly apparent in his illustrations for *A Tree Is Nice,* this year's winner of the Caldecott Medal.

Janice Udry's words are few and each one bears the impact of a simple truth that is beauty, too. Who can dispute her statement " Trees are very nice. They fill up the sky " ? Marc's picture for this is a gay splash of wood and greenery with a small recumbent boy in the foreground to emphasize the fact that trees are worthy of a dream. When Miss Udry says that " We can climb a tree," Marc has filled a broad-limbed tree with exploring youth, each one engaged in the pursuit of an imaginative game. The pictures in every case are an extension and embroidery of the author's theme — that trees are nice. It is empathy that adds that extra twist of imagination and lends new enchantment to the text. An illustrator of children's books whose readers are sternly literal as well as highly fanciful must have this attribute in large degree.

Young readers are not the only people whom Marc has touched with this magic attribute. He has always to consider his authors, a touchy tribe with a nervous dread that people may not properly appreciate their point of view. James Thurber, an artist and writer capable of evaluating the aspects of this and most other questions, says this about Marc:

" Marc Simont not only illustrated *The Thirteen Clocks* but also my new book, *The Wonderful O,* which Simon and Schuster will publish in June. The fact that I have no other illustrator is proof of my admiration for his artistry, his humor and his perceptive grasp of the not inconsiderable problem of dealing with the people and animals of my strange world."

Humor is Mr. Thurber's province, an elevated area which he maintains as his private preserve. Humor is one of Marc's strongest characteristics and it seems quite natural to those who know him that he should be able to make a picture for *The Thirteen Clocks* of that thing that was " the only one there ever was " and the thing "that would have been purple if there had been any light to see it by."

Marc's humor and his gift for gaiety are facets of his personality that his friends find most engaging. These qualities, added to the empathy I have mentioned, make conversation with Marc something that puts the feeblest thinkers in a comfortable glow of self-appreciation. His lightning response to a word and even his eyebrows make them feel that they, too, belong to the company of wits.

For Marc himself is a wit with words and his stories are legend in Cornwall. He can turn an everyday event into a tale that literally rocks his hearers. Cornwall offers a fertile field for these talents, for the town relies heavily on amateur entertainment to maintain its civic improvements. At these events Marc is often the star performer. As an aging opera *diva* chasing a lost note, or a professor of elocution pursuing his muse, he has no rival in the opinion of a Cornwall audience. Some who have heard these rollicking absurdities feel that Marc, like Sherlock Holmes, missed his calling by not going on the stage.

But over thirty books, five of which he has written as well as illustrated, bear witness against this theory. *Good Luck Duck* by Meindert De Jong, *The Happy Day* by Ruth Krauss, and *A Tree Is Nice* are tangible evidence that Marc is first and foremost an artist.

Ruth Krauss who has worked with him on three books is a writer vehemently certain that he is dedicated to the graphic arts.

"I never knew an artist like him," she says. "He doesn't seem to care about money. All he wants is to get the pictures right and he'll spend hours and days doing it."

The Happy Day was the result of such work. The black and white drawings of bears, woodchucks and squirrels under the snow, their faces wreathed in contented smiles, are perhaps Marc's happiest contribution to art for children.

"Pictures for children have to tell something," he says. "Kids like bright colors, sure, but the most important thing to them is — what's happening?"

In my own case I have an example of how Marc was able to "tell something." He has, I am proud to say, illustrated two of my books and in one of them there is a young lady, a secondary character, named Janey. The exigencies of writing being what they are, I didn't need to describe her very fully, but I knew what she should look like. So did Marc. He drew a picture of Janey, freckled nose upturned, elbows akimbo, standing in the middle of a blackberry bush where the story had landed her. She was exactly right, a budding Lucy Stone, just as I had meant her to be and the picture told you so.

Perhaps if Marc has any hallmark in his drawings it is a character like that, be it male or female. You see him in *A Tree Is Nice*, sitting in the crotch of a tree with folded arms, obviously "in wrong" and defiant. His son, Doc, may be partly responsible for the appearance of the young sprout of Democracy in so many of his pictures. The adventures of Doc are a saga in themselves. Marc tells of the time a group of people were admiring a sunset and Doc and a water pistol appeared on the scene. But it is kinder to end this story here.

The fact that Marc writes stories for children, as well as illustrates them, is not surprising to those who have heard tales such as the unfinished epic above. *Polly's Oats, The Lovely Summer, The Plumber out of the Sea,* and *Mimi* are well written and amusing and have the added advantage of being illustrated by the author.

People who know Marc are apt to feel that he can do anything. Skating, skiing, singing, playing tennis, these are sidelines with him. But they show his most American side. He loves sports and baseball in particular. Red Smith, with whom Marc collaborated on a book called *How to Get to First Base*, reports that "when he was doing the book of baseball sketches, he'd go to Yankee Stadium and get so wrapped up in the game that he would leave the park without a line drawn in his notebook. Artists you can shake out of any tree but baseball fans like that are hard to come by."

No matter what Mr. Smith thinks of the blossoming abundance of artists, he does concede that "Marc is an extraordinarily gifted

guy, blessed with a quality of humor that few other artists have."
The two books on sports that Marc did with Red Smith and a
memorable volume called *Opera Soufflé* show a fine flair for cari-
cature, an art that requires quickness of mind and eye and the
power of making one line do the work of fifty. Red Smith was
particularly pleased with a portrait of Yogi Berra. After being
touched with the magic of Marc's pencil, " Yogi," says Mr. Smith,
" looks more like a bundle of old laundry than you would want
your old laundry to look like." Those who have seen Mr. Berra
behind home plate will readily appreciate that Marc and Red
Smith between them have done full justice to Yogi's sartorial
splendors.

From caricatures to portraits might seem a long step to some
artists, but Marc has done a great many portraits without having
his sitters complain that the result fell into the former category.
Children are a specialty with him and his success with them may
be due in large part to the fact that his young sitters have such a
good time with Marc that the finished portrait reflects that cheerful atmosphere.

Marc paints animals, too. One portrait of a Nubian ram was
received with such enthusiasm that Marc has been advised to
devote himself exclusively to goats. The number of Nubian goats
who wish to have their portraits painted is perhaps somewhat
limited, however, and Marc has not considered this suggestion
too seriously.

For the past two years the Simonts have lived in New York in
the winters and Cornwall in the summers. " Living in New York
hath charms," he says. " Granted, the snow isn't so white as it is
in the country, but on the other hand, you don't have to shovel it."

Whether it is this freedom from the hazards of country living
or the fact that he finds New York a stimulating place to work,
Marc has won for himself a high place in that field of art which
he most enjoys — illustrating books and especially children's books.

" Juvenile editors don't bind you to an idea," he says. " They
leave you alone."

This lack of interference is a priceless boon to a creative person.

Like every artist, Marc understands the difficulty of making that first shining idea grow and come alive in a finished picture. He once wrote an editor, " I'm never happy when I finish a job because I always feel I could have done better . . . my feeling is always, ' This should have been done completely differently.' "

But juvenile editors are wise in the ways of writers and artists; they know that they always feel this way — even a winner of the Caldecott Medal.

" That prize," says Mr. Behn, who shall have the last word, " it won't change Marc at all. He's some feller."

by *Esther Averill*

What Is a Picture Book?

THE time has come to attempt a critical appraisal of the twenty books which have won the Caldecott Award for their illustrators. I almost wish the task had fallen to another person, for these volumes, grouped together for inspection, have somewhat disconcerted me. I had anticipated a different kind of impact — one in keeping with the happiness I've always felt in realizing that the Caldecott Award exists to pay honor to our gifted artists.

Lovely books are in the group, but these parts seem greater than the whole. As a body of published work, the Caldecott Award books seem to lack a common bond. This may be due partly to the fact that some of them are not really picture books.

Most of us assume that a Caldecott Award book should be a picture book. "*Awarded the Caldecott Medal for being the Most Distinguished Picture Book of the Year.*" These words are quickly printed on the jacket of a prize-winning book as it goes forth afresh to meet its public. Has the public sometimes wondered: What is a picture book? What is a distinguished picture book?

For, to the public's confusion, picture books and illustrated books alike have won the Award, and there is a basic difference between the two. In an illustrated book the pictures are, as the term "illustrated" implies, a mere extension — an illumination — of the text. In a picture book, as the term also implies, the pictures play a livelier role, and are an integral part of the action of the book.

Definitions in the book-making arts serve merely as a take-off. One must really learn by looking, and to get the feel of the picture book style one may well turn to the works of Randolph Caldecott, the great English illustrator for whom our own Award has been named.

I have at hand a copy of Randolph Caldecott's Picture Book No. 7, *The Queen of Hearts*. Once again I am aware that the delight this book invariably gives me stems not only from the vivacity and draughtsmanship of the drawings, but also from their arrangement. They are so placed that they give visual action to every page, sometimes as full-color illustrations, or again as smaller, monotone sketches around which the white of the paper affords relief to the eye.

Scattered through the thirty-two pages of *The Queen of Hearts* are the twelve lines of the nursery rhyme, the words appearing where they best sustain the pictures. It is this deft balance between text and pictures which helps to motivate the picture book and puts it in a class quite apart from the illustrated book. Techniques for making picture books are, of course, infinite in number.

Among the fine picture books on the Caldecott Award list is Robert McCloskey's *Make Way for Ducklings*, long a favorite with American children. In *Make Way for Ducklings* we find the modern technique of "bleeding" illustrations off the pages in order to obtain a maximum of pictorial effect. There is no white space in this book. McCloskey sweeps his pencil across the double-spreads which make up his story, so that there is great dramatic action. And there is detail, too, buildings, cars, people and the ducks themselves. Children, whose eyes are microscopic, never tire of such detail.

Whereas *Make Way for Ducklings* is printed most satisfactorily in monotone, several other Caldecott Award books employ color to heighten their emotional impact. This is true of Virginia Lee Burton's *The Little House*, Leonard Weisgard's *The Little Island*, Roger Duvoisin's *White Snow Bright Snow* and Nicolas Mordvinoff's *Finders Keepers*.

Each of these four books makes a definite contribution to the technique of picture book making, although this contribution may sometimes seem to be of an experimental nature. Burton has done in color what Wanda Gág did long ago in black and white in *Millions of Cats* (1928). Weisgard and Duvoisin use pictures that stand like paintings to establish a mood for the child as he listens to the lyrical texts of Margaret Wise Brown and Alvin Tresselt. Mordvinoff, on the contrary, achieves a tight-knit, dramatic effect, since his author, William Lipkind, has reduced the text to a bare minimum. How difficult it is to achieve such verbal economy! How taxing it is for all concerned to create any kind of decent picture book! The layman will never know the backbreaking work that goes into them. Rest assured, the simpler they seem, the harder they've been to make.

Unfortunately, not all of those books in color represent the artists at their best. This is less the fault of the jurors than of the prize-giving system which demands that selection be made from the crop of a given year. Certain remedies might help the best books get their chance when their time comes. One would be (as I have already suggested) to eliminate the illustrated book (in contradistinction to the picture book) from the contestants. A second would be to judge a book on its individual merit, rather than on the past performance of its artist.

Past performance appears to be the factor which has most constantly weakened the Caldecott Award list. Of course, the desire to pay tribute to a well-loved illustrator because of his earlier contributions is an endearing trait. But in such a case, the honor falls to the man rather than to his work.

Surely such a charming and spirited artist as the late Robert Lawson would not choose to be remembered for that rare, dull lapse of his, *They Were Strong and Good*, which won the Caldecott in 1941. One feels the jurors were honoring Lawson's share in the famous *Story of Ferdinand* (1936).

Bemelmans' *Madeline's Rescue* may be another case in point. Certainly this book, with its sophisticated overtones, cannot compare with the original *Madeline* (1939), which offers such a delightful, unadulterated excursion into a child's world.

Into one's mind creep memories of certain picture books, absent from the Caldecott Award list, which have stood the test of time and become classics. Among the earlier absentees are: Dr. Seuss' *And To Think That I Saw It on Mulberry Street* (1937), James Daugherty's *Andy and the Lion* (1938) and in the same year Wanda Gág's picture-storybook *Snow White*, Warren Chappell's *Peter and the Wolf* (1940), Jean Charlot's *A Child's Good Night*

Book (1943), and Marie Hall Ets' *In the Forest* (1944). Obviously, for chronological reasons, some of these could not have won the Award. Am I wrong in believing others might have?

Let us turn now to certain picture books in which there was general rejoicing when the Caldecott came their way. I have put them in a group by themselves, since they seem to me to be picture-storybooks, rather than simple picture books. Once I had occasion to define the picture-storybook as a genre in which the textual story is fully developed but the pictures are so important one can hardly imagine the story without them. It falls legitimately into the picture book category.

The most recent example of the picture-storybook is Marcia Brown's *Cinderella* with its delicately colored illustrations so provocative of courtly life in times gone by. The line of the drawings is well matched by the type, and there is emotional harmony between the pictures and the text which accompanies them on each page. The book as a whole has typographic unity.

Louis Slobodkin's illustrations for Thurber's *Many Moons* are not so happily arranged. Turn the pages of this volume rapidly and you will find your eye jerked hither and yon.

Ingrid and Edgar Parin d'Aulaire are among the artists not easily caught off their typographic guard. In all their work they show deep concern for balancing the type page with those lovely colored images they execute in a kind of modern folk style. *Abraham Lincoln* is a definite contribution to the art of picture book making.

One of the loveliest of the picture-storybooks is *Mei Li*, written and illustrated by the late Thomas Handforth. It appeared early in the history of the Caldecott Award, and reminds us that the art of picture book making has not kept pace, on the whole, with the vast expansion in the children's book industry.

Handforth was a traditionalist in his approach to drawing. From his sound knowledge of anatomy, costume and architecture he selected just the right amount for children. And he handled his pictures so that they are not mere illustrations — an extension of the text — but an integral part of the action of the book. Watch their lively flow from left-hand page to right. See how they walk pleasantly hand in hand with the text. And what good ink the printer used. These black and white drawings fairly sparkle with color. In short, *Mei Li* may be placed alongside the best for adults and hold its own. This is a final test for any child's book.

We come now to the first of the Caldecott Award books, Dorothy Lathrop's *Animals of the Bible.* Because of its unobtrusive typography, this volume at first glance might appear to be an illustrated book rather than a picture book. But the more one studies it, the more one realizes that the lovely pictures are its *raison d'être*, and that there is perfect balance, both spiritual and typographic, between pictures and text. Since the text is the King James version of the Bible, this is no trivial accomplishment.

Only one other Caldecott Award book deals with a religious theme. This is Rachel Field's *Prayer for a Child*, illustrated by Elizabeth Orton Jones. I should call it an illustrated book, rather than a picture book, for the pictures contribute little to its action. The reverent, mystical mood the prayer might awaken in a young person is not sustained by drawings of such a realistic nature. They appeal more to adults who enjoy looking with sentimental eyes at childhood scenes.

Three other Caldecott Award books seem to me to fall short of picture book standards. The pages of *The Rooster Crows* are in no way animated by the pedestrian drawings of the Petershams, who on previous occasions have gladdened us with works of true distinction. *The Egg Tree* by Katherine Milhous and *Song of the Swallows* by Leo Politi have a fault in common: the pictures, though pleasing, are used too profusely in conjunction with the text. The pages look too " busy."

As for *The Big Snow* by Berta and Elmer Hader, other illustrations among the Award books may have been rendered with greater brilliance. But the Haders' pictures have a sincerity that lends a special kind of conviction, and they have been well thought out in relation to the text. The result is a picture book worthy of recognition.

The picture books by Lynd Ward and Feodor Rojankovsky

have a heavy air which, when one considers the fine talents of these two men, seems rather unnecessary. Ward's drawings in *The Biggest Bear* are distinguished in draughtsmanship, but somber in their effect, and they fall always on the right-hand page with never a doublespread or an extra spot to break the monotony. Compare *The Biggest Bear* with an earlier book of similar format, *Andy and the Lion*. In *Andy* the pages are vivacious; even the white spaces glow.

Rojankovsky's drawings for *Frog Went A-Courtin'* lack his usual verve. Even at that, the book would be more spirited if there were greater variety in the disposition of the pictures. Compare *Frog Went A-Courtin'* with Randolph Caldecott's *Frog He Would A-wooing Go*, in which (as in *The Queen of Hearts*) the illustrations are so grouped that they contribute a special action to the book as a whole. Or if you prefer a modern example of fine picture book making, turn to *I Play at the Beach*, which was illustrated by Rojankovsky and published in the same year as *Frog Went A-Courtin'*. Here is a radiant little volume of fine drawings, handsome color printing and subtle typography.

This year's Award book, *A Tree Is Nice*, illustrated by Marc Simont, places me in a dilemma. The reason is a literary one. Although I'm not sure how important literary merit is in judging an Award book, I have a feeling it should count. At least it counts with me to the extent that even the title, *A Tree Is Nice*, disconcerts me. It belongs to a new school of writing for children, a school I don't quite understand — and therefore cannot judge fairly.

As for the graphic aspects of *A Tree Is Nice*, I admire Simont's color spreads and also his monotone drawings. There is plenty of diversity in the make-up of the pages. But to my way of thinking, there is so much diversity that the book does not hang together as a unit. Not only is the make-up extremely varied, but the drawings themselves seem occasionally to change in style. This may be intentional on the artist's part. I myself prefer the wonderful harmony he achieved in his earlier work for *The Happy Day* — a harmony to be found not only in each drawing, but in each drawing in relation to its page, and each page in relation to the book as a whole.

Throughout this chapter I've been groping in the area of book design. Some of you may argue that the Caldecott is awarded solely on the merits of the illustrations. But illustrations are only one of the several elements of a book. Can illustrations really be good (in the sense that they function adequately) unless good book design is at their service?

The American Institute of Graphic Arts, with its various exhibits of children's books selected on typographic and artistic merits, has set many of us to thinking along new lines. In a 1951 catalogue* for one of these exhibits, James Johnson Sweeney, formerly Director of the Museum of Modern Art, has thrown light upon a matter which is obscure to many of us:

"A child's book is essentially a work of visual art — something that speaks directly to the eye and through the eye. It is a source of education to be sure, but never merely a vessel for the conveyance of information. Its real role is that played by a Gothic stained glass window in the Middle Ages, or a mosaic in the apse of a Romanesque church. It should be aimed primarily to stimulate the imagination through the eye — to educate in the true sense, by drawing something out of the observer — to mature the observer through stimulation, to exercise the imagination and develop the power for creating images. It is a work of visual art and should be approached, in the making, as one, and weighed on its completion by the same standards."

It is Mr. Sweeney's contention that illustrations which do not function harmoniously with the whole book become mere decorations:

"Where there is not a fusion of all the elements of a book — text, illustrations, format, typography — one element, or several, risks giving the appearance of a decoration, an applied embellishment in relation to the others. It may be the text, in the case of a young

*Children's Book Show 1945-1950. American Institute of Graphic Arts. New York, 1951.

child's book, it may be the illustrations, in an older one's, it may be the type employed, or even the typographical decorations themselves."

I believe Mr. Sweeney would enjoy William Pène Du Bois' *Lion,* one of 1957's five Caldecott Honor Books, or runners-up. I do know that many who love the graphic arts wish a special Caldecott Medal might have been struck off to honor a book which makes fine typography such an integral part of the action. The lines of the drawings and those of the type seem made to match one another. The type page is handsome and enlivened with capitals and red letters. The paper is excellent, the margins are generous and the colors pure. I venture to say that a child who loves this book will never again be content with shoddy design.

Children, even though inarticulate, are capable of appreciating the niceties of good book making. For this reason one wishes that in the years to come the Caldecott Award list might be more representative of picture books judged as " works of visual art."

In closing I take the liberty of quoting an incident related by Frances Clarke Sayers when she was Superintendent of Work with Children in the New York Public Library. Mrs. Sayers had had occasion to serve with Mr. Sweeney on the 1951 jury for the American Institute of Graphic Arts. In the catalogue of the exhibit she wrote:

" The librarian-juror, all the while she chose books with her fellow jurors, was haunted by the memory of a thirteen-year-old boy in a branch library. He was picking out his Saturday's quota of reading. 'If there's anything I hate,' he said, flipping through the books he was examining, and apropos of nothing that had gone before, 'if there's anything I hate, it's a cheap-looking book.'"

It may well be that when he was little the boy's taste was formed by some of the fine books mentioned in this article. In any event, the incident serves as a reminder that picture books enter a child's life during his earliest impressionable years, and the best is none too good for him.

Indexes

Index of Titles Mentioned

Index by Author
of Books Mentioned